What Shall We Do Tomorrow® *at* LAKE TAHOE

1998-99 EDITION

A COMPLETE ACTIVITIES GUIDE
FOR LAKE TAHOE, TRUCKEE
AND CARSON PASS

BY
ELLIE HUGGINS

Coldstream Press
Truckee, California

Cover Photo: An April day at Sand Harbor. © Ellie Huggins
Back Cover Photo: Skiing at Heavenly Lake Tahoe. © John Kelly. Courtesy of Heavenly Ski Resort

Book Design: Ellie Huggins
Cover and Logo Designs: Deviated Design
Drawings: Andrea Hendrick
Maps: Sue Irwin
Editors: Laurel Hilde Lippert, Dan Wendin
Contributing Editor: S.E. Humphries
Printing: Gilliland Printing

Publisher's Cataloging-in-Publication
Huggins, Ellie
    What shall we do tomorrow at Lake Tahoe : a complete guide for Lake Tahoe, Truckee and Carson Pass / by Ellie Huggins.— 4th, 1998-99 ed.
    p. cm.
    Includes index.
    Preassigned LCCN: 98-70506
    ISBN: 0-9633056-7-0
    1. Tahoe, Lake, Region (Calif. and Nev.)—Guidebooks. 2. Truckee Region (Calif.)—Guidebooks. I. Title.

F868.T2H836 1998   917.94'380453
                                   QBI98-445

"What Shall We Do Tomorrow" is a registered trademark owned by Eleanor Huggins.

Second Printing

Copyright © 1998 by Eleanor Huggins
All rights reserved
Printed in the United States of America

 Printed on recycled paper.

Published by:
    Coldstream Press
    P.O. Box 9590
    Truckee, California 96162
    voice: (800) 916-7450
    fax: (530) 587-9081
    e-mail: dwendin@coldstreampress.com
    www.coldstreampress.com

TABLE OF CONTENTS

Area Bus Service 2
Resource Phone Numbers 4
Introduction 7
    History 10
    Natural History 23

Summer Activities 29
    Adventures 31
        Parasailing 31
        Balloon Rides 32
        Gilder Rides and Scenic Flights 33
        Rock Climbing and other Challenges 34
        Bungee Jumping 36
        All-Terrain Rides, Hay and Carriage Rides ... 36
        Guided Hikes 37
    Excursions 38
    Water Sports Rentals 46
    Beaches 48
    Boating 58
    Cruising Lake Tahoe 63
    Fishing 67
    Fishing Charters 76
    Fly-Fishing Guides 80
    Rafting 84
    Bicycle Rentals 86
    Bicycling 88
        Mountain Bike Parks 94
        Mountain Bike Roads 96
    Horseback Riding 100
    Tennis 103
    Golf 106
        Miniature Golf 112
    Historical Walks 113
    Special Hikes 127
    Just For Kids 162
    Ranger Programs 166

Winter Activities **168**

Downhill Skiing 170
X-Country Skiing 185
    X-Country Ski Areas 185
    Sno-Park Ski Trails 194
    Back Country Trails 198
Ice Skating 203
Snowmobiling 204
Snowplay 208
Winter Adventures 212
    Sleigh Rides 212
    Special Ski Classes 214
    Dog Sled Rides 216

Year-Round Activities **218**

Dining Out 219
    The Casino Hotel Buffets 247
Kids at Casinos 249
Art Galleries 251
Shopping 259
Museums 263
Photo and Vista Points 270
Special Events 273
Historic Inns and B & B's 279
Lodging Reservations 297

Index **301**

Winter dawn at Donner Lake.

Area Bus Service

Lake Tahoe and Truckee have year-round bus service that connects in winter with shuttles to ski areas and in summer to the special summer trolleys. The Lake Lapper Bus goes around Lake Tahoe weather permitting. Schedules for all services are at Visitor Information Centers, retail outlets and bus stops. Hornblower Cruises is negotiating for a water taxi service between Ski Run Marina and Tahoe City for summer 1998. The service will definitely be running in 1999. Hours: 10:00 a.m. to 8:00 p.m. (530-541-3364)

Year-Round — North Lake Tahoe and Truckee

TART buses run from Sugar Pine Point north around the lake to Crystal Bay at Stateline on the North Shore every hour from 10:30 a.m. to 5:30 p.m. seven days a week. Evenings there are hourly runs from 5:30 p.m. to 1:00 a.m. between Crystal Bay and Tahoe City with connections to Squaw Valley. There is regular TART service between the Truckee Train Depot and the Tahoe City Y. In July and August San Francisco-style trolleys run hourly between the West Shore and Carnelian Bay and every half-hour between Carnelian Bay and Crystal Bay. (530-581-6365)

The TRUCKEE TROLLEY connects town and Northstar-at-Tahoe via the airport and roams from the Depot in Downtown Truckee out Donner Pass Road to Gateway and Crossroads Shopping Centers, to the Factory Stores and Donner Memorial State Park. Evenings the trolley connects Truckee and the Stateline casinos. In summer the trolley extends to West End Beach at Donner Lake. (530-587-7451)

Year-Round — South Lake Tahoe

STAGE buses have regular service every fifteen minutes on two routes up and down Highway 50 between the South Tahoe Y and the casinos, along Pioneer Way and up Ski Run Boulevard. Maps are on the buses. (530-573-2080)

Area Bus Service

Winter — Truckee and North Lake Tahoe

The TRUCKEE TROLLEY offers service between Northstar-at-Tahoe and Truckee downtown. TART connects with shuttles to Alpine Meadows and Squaw Valley. TART. (530-587-7451)

Summer — South Lake Tahoe

The NIFTY 50 TROLLEY runs two routes from 10:00 a.m. to 11:00 p.m. every hour. Route A runs from the casinos and motels along Highway 50 to the Factory Stores at the South Tahoe *Y* and out Emerald Bay Road to Camp Richardson's Resort, the Tallac Historic Site and the U. S. Forest Service Visitor Center. Route B offers service from Zephyr Cove to the Casinos and up to the Heavenly Valley Tram. (530-542-6077)

Winter — South Lake Tahoe

Free shuttles run from the casinos and all major hotels to Heavenly all day. Sierra-at-Tahoe has shuttles that leave in the morning from the hotels and return in the afternoon. Reservations are required for the shuttle service to Kirkwood. Call 209-258-6000. Zephyr Cove Resort offers free shuttles between the casinos and their snowmobile rides.

The Lake Lapper

Two buses go around Lake Tahoe in opposite directions stopping at 20 destinations. Color coded for direction, the green route goes clockwise, the blue route counter clockwise. Buses run from 8:00 a.m. to 7:45 p.m. Sunday through Thursday, 8:00 a.m. to 10:45 p.m. Friday and Saturday. The complete trip around the lake takes 2 $3/4$ hours. (530-542-5900)

Beach Shuttle — East Shore Beaches

When this book went to press, parking will probably be limited to official parking lots on the East Shore (no roadside parking). A beach shuttle will operate all summer between the junction of Highway 50 and Highway 28 and Incline Village.

Resource Phone Numbers

TRANSPORTATION

Amtrak	800-872-7245
Caltrans Highway Information Network	800-427-7623
Greyhound Bus Lines – South Lake Tahoe	702-588-4645
Greyhound Bus Lines – Truckee	530-587-6153

Local Bus Lines

TART – Tahoe Area Regional Transit	530-581-6365
North Tahoe TMA	530-581-3922
South Tahoe TMA	530-542-6076
Truckee Trolley and Dial-A-Ride	530-587-7451
STAGE – South Tahoe Ground Express	530-573-2080
Bus Plus (on demand service - So. Lake Tahoe)	530-542-6077

Taxi Companies

Ace Taxi - South Lake Tahoe	530-5444798
Paradise Taxi– South Lake Tahoe	530-577-4708
Sierra Shuttle Service (Airport taxi)	530-525-9110
Sunshine Taxi Company	530-542-1234
Tahoe Truckee Taxi	530-583-8294
Tahoe Keys Taxi – South Lake Tahoe	530-544-7777
Yellow Cab	
North Lake Tahoe	530-546-9090
Incline Village	702-831-8294

PARKS

California State Parks

Sierra District California State Parks	530-525-7232
Donner Memorial State Park	530-582-7892
Tahoe State Recreation Area (Summer)	530-583-3074
Kings Beach State Recreation Area	530-546-7248
D.L. Bliss State Park (Summer)	530-525-7277
Emerald Bay State Park (Summer)	530-525-7277
Sugar Pine Point State Park	530-525-7982

Resource Phone Numbers

Nevada State Parks
    Lake Tahoe Nevada State Park   702-831-0494
    Kahle Park   702-588-0271

Regional Parks and Parks and Recreation Departments
    Truckee Donner Recreation and Parks   530-582-7720
    North Tahoe Regional Park   530-546-7248
    Tahoe City Parks   530-583-3796
    Incline Village IVGID   702-832-1100
    South Lake Tahoe Recreation and Parks   530-542-6055

Unites States Forest Service
    Big Bend Visitor Information (Summer)   530-426-3609
    Truckee Ranger Station   530-587-3558
    Tahoe National Forest   530-265-4531
    Lake Tahoe Basin Management Unit   530-573-2600
    Visitor Information Center (Summer)   530-573-2674
    Desolation Wilderness Permits   530-573-2600

VISITOR INFORMATION

Visitors and Convention Bureaus
    North Tahoe   530-583-3494
    Truckee   530-587-0476
    North Tahoe Resort Association   800-824-6348
    Incline Village Crystal Bay   702-832-1606
    Tahoe Douglas Visitor Center   702-588-4591
    South Lake Tahoe Reservations   800-288-2463
    South Lake Tahoe Chamber of Commerce   530-541-5255

Important Note:
After Dec. 15, 1998 all 702 area code numbers are changed to 775.

"As it lay there with the shadows of the mountains photographed upon its surface, I thought it must surely be the fairest picture the whole world affords."
Samuel Clemens, alias Mark Twain, 1861.

Introduction

You have come to Lake Tahoe to ski; it's storming and you wonder what you can do. You're attending a conference. You have a free day and want to go out on the lake. Who rents boats, or offers a tour of the lake? You're renting a cabin for two weeks, and the kids are tired of the beach. What can you plan for them tomorrow? Where can you find out more about the emigrants who brought their wagons over Donner or Carson Pass, visit a museum or drive somewhere interesting for a picnic?

This book will help you discover the many options that will make your visit to Lake Tahoe, Truckee and the Carson Pass region an enjoyable and fun-filled time. Would you like to take a balloon ride, or kayak on the lake? Do you want to try your hand at fishing, rent bikes for a day, find a meadow with wildflowers, or cross-country ski free? In short, What Shall We Do Tomorrow? The many choices open to you are described in this book.

The book is arranged in four chapters, one each for summer, winter and year-round activities and a chapter with descriptions of historic lodges and B&B's and lodging reservation services for condominiums or homes. Each category of activity has a logo, shown on pages 8 and 9. Just turn to the pages with the logo at the top to find out where to rent a bike, take a cruise, cross-country ski, hike or do any one of 31 different activities covered in this book.

The left-hand column of each page includes fees, season and hours of operation plus addresses and phone numbers. Separate pages list the shops that carry rentals of bicycles and water sports equipment.

The locations of all activities are listed in the following geographical order: Donner Summit, Truckee, Highway 89 South, Tahoe City, North Shore, West Shore around the South Shore north to Sand Harbor, then Echo Summit and Carson Pass.

Summer Activities

 Adventures

 Excursions

 Beaches

 Boating

 Cruising Lake Tahoe

 Fishing

 Fishing Charters

 Fly-Fishing Guides

 Rafting

 Bicycling

 Horseback Riding

 Tennis

 Golf

 Historical Walks

 Special Hikes

 Just For Kids

 Ranger Programs

Winter Activities

Downhill Ski Areas

X-Country Skiing

Ice Skating

Snowmobiling

Snowplay

Winter Adventures

Year-Round Activities

Dining Out

Kids at Casinos

Art Galleries

Shopping

Museums

Photo and Vista Points

Special Events

Lodging Information

Introduction

History

The Region's Earliest Inhabitants

Human history of the Truckee, Lake Tahoe and Carson Pass region goes back many thousand years when the Washo and Paiute tribes of Nevada traveled to the mountains to hunt and fish and escape the summer heat of the desert. Evidence of Paiute summer encampments can be found in various places near Truckee. Perhaps as early as five thousand years ago, Native Americans from Nevada created petroglyphs on the granite rocks just east of Donner Pass, and obsidian arrowheads have been discovered on the west shore of Donner Lake. The Paiutes worshiped the rocking stone perched on top of a flat rock above Truckee. This rock was so perfectly balanced that the wind could set it to rocking. The Paiutes believed that the wind spoke to them through its movements. It is presently enclosed in a cupola located next to the Veterans Building. At the turn of the century the town fathers cemented the rocking stone into place to prevent it from rolling down upon unsuspecting citizens.

For thousands of years Washo tribes came to Lake Tahoe every summer to meet and reaffirm their tribal unity. The Washo climbed up from the Carson Valley to their summer villages along the shores of the lake. They called these places *da ow a ga*, which means "edge of big waters." Although the Washo believed that the remains of Ang, a much-feared, monstrous bird, lay at the bottom of the lake, they still believed that *da ow* was sacred. The lake was the giver of life, for it fed fish, animals and humans. The tribes fished and gathered seeds, roots, strawberries, gooseberries and sugar pine sap. Deer and rabbit were favorite meats. In the fall they moved to lower elevations along the eastern slope of the mountains. Here they gathered the nuts of the piñon pine. By winter they retired to villages in the Carson Valley where the women spent long hours weaving beautiful baskets and the men prepared arrowheads.

The arrival of white men signaled serious changes for the Washo. Settlers claimed their hunting and fishing grounds, felled their piñon trees for building and fuel, and brought cattle that destroyed the meadow plants upon which the Washo depended. Unable to withstand the invasion, the native population dwindled. Most tribes stopped coming to the lake for the annual migration and stayed in Carson Valley. Their descendants settled in small colonies on their ancient lands. In recent years the tribes have been instrumental in creating a Washo Indian Cultural Exhibit at the Tallac Historic Site. The exhibits not only help Washo tribes maintain a sense of their heritage but give visitors an understanding of the culture of these early people of Lake Tahoe.

Opening the Trail to California

The Spaniards who settled in California in the eighteenth century did not venture into the mountain range they called the *Sierra Nevada*, or Snowy Range. When Americans began looking westward to settle California's fertile valleys, emigrants attempted to find a route west across the Sierra Nevada to Sutter's Fort. The first group to succeed crossed the forbidding barrier in 1841, but without their wagons which they had abandoned in the Nevada desert. Their route is believed to have been near Sonora Pass.

The California Emigrant Trail was opened in 1844 by a group known as the Stephens-Townsend-Murphy party, led by Elisha Stephens. Their herculean effort must be admired, for this wagon train had traveled in unknown country ever since leaving the established Oregon Trail in Idaho. While traversing the Nevada desert, they encountered a Paiute who scratched a map in the sand that showed a route following a river (the Truckee) to the summit. In 1994, to celebrate the sesquicentennial of the first wagons over the Sierra, a mountain overlooking Donner Pass was named Mount Stephens, thus finally putting Elisha Stephens' name on the land he struggled to cross.

The Stephens party reached the site of present-day Truckee on November 14, discovering to their dismay that the Truckee River bent south, not west toward the visible summit. They discussed the problem, deciding to split up. Six men and two women on horses and mules followed the Truckee River south, and it can be assumed that they were the first Americans to walk along the shores of Lake Tahoe. Their probable route to the Sacramento Valley followed the Rubicon River, bringing them safely to Sutter's Fort in early December.

The other group of emigrants decided to leave all but five wagons on the shores of Donner Lake. Moses Schallenberger and two other young men offered to stay with the abandoned wagons and their contents until they could be brought over. As winter storms raged and their supplies dwindled, Schallenberger's two friends decided to attempt the pass on crudely fashioned snowshoes. Moses, too weak to accompany them, was left entirely alone until his rescue in February.

The weary emigrants and five wagons made it over the pass in two feet of snow but only reached Big Bend before they were forced to make camp for the winter. A baby was born to one of the Murphy women, and the women, children and two men were left at this campsite. The able-bodied men continued on foot to Sutter's Fort.

Moses Schallenberger and those at Big Bend were not rescued until late in February. The miracle of this tale is that all survived. Because of the determination of the group and the cool leadership of Elisha Stephens, a route to California was found.

Hauling a wagon over the granite walls of Donner Summit.

The Ill-fated Donner Party

The tragic story of the 1846 wagon train known as the Donner Party is memorialized in the names Donner Lake, Donner Summit, Donner Peak and Donner Memorial State Park.

Illinois farmers George and Jacob Donner and their friend James Reed set out for California in the summer of 1846. They were taken in by glowing reports in Lansford Hastings' *The Emigrants' Guide to California and Oregon* that described wild clover five feet high and hollyhocks and sweet william blooming everywhere at Christmastime. Illinois harsh winters and summers filled with sickness convinced the Donners that California was the only place to spend the remaining years of their lives. These neophytes on the trail did not employ a guide, preferring instead the written word of author Hastings that promised to shave 200 miles off any previously used route. Nor did they accept the advice of experienced mountain men who warned them that no wagons could pass through the country described in Hasting's guidebook. This decision cost them dearly, for they spent a month hacking their way foot by foot through steep canyons of Utah, taxing men and animals almost to the breaking point. A disconsolate wagon train with no leader crossed the Nevada desert weeks later than planned.

It was early November with snow already on the peaks at the pass when the group began the ascent from Truckee Meadows (Reno) toward the summit of the Sierra. They were forced to return to Donner Lake after failing to cross Donner Pass during a fierce snowstorm. One family used Moses Schallenberger's cabin and others made crude shelters nearby. Their suffering is hard to comprehend. Many died either from starvation or attempting to cross the mountains.

The Donner family and their drivers were the last to leave Truckee Meadows. Six miles northeast of Donner Lake a wagon overturned as it descended toward Alder Creek. While fixing the broken axle, George Donner cut his hand badly. The injury and a snowstorm forced the group to make camp immediately. Here, all but a few children would spend their last days, starving to death in cold, inadequate shelters.

Archaeologists and historians continue their research of this tragedy and identification of the sites of the various winter encampments. Donner Memorial State Park and the U.S. Forest Service Donner Day Camp both offer interpretive exhibits describing the travails of these ill-fated emigrants.

Early Days in Truckee

In 1863, seventeen years after the Donner tragedy, Truckee was first settled when Joe Gray built a cabin near the turnpike road on which he arrived. This was the year that the Central Pacific Company began building the country's first transcontinental railroad. The cabin was known as Gray's Station and became a way station to travelers over the Sierra. The next year J. McConnell built another cabin not far away which he sold to S. S. Coburn before the year was out. Coburn added more buildings, and the little town became known as Coburn's Station serving the construction crews of the Central Pacific Railroad between 1864 and 1868.

The Dutch Flat to Donner Lake Toll Road was built along sections of the former emigrant road and the railroad right-of-way in 1866. It brought railroad workers and supplies and even a few hardy tourists to see the beauty of the Sierra Nevada up close. At the east end of Donner Lake, a small town soon boasted two hotels, a general store and sawmill. This cluster of establishments had the proud name of Donner Lake City.

Ten thousand Chinese laborers braved summer dust and winter snows in 1867 and 1868 to lay the tracks and hack thirteen tunnels through the granite at a rate of seven inches a day. The Chinese, as well as lumbermen and construction workers, built their shanties along the Truckee River near Coburn's Station.

When the first trains rolled through town in June of 1868, thousands lined the tracks to cheer. A month later, the town burned to the ground. It was soon rebuilt and christened Truckee, in honor of the Paiute who showed Elisha Stephens where to find the pass over the Sierra.

Gold in California

When gold was discovered in 1848, the world rushed to California. Those already in the West headed for the hills to pan for gold, among them a group of Mormons. They did not stay long, however, for Brigham Young called them home to Salt Lake City. Their journey east established the route over Carson Pass that soon became the preferred trail to reach Hangtown (Placerville). Thousands of wagons were hauled over the Sierra via the Carson Emigrant Trail which followed the Carson River from Carson Valley into Hope Valley. From there it skirted the shores of Red Lake to a fearful climb over the first pass. A second summit was traversed at a point between Thimble and Covered

Wagon Peaks in present-day Kirkwood Ski Resort. This pass above 9,200 feet is the highest crossed by any wagons on the trek west.

The town of Genoa, Nevada, at the eastern edge of the Sierra became an important trading post for thousands of emigrants. This small settlement was also home to one of the area's legends, "Snowshoe Thompson," who strapped on his 10-foot skis and carried the winter mail across the mountains between Genoa and Placerville from 1856 to 1876.

Settlers Come to South Lake Tahoe

The first major road between Placerville and the Nevada territory opened in 1857. Known as "Johnson's Cutoff," it was named for John Calhoun Johnson, a rancher who found a route across the Sierra (now Echo Pass) toward the South Shore of Lake Tahoe. From this point the road crossed Luther Pass to the west fork of the Carson River and on to what is now the town of Woodfords.

When silver and gold were discovered in Virginia City in 1859, commerce picked up as wagon masters and ranchers ferried supplies to feed the miners of the Comstock mining bonanza. A toll road, known as the Bonanza Trail, crossed the Tahoe Basin along the route of today's Pioneer Trail to Daggett Pass (Kingsbury Grade) and north to Genoa in the Carson Valley. By 1863 a road was built over Spooner Summit. In that year it was estimated that 5,000 teamsters were employed hauling everything from machinery and dairy products to silk for ladies' gowns through South Lake Tahoe to Virginia City. That same year Glen Brook House opened its opulent rooms to travelers along the road and remained one of Tahoe's most famous hostelries for a decade. In the 1870s Glen Brook House advertised that you could reach its front portal in 20 short hours from the Bay cities. When the Central Pacific Railroad through Reno was completed in 1868, a faster more reliable way for goods and people to reach the mines signaled the end of the Bonanza Trail.

Lumbering Decimates Tahoe's Forests

The abundance of timber surrounding Lake Tahoe encouraged small operators to establish lumber mills for building in the local communities along the lakeshore. But it was the insatiable demand for wood to shore up the Virginia City silver mines that brought entrepreneurs to the area. Among the most famous was the Bliss family who founded the Carson and Tahoe Lumber and Fluming Company. Trees were felled at a horrifying rate, sent downhill in flumes, then rafted across the lake to the Bliss mill at Glenbrook. Here Bliss built a railroad up to Spooner Summit where logs were rolled into other flumes for a speedy journey to the Carson Valley. There they were loaded onto the Virginia and Truckee Railroad bound for Virginia City. Incline Village takes its name from the Sierra Nevada Wood and Lumber Company's Incline Tramway. With a length of 4,000 feet and vertical lift of 1,400 feet the tramway carried lumber from the shores of the lake east up to the summit on the first leg of the journey to the Virginia City mines. It is estimated that 30 million board feet of lumber was supplied by the Glenbrook and Incline mills annually during the 1870s. At the same time four local lumber companies invested $3.5 million in 21 miles of pipeline and 45 miles of flumes to carry millions of gallons of water daily from Marlette Lake to the Virginia City mines.

By the end of the century the character of the forest around the lake had been changed forever. Sugar pines disappeared and the finest fir, yellow pine and Jeffrey were cut, leaving many areas absent of seed stock for new pines and open to an invasion of chaparral brush. Smaller white fir, not desirable for lumber, remained. Their seedlings proliferated, growing well in shade and leading to the single species forest seen in many South Shore locations today. It is estimated that more than 60 percent of the white fir are victims of the eight-year drought from 1987 to 1994. The task facing the U.S. Forest Service and the communities of the lake is to find a way to remove the dead trees without producing scars on the land and roads that create erosion runoff that will reduce Lake Tahoe's famous water clarity.

The Railroad Center of Truckee

Truckee has known good times and hard times over the years, but because of the railroad, it has remained a center of commerce in the Sierra Nevada. In the 1870s lumbermen swarmed to the area to fell local forests to feed the steam engines of the railroad and to support the deep silver mines in Virginia City, Nevada. In winter, frozen ponds provided ice to keep fruit shipments cold on their trip to market and to cool miners in the hot tunnels of Virginia City's mines. When the hills near town were barren of trees and the silver mines played out, Truckee was in a decline. One of the town's leading citizens, C.F. McGlashan, decided to put Truckee on the map as a tourist mecca. He created an ice palace in the center of town and talked the railroad management into running excursion trains to Truckee for winter carnivals. The Dutch Flat to Donner Lake Road was taken over by the state to create a proper road for the fast growing number of automobiles. In 1928 the automobile era began in earnest when State Highway 37 was realigned and paved to create U.S. 40. This transcontinental highway brought traffic jams to Truckee's main street. The area became a stopping place but not a particularly desirable resort. Recession and war brought tough economic

Truckee Ice Palace.

Courtesy of Donner Memorial State Park

Introduction

times until the 1960 Winter Olympic Games at Squaw Valley ushered in modern ski development. When Interstate 80 was completed in 1964, traffic bypassed the town bringing peace to Downtown Truckee and to summer vacationers at Donner Lake.

Lake Tahoe Beckons Summer Visitors

Meanwhile, along Lake Tahoe's South Shore, deforested land became available for grazing or small summer settlements. While the end of the logging era depleted the permanent population of the area, the lake was being discovered as a summer tourist haven. Bliss dismantled his Glenbrook railroad operations and moved them to Tahoe City where he soon established the Lake Tahoe Railway and Transportation Company to carry passengers from the Central Pacific in Truckee to Tahoe City. He brought in *The Tahoe*, a lovely 169-foot steamship which soon became the "Queen of the Lake," carrying passengers and mail to homes and hotels along the shore. In 1900 rail service from Truckee to Tahoe brought tourists to the Tahoe Tavern, a magnificent hotel that opened in that year. The railroad connection provided yet another summer excursion possibility. Travelers could ride the train from San Francisco to Truckee then on to Tahoe City where a steamer delivered them to Glenbrook and a stagecoach bound for Carson City. Here the Virginia and Truckee Railroad offered service back to the main rail line in Reno.

With ship transportation around the lake assured, fine hostelries and more modest summer camps appeared. Rubicon Park Lodge and Lucky Baldwin's famous Tallac Hotel opened their doors to wealthier tourists. There were dance floors built over the water and casinos for evening entertainment, while boating on the lake, swimming, fishing and horseback riding were the sports of the day. Tallac Hotel was known as the "Saratoga of the Pacific." By 1927, however, Lucky Baldwin's heirs demolished the buildings, sold off the salvage and placed "Keep Out" signs on the neighboring property. Years later the land was sold to the U.S. Forest Service, along with other private lodges and buildings on nearby properties. This entire section of the South Shore between Highway 89 and the lakeshore is now the Tallac Historic Site. Just east of the historic site, Richardson's Resort at Camp Richardson continues to host visitors as it has since 1926.

Automobiles and Roads Bring a New Influx of Tourists

The advent of automobiles and paved roads to the lake brought a new wave of summer tourists. Summer cabins were built at Fallen Leaf, Angora and Echo Lakes. The developments at both Fallen Leaf and Echo Lakes were owned primarily by professors' families from both Stanford and the University of California. At Fallen Leaf, a lodge was created with rustic accommodations and a central dining hall. Now known as the Stanford Camp, it is run by the Alumni Association of Stanford University and the cabins in all these locations have been passed down to descendants of the original owners.

Early motoring at Lake Tahoe.

Winter Tourists and Gaming at the Lake

Before the Second World War, hardy skiers had been coming to Tahoe Tavern and Granlibakken Ski Area near Tahoe City to enjoy skiing with rope tows. The Sierra Club Clair Tappaan Lodge hosted skiers at the Ski School Klein, started by Bill Klein and his brother, Fred. In 1939, Sugar Bowl opened its pioneer ski resort with the area's first chair lift. After the war, Sierra Ski Ranch offered downhill skiing on the South Shore. But it was the 1960 Winter Olympic Games at Squaw Valley that ushered in ski development on a large scale. On the North Shore developers built lifts and homes in beautiful Alpine Meadows, and Northstar-at-Tahoe was built as the area's first full-service resort, complete with golf course, homes, condominiums, and recreation facilities. Heavenly Valley Ski Area became well known when its founder Chris Kuraisa invited Stein Eriksen to direct the ski school. Kuraisa also put in the area's first tram to open runs with some of the best views of Lake Tahoe. The Killebrew family bought the resort from Kuraisa and expanded it to include trails on the Nevada side of the mountain. After a few years of Japanese ownership, the resort, one of the premier ski resorts in the world, is now owned by Les Otten's American Ski Corporation.

Year-round tourism created a 1960s and 1970s building boom of condominiums and homes. Highrise casino hotels sprang up filling the skyline on the Nevada side of the South Shore. When citizens discovered degradation of Lake Tahoe's famous water clarity, they mobilized to form the League to Save Lake Tahoe. The organization has worked hard to make the Tahoe Regional Planning Agency live up to its charter to protect the environmental health of the Tahoe Basin. The South Shore grew so rapidly in the 1970s that a new California city, South Lake Tahoe, was established by the voters, and in 1993, Truckee, the oldest town in the Sierra, finally became an incorporated city with a current population nearing 12,000. The Truckee Donner Land Trust was founded in 1990 to preserve the area's historical, recreational and scenic lands. To date the group has added 131 acres to Donner Memorial State Park and preserved sections of the Emigrant Trail in Coldstream Valley.

The Tahoe Conservancy

To fund efforts needed to keep Lake Tahoe blue and clear, California voters created the Tahoe Conservancy. In 1985 the Conservancy began active operation. It has dispensed more than $100 million to acquire 5,800 acres of environmentally sensitive lands and wildlife habitat as well as to provide funding for erosion control projects to prevent further degradation of the legendary blue waters. Lands are being restored and public access to lakefront areas has been provided in 22 projects. Recognizing the need for expanded recreation opportunities in the basin, the Conservancy has helped with acquisition of rights-of-way and construction of 28 miles of hiking, biking and cross-country ski trails.

President Clinton attends Tahoe Summit

In the summer of 1997 President Clinton and Vice President Gore attended the first environmental forum for the future of Lake Tahoe. The President was very impressed with the coalition of ski resorts, conservationists, casinos, and state and local officials concerned with the lake's future. Thus the meeting ended with a precedent-setting pledge from the federal government of $50 billion in the next five years to fix drought-damaged forests and continue the efforts of the Conservancy to keep the lake's fabled blue waters clear.

Carson Pass and Hope Valley — Offering a Wilderness Experience

Carson Pass and Hope Valley have remained relatively untouched by development and, with the exception of the Kirkwood Resort just west of Caples Lake, the area is known best for its beautiful scenery, superb hiking and fishing. Two small lodges, Caples Lake Lodge and Sorensen's Resort, continue to attract overnight guests who want a quiet retreat in a wilderness setting. Kirkwood Resort has become a premier ski resort offering tennis, swimming, riding, mountain biking and hiking to a growing number of summer visitors.

Naming Lake Tahoe

Lake Tahoe was of only passing interest to early emigrants who struggled over the Sierra Nevada in the 1840s. It was first mentioned by John Charles Frémont in the report of his 1844 expedition. While struggling over Carson Pass, Frémont named the distant body of water Lake Bonpland in honor of a French botanist. Maps of the 1850s and 1860s carried the name Lake Bigler, honoring a governor of California. There were those who did not like the name, however. It seems that Governor Bigler was a sympathizer of the South in the Civil War, and Unionists did not want the lake named after him. Finally, citizens, with support from several newspaper editors, christened the lake "Tahoe," a corruption of a Washo Indian word meaning *big waters*. But, it was not until 70 years later in 1945 that the California State Legislature officially changed the name to Lake Tahoe.

Donner Lake from Donner Summit.

Natural History

Geologic History

The geologic story of California began when the sea covered the land. Three times, over eons, the mountains rose, were eroded, and sank beneath the sea. The last period of great uplift produced the Sierra Nevada we see today. The 400-mile Sierra Nevada is one of the longest single mountain ranges in the world. For this reason it is correct to use the singular *Sierra*. The southern peaks are the highest and include Mount Whitney at 14,495 feet.

The granite bedrock of the Sierra was formed when two plates of the earth's crust, an ocean plate (Pacific Plate) and a continental plate (American Plate), moved toward each other. A process called subduction began. The thin but heavy plate of ocean floor slid under the lighter, higher riding continental plate and remelted in a crustal recycling system. The resulting molten rock either rose to the surface in volcanic eruptions or cooled slowly underground into a mass, or pluton, of crystalline rock. In this way, the batholith of granite became the bedrock of the future Sierra Nevada range.

The plates of the earth's crust are never still. They continue to move up and down, slide past each other, and thrust upward as in the devastating 1994 Los Angeles earthquake. The Sierra Range is still rising, a few centimeters a year, not so that we would notice, but in mostly small quakes that only sensitive instruments can detect. Occasionally though, the earth rumbles and you can feel a quake. In 1872 a major quake produced a vertical displacement of 17 feet in the Owens Valley. The mountains of California are beautiful because of the past activity of its earthquakes.

Between 15 and 30 million years before humans settled California, a series of cataclysmic events took place. Volcanoes along the Sierra crest spewed clouds of ash and sent rivers of lava and volcanic mud across the landscape. Many of the peaks in the Truckee and Carson Pass area are remnants of those ancient volcanoes. Then a series of movements along faults uplifted the entire block of the range, creating a steep escarpment along the eastern edge. About three million years ago, a block of the earth's crust dropped down creating a deep rift where Lake Tahoe now lies. Subsequent lava flows dammed its drainage, setting the stage for filling the lake.

Starting one million years ago, the Ice Ages brought a series of glaciers to the region scooping out bowls at Donner Lake, Emerald Bay, Fallen Leaf and Cascade Lakes. These same glaciers scraped across the bedrock granite of the Desolation Wilderness, polished it smooth and left erratic boulders dotting the granitic landscape like giant bowling balls. Moraines of rock and rubble at the outermost edges of the glaciers dammed the outlet of Lake Tahoe. In one glacial period an ice dam formed at the outlet to the Truckee River, allowing the water level to rise 600 feet. The ice dam broke and a flood of water, rock and ice cascaded down the Truckee River, carving the canyon north and east toward Reno. Only 10,000 years ago, the last of the great glaciers began to melt, sending torrents of water to fill Lake Tahoe and gouge out river valleys flowing east and west from the crest. The stage was set for the arrival of the flora and fauna we see today.

Plants and Animals of the Region

The land in this region varies in elevation from about 6,000 to 10,000 feet, forcing plants and animals to survive with an average growing season between 60 and 120 days. Snow can cover the ground from early November until mid-July. At lake level the dominant tree species are white fir, Jeffrey and lodgepole pine. Between 1860 and 1900 loggers clear-cut the basin of the finest fir, yellow pine and Jeffrey pine that shared the forest with the sugar pine, a stately tree with outstretched branches holding foot-long cones. Sadly, only a few virgin stands of sugar pine remain today. Above the lake at 7,000 feet red fir trees grow forming a cathedral-like canopy that does not allow much undergrowth, making it a perfect place to hike or ski. Graceful hemlocks and western white pine grow in clusters at tree line along with lodgepole and whitebark pine. For those willing to climb, beautiful gardens of miniature alpine flowers hug the rocky terrain above 9,000 feet, turning it into a painter's palette of color during July and August. The Sierra juniper, that ancient giant that stands sentinel on windswept ridges, can be found along the Pacific Crest Trail. Summer visitors to the area will most often be greeted by fields of blue lupine near roadsides and along trails, while open meadows

sugar pine

red fir

hemlock

Introduction

glow with yellow mule ears. Wildflower lovers will find many trails into the high country where they can enjoy a multitude of colorful gardens to please the eye and thrill any photographer.

The animals who remain all year must be hardy, hibernating in winter or able to store or find food when snow covers the ground. Most-often encountered are perky chipmunks dashing across the forest floor and ground squirrels standing outside their holes ever-watchful for danger, a well as an occasional marmot or porcupine. Mule deer are everywhere in the summer, and black bears raid unprotected garbage cans. Coyotes and raccoons are frequent foragers in residential areas. They appreciate the easy dining on dog food and garbage. Very occasionally, you might be surprised by the winter visit of a bobcat. (See below) Resident ducks and Canada geese are omnipresent, while overhead, the lucky observer may spot an osprey or bald eagle. The eagles nest in some locations along the southwest shore of Lake Tahoe, while ospreys can be seen on top of pine snags along the West Shore and in Emerald Bay. The nests can be seen from some vantage points in D.L. Bliss State Park or from an Emerald Bay cruise.

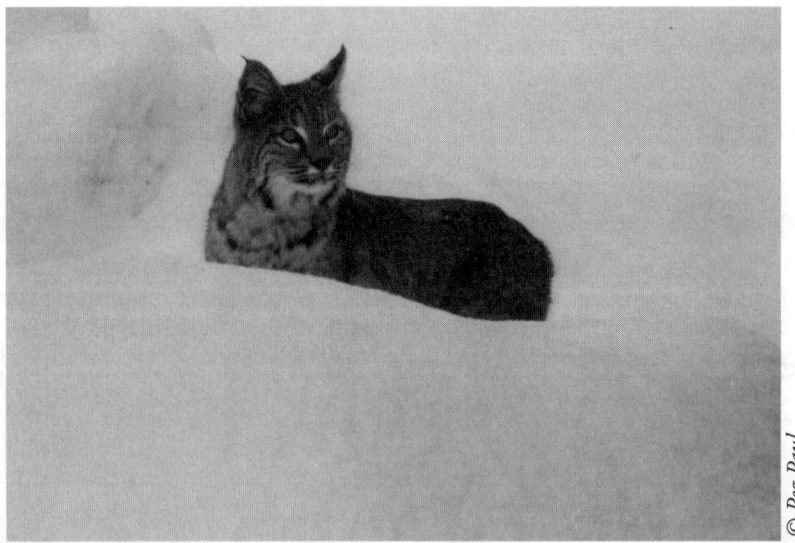

Rare winter visit of this handsome bobcat at the author's house. Notice the tufts on the ears. This is its identifying feature.

Lake Tahoe Facts

Lake Tahoe is not the highest nor is it the deepest lake in the world, but its setting, nestled in a deep valley between towering mountains, makes it one of the most beautiful. The clarity of its water is legendary, taking on the color of cobalt during summer days.

Lake Tahoe lies at 6,223 feet with one third of the lake in the state of Nevada and two thirds in California. It is 22 miles long and 12 miles wide with a maximum depth of 1,645 feet. When full it holds approximately 122 million acre feet of water, enough to cover Texas 8.5 inches deep or the state of California 14.5 inches. The Lake Tahoe Basin is roughly 480 square miles, larger than the state of Rhode Island. Average snowfall is 300 inches. With an estimated 250 sunny days per year, it is a vacation paradise.

Starting in 1986 and continuing through 1992 a drought forced the ski industry to install snowmaking, a costly endeavor for resorts that used to rely on Mother Nature for 10 to 12 feet of snow per season. Lake Tahoe fell to an historic low below the natural rim in 1991, drying up the Truckee River below Tahoe City. The winter of 1994-95, however, became one of the wettest winters in recorded history, only 1951-52 and 1982-83 being wetter. The winter of 1996-97 brought another disaster; so much rain between Christmas and early January that the Truckee River jumped its banks, flooding homes, carrying away trees, propane tanks and parts of decks and forcing evacuation of riverside residents. Donner Lake rose so high that many docks were destroyed. Roads washed out and Reno experienced the worst flood in history, closing casinos.

The snow pack and its water content are important not only to the plants and animals of the region, but as water supplies for thirsty Nevadans. A fact not usually understood is that Lake Tahoe has been dammed to raise the water level six feet above the natural rim of 6,223 feet above sea level. Water released from the dam is a primary source for residents of Reno and farmers of Fallon. In 1993 the lake spilled over the natural rim for the first time since September 1991 and regular releases followed the wet winter of 1994-95. However, the dam could not hold back enough water to prevent the floods of 1997.

Kayaking in Emerald Bay.

Prize catch, circa 1890.

Summer Activities

Lake Tahoe is world-renowned for the azure color of the water and the beauty of its setting. There are dozens of beaches for sunning and picnics. Although the average summer water temperatures seldom climb to 68°F, some beaches feature shallow water that warms enough for swimming. Lake Tahoe is a boater's paradise. You can paddle along the shore in a kayak or canoe, take a high speed run in a powerboat, sail, or enjoy a cocktail cruise on a sternwheeler to Emerald Bay.

Donner Lake near Truckee is favored for watersports and fishing. Being a smaller lake, the water temperatures can climb above 70°F.

The Carson Pass and Hope Valley area is true wilderness. Here you can hike trails to high mountain lakes and meadows where wildflowers abound or along rushing streams. The West Fork of the Carson River, Caples Lake and Blue Lakes are well-stocked with trout. For those with an interest in history, you can walk along the traces of the Emigrant Trail or stop at a Pony Express station.

Watersports are not the only Lake Tahoe attraction. Trails into the surrounding mountains take you to wildflower gardens of incredible beauty and to peaks with 360-degree views. If you seek adventure, you can take a glider ride out of the Truckee Tahoe Airport, ride high above the lake in a balloon, try parasailing or take a rock climbing class. Summer visitors will also find championship golf courses, tennis courts, and riding stables offering horseback tours into the mountains.

Simply said, there are activities to please every member of the family during the day, and music, fine dining or gambling in the evening.

Special events are held throughout the year: concerts, a Shakespeare festival, summer music at the Tallac Historic Site, art shows, boat shows and the Truckee rodeo. These are all listed in the "Special Events" section. You will want to check the free *North Tahoe Truckee Week* magazine or the entertainment sections of the *Sierra Sun, Tahoe World, The Bonanza* and the *Tahoe Daily Tribune* for exact dates and times.

Waterskier on Donner Lake.

Coming in for a safe landing with Lake Tahoe Parasailing.

Adventures

This section tells of activities for the adventurous. In a balloon, glider or airplane, you can soar above the Tahoe Basin or you might want to learn rock climbing or try scuba diving. These activities are not cheap. "Excursions" (page 38) are a more modest price.

Parasailing

700 North Lake Blvd., Tahoe City
530-583-SAIL

Lake Tahoe Parasailing will lift you high above the lake. All rides take off from the flight deck aboard their specially designed boat.

On the pier behind Safeway.
530-583-6000

Lighthouse Watersports will launch you from the flight deck at the stern of their specially designed parasail boat. You stay dry while you glide safely above the north shore of the lake.

Kings Beach State Beach
530-546-2782

Kings Beach Aqua Sports offers stay-dry flights from their parasail boat. They also have a waterski school, and while some of your party parasails, the rest of the family can enjoy the beach.

Reservations.
Incline Village
702-831-4386
After 12/15/98
775-831-4386
So. Lake Tahoe
530-544-5387

Action Water Sports of Tahoe offers parasailing adventures from two locations. You can reserve flights from either the Hyatt Beach at Incline Village or from Timber Cove Marina in South Lake Tahoe. All flights are from a boat so you won't even get your feet wet.

Summer   *31*

_____ Adventures

Reservations required.
Ski Run Marina, or Camp Richardson
530-544-PARA

South Shore Parasailing arranges lift-off and landing on the deck of specially designed parasailing boats that leave from either Richardson's or Ski Run Marina near the casinos. Early bird specials are available for those who want to fly before 10:00 a.m.

Reservations recommended.
Zephyr Cove Marina, NV
702-588-3530
After 12/15/98
775-588-3530

Captain Kirk's Beach Club will launch you off the boat or dry land to parasail high above the lake and take in the incredible views. With the many activities at Zephyr Cove, the whole family can come, rent boats or jet skis, take a cruise to Emerald Bay, or just lie on the beach and swim.

Balloon Rides

Reservations required.
530-587-6922
888-GO-ABOVE

Mountain High Balloons rise above the Truckee area providing passengers with a thrilling and memorable view. Flights lasting several hours leave early in the morning (meeting time 7:00 a.m.) and some evenings. Each ride will take two to five people. Lift-off location varies.

Reservations required.
530-544-7008

Balloons Over Lake Tahoe will pick you up anywhere in the South Lake Tahoe area and bring you to your flight that begins before sunrise and ends about four hours later with a tour over the lake. Your adventure ends with a champagne and orange juice toast along with great pastries and fruit.

Lampe Park, Gardnerville
800-386-2563

Dream Weavers Hot Air Balloon Company usually launches from Lampe Park in Gardnerville, but will consider alternative launching sights. The flight lasts about one and a half hours high above the Carson Valley.

Adventures

Reservations required.
530-544-1221
800-872-9294

Lake Tahoe Balloons' pilot and owner has 15 years experience in the business and offers flights year-round. You lift off from an aircraft carrier at Tahoe Keys and fly high above the lake with close-up views of Emerald Bay and Cascade Lake. Flights are for up to six people and last one and a half hours ending with a champagne brunch.

Glider Rides

Truckee Tahoe Airport,
Truckee
530-587-6702

Soar Truckee will take you up in a glider for a unique view of the Truckee and Tahoe Basins. Soar high above Martis Valley and view Lake Tahoe to the south.

Seaplane Tours

Reservations recommended.
Tahoe City Marina
530-583-0673
888-732-7526

Commodore Seaplanes will carry you high above the lake to various points of interest. A minimum of two persons is needed. You may also charter fishing or picnic trips.

Scenic Flights

Reservations required.
So. Lake Tahoe Airport
800-251-4748
702-588-4748
After 12/15/98
775-588-4748

Alpine Lake Aviation owner Jerry Capps operates charter flights and tours out of South Lake Tahoe Airport. You can charter a flight to anywhere or take one of two wonderful tours. He will fly up to seven passengers on a 45-minute to one-hour flight around Lake Tahoe. He tells the history, tall tales and Indian legends through individual head sets as you fly across the casino area, over Sand Harbor to the North Shore and down the West Shore to Emerald Bay and Fallen Leaf Lake before returning to the airport. A special one and one-half hour flight circles all the sights of Yosemite Valley and the high country and returns to fly around Lake Tahoe, too.

Adventures

High Country Soaring

Reservations required.
Minden, NV.
702-782-4944
After 12/15/98
775-782-4944

Seven days a week, this company will take you on scenic 45-minute rides over Heavenly Ski Resort with views of Lake Tahoe and the Carson Valley. If you are so inclined, you can ask the pilot to do a few aerobatics on the way home. They also offer rides in their two passenger gliders (you and a pilot). If you wish to learn to fly a plane or glider, the company has fully licensed instructors for all levels of flying.

Reservations required.
Truckee Tahoe Airport, Truckee
530-587-4465

Todd Aero offers scenic flights over the Lake Tahoe Basin, leaving from the Truckee-Tahoe Airport. Regular hours are Wednesday through Sunday but flights can be arranged for any day.

Rock Climbing and other Challenges

Donner Pass Rd., Donner Summit
530-426-9108

Alpine Skills International at Donner Summit offers weekend rock climbing instruction for all levels. If you want to watch a class in session, check out the cliffs along Old Highway 40 west of Donner Lake.

Squaw Valley
530-583-7673

Squaw Valley Climbing Wall is located in the cable car building and operates year-round. Here you can practice the art on this interesting wall before trying the real thing. Experienced trainers lead you through the steps. It's safety first, and all ages can participate.

Reservations required. Summer only.
Northstar-at-Tahoe
530-562-2285

Northstar-at-Tahoe offers an adventure challenge course once a week and an orienteering course five days a week. A 24-foot climbing wall is open daily with rental shoes available to those who want to try this challenge for the first time. You might even get hooked on the activity and buy your own.

Rock climbing lesson near Donner Pass.

Adventures

Bungee Jumping

Fee for cable car. No reservations needed.
High Camp, Squaw Valley
530-583-4000

Bungee Squaw Valley is right at the edge of High Camp Bath and Tennis Club. Operating all year, here's your chance to say you've done it from 8,200 feet in summer shorts or your ski clothes. They sell bumper stickers, hats, T-shirts and videos as memories of this super thrill.

All-Terrain Vehicle Rides

Reservations required.
*2286 Utah
So. Lake Tahoe*
530-541-5875

Lake Tahoe Adventures has a variety of tours from easy to challenging, rugged tours of the Rubicon Trail west of the lake. Follow your guide to an adventurous experience in the Rubicon area. Children 14 to 18 years old are welcome, but must be accompanied by a parent or guardian. Rides vary from two to three hours to half-day scenic tours or full-day rough rides. You can also take a 3-day adventure into the wilderness, crossing rivers and climbing over rocks.

Hay and Carriage Rides

Reservations required for hayrides.
530-541-2953

Borges Carriage Rides leave regularly on a first-come first-served basis from the Horizon Casino Resort. Drawn by gentle equine giants, Blond Belgians or the rarer Baskir Curleys from Russia, you will ride in style for 30 minutes down to the Edgewood Tahoe Golf Course and along the lakefront back to the Horizon.

Hayrides in the evening leave near the side entrance to Caesars Tahoe. You must have six or more people. They also offer sleigh rides in the winter. See page 213 in "Winter Adventures" for the description.

Adventures

Truckee Carriage and Coach Company

Fee per person.
Hyatt Lake Tahoe Hotel, Incline Village
Mobile phone: 530-591-3867
Truckee: 530-587-3867

In a reproduction of a French turn-of-the-century carriage, this company will take you out in the afternoon and early evening from the Hyatt Lake Tahoe Hotel and Casino. In the winter they take groups on sleigh rides at the Resort at Squaw Creek. (See page 212 in "Winter Adventures" for a description.)

Guided Hikes

Tahoe City
530-583-4506

Tahoe Trips and Trails takes groups of 10 to 16 into the Lake Tahoe area mountains on hikes for all abilities. With two guides for each trip, you can choose a faster or slower pace. Their guides have a broad knowledge of local flora, fauna and geology as well as stories of the old timers. Lunch and healthy snacks are provided. This year they have added mountain biking tours and multi sport samplers with hiking, biking, rafting, kayaking and horseback riding. August trips usually feature one night at the Shakespeare Festival at Sand Harbor, complete with pre-curtain gourmet picnic. Special family trips are listed on page 162 in "Just For Kids."

Hiking above Lake Tahoe with Tahoe Trips and Trails.

Summer

Excursions

If you have had too much sun, or the kids want a change of scenery, there are many interesting places to go for a special day-long excursion. You can visit Nevada's oldest town, go to the National Automobile Museum or visit one of the many hot springs on the east side of the Sierra. These excursions need a whole day, so pack a picnic, bathing suit, map of Nevada and pile into your car, for there are adventures over the hill. This section also lists three companies that will do the driving for you and tell you about the area's interesting history along the way.

Squaw Valley High Camp Bath and Tennis Club

Fee to ride the cable car. 10am–10pm. Squaw Valley 530-583-5585

Ride the cable car to High Camp at 8,200 feet above sea level to hike around the plateau, or, if you are feeling energetic, you can take the Pioneer Trail and climb the trail to Emigrant Pass in order to see over into the North Fork of the American River. The views of the Lake Tahoe Basin are spectacular from the decks. Restaurants at High Camp include Alexander's for a sit-down dinner, the Poolside Café and a deli. This is an excellent way for families with small children to "climb" a mountain and get the views. For those who are sports-minded, facilities include a skating rink, spa, and heated swimming lagoon, all open to the public for additional fees. The skating rink is covered and you may rent skates or bring your own for a one-hour session. This is also a great spectator sport, especially when the pro is giving a lesson to an aspiring star. You can bungee jump here too. See "Adventures" on page 36 for information.

Excursions

Ponderosa Ranch

Admission fee. Daily, Year-round 10am–6pm. Just south of Incline Village on Hwy. 28. 702-831-0691 After 12/15/98 775-831-0691

You'll step back into time when you visit the site used in the famous 1970s TV series, "Bonanza." You can search the town for memorabilia of the Old West, order barbecue food, and taste real sarsaparilla. The owners of the ranch collect all kinds of antique machinery including old steam shovels, World War II vehicles, and antique cars of every age and description. There are animals to look at and pet, and you can take a guided tour of the Cartwright's ranch house. Hayride breakfasts are held every day for only $2 above the price of admission to the park.

Grover Hot Springs State Park and Markleeville

Fee per vehicle, fee per person for use of hot spring pools. All year, but pool hours vary with season. Take Hwy. 89 south from Meyers to Hwy. 88. Drive east on Hwy. 88 to Woodfords and south on Hwy. 89 to Markleeville and follow signs to the park. 530-694-2248

Grover Hot Springs State Park is outside Markleeville on the eastern slope of the Sierra Nevada under Hawkins and Markleeville Peaks. The park is best known for two concrete pools that are fed from the runoff of six mineral springs and are regulated at 102°F to 104°F, just the right temperature to soak out tired muscles after hiking or cross-country skiing. In summer the campgrounds attract hikers and anglers who wish to climb the nearby peaks or fish in the creeks that run through the park or in the nearby Carson River. In winter cross-country skiers come to enjoy the miles of trails through the 519-acre park before a dip in the hot springs.

Families may want to visit the Alpine County Historical Complex on the knoll above Markleeville where the Webster School, built in 1882, has been restored. The Old Log Jail and a museum with rooms full of exhibits will be of interest to all in your party. Markleeville, the county seat for tiny Alpine County, has a long and colorful history.

Summer

Excursions

Historic Bowers Mansion and Hot Spring

Fee to tour mansion and use the pool.
Take U.S. 50 to U.S. 395, then north to Hwy. 429.
702-849-1825
After 12/15/98
775-849-1825

This is a nice place to spend the day with the family, to picnic on the green lawns of Bowers Mansion Park, dip in the pool and tour the mansion. The pool is kept at about 80°F with a wading pool for toddlers. The fancy mansion was built by Sandy and Eilley Bowers who made their fortunes from the Comstock mines.

Nevada State Railroad Museum

Fee to visit museum.
Wed.-Sun. all year. Train rides certain weekends Memorial Day through Labor Day, some weekends in October.
On Fairway Drive off U.S. 395, one mile south of Carson City.
702-687-6953
After 12/15/98
775-687-6953

This museum is a tribute to Nevada's Virginia and Truckee Railroad that served Virginia City in its glory days. Not far from the museum millions of logs from the mills in Glenbrook on the east shore of Lake Tahoe ended their flume ride here from Spooner Summit and were loaded onto the trains. The logs were used to shore up the tunnels of the Virginia City silver mines. Two engines and cars from the V&T have been lovingly restored by state employees. Volunteers drive a steam train and a 1920s motorcar for those who wish to step back in time on these grand machines. Times vary, so check with museum for days and hours. There is something for every train buff in the museum gift shop.

Nevada State Museum at Carson City

Admission fee.
Daily, 10am-4pm.
Take U.S. 50 to U.S. 395. to Carson City across from The Nugget casino.
702-687-4811
After 12/15/98
775-687-4811

The museum was formerly a U.S. Mint with its nineteenth-century machinery still intact. The 100-year-old coin machine stamped out 118 million quarters, dimes and pennies in its last three years of life when it was loaned to the Denver Mint to alleviate a coin shortage.

Extensive natural history dioramas let you see the animals and birds of the region in their natural habitat. Don't miss

Excursions

the skeleton of the giant mammoth that lived in Nevada only 17,000 years ago, as well as fossils of creatures from dinosaur times. The exit is through a re-created silver mine where you walk along the mine rails and stand in the cage that took miners deep into the earth.

Genoa and the Mormon Station

From South Shore take Hwy. 207 east over the pass (Kingsbury Grade) to Hwy. 206 (Foothill Rd.) and drive north 2.5 miles to Genoa. From Carson Pass take Hwy. 88 east to junction with Hwy. 206 and drive north about 12 miles to Genoa.

Genoa was the first permanent settlement in the state of Nevada. Because the site was an ideal resting place for thirsty emigrants before they tackled the Sierra Nevada, a trading post was established in 1850 by Hampton Beatie and six Mormons from Salt Lake City. The first year it was merely a log structure that was abandoned in the winter. The next summer a new Mormon proprietor built a two-story log cabin in an "L" shape that formed two sides of a five-sided stockade. This became known as Mormon Station and served weary emigrants and, later, miners on their way east to the Nevada mines.

During the 1850s Mormon Station was still a part of the Utah Territory. Brigham Young appointed Mormon apostle Orson Hyde to serve as probate judge and spiritual head of the Mormon community. Judge Hyde arrived in 1855 and named the town Genoa because the area reminded him of the mountains near Genoa, Italy.

You can wander around the now sleepy town and visit the re-created Mormon Station. Across the street is the Genoa Country Store in the rebuilt former Pony Express Station. You can buy picnic fixings or an ice cream cone, spread your blanket on the lawn or use the tables at the Mormon Station — an ideal way to stretch and relax. Across Main Street you can peek in Nevada's first bar which has hosted many gun-toting cowboys and even an outlaw or two.

Excursions

The building has been used for Hollywood films, including John Wayne's last picture. History buffs will want to visit the Courthouse Museum for the story of Carson Valley. Be sure to walk up Mill or Nixon Street to the cemetery. Here you will be able to find the grave of one of the Sierra's most colorful characters, John "Snowshoe" Thompson. On a cold winter day in January 1856, a stranger schussed down out of the mountains on 10-foot skis with a canvas sack full of mail. No resident of the town ever expected to see outsiders once the snow had fallen on the mountain passes, much less to receive mail from home via California. On that day "Snowshoe" Thompson, an immigrant from Telemark, Norway, began a 20-year career carrying the winter mail twice a month between Placerville, California, and Genoa, Nevada. It took him an average of five days to cross the Carson Pass on the general route of the Emigrant Trail, and he seldom missed a delivery. Although he was never paid by the U.S. Government for his services, he bought a homestead in Diamond Valley, near Markleeville. You can see a "Snowshoe" Thompson exhibit in the Courthouse Museum. To finish your day in great style, stop at nearby Walley's Hot Springs for a dip in one of the many pools.

Walley's Hot Springs

Twelve miles east of Lake Tahoe at the foot of Kingsbury Grade on Hwy. 206 near Genoa, NV.
702-782-8155
After 12/15/98
775-782-8155

In 1862, David and Harriet Walley built an elegant hotel and spa and offered refined accommodations for the silver barons and other society of that time. Even Mark Twain was once a guest here. A tradition of relaxed elegance brought guests a hundred years ago and continues to attract visitors today. The hot mineral spas are not the only offering, for Walley's now has a swimming pool, fitness center and tennis court as well as cottages for overnight visitors.

Excursions

Children under twelve are permitted to dip in the pools on Sunday from 10:00 a.m. to 4:00 p.m. only. You can indulge in a dip in the hot pool any time, but if you are looking for a romantic getaway in the Carson Valley at the foot of the Sierra, consider a special overnight in this oldest of Sierra resorts.

National Automobile Museum

Mon.-Sat., 9:30am-5:30pm.
Sun., 10am-4pm.
Closed Thanksgiving and Christmas days.
Corner of Lake Street South and Mill Street, Reno
702-333-9300
After 12/15/98
775-333-9300

We all have the citizens of Reno to thank for creating a foundation to keep the fabulous automobile collection of William Fisk Harrah in town after he died. Old and young, men and women, all will find something of fascination at this spit and polish museum of automobiles and related history from the 1880s to the present. You can't miss this museum on the banks of the Truckee River painted the 1957 Chevrolet color known as Heather Fire Mist — it looks like mauve to us. Four halls house beautifully displayed autos of every description, from carriages cum auto of the late 1800s to the corvette designed for John Wayne — 200 vehicles in all.

Appropriate gowns, hats and jewels worn by automobilists at the turn of the century are in cases along the walls. Walk down a 1930s street or remember the fins of the 1950s in the hall devoted to this era. Docent-led tours follow a 22-minute, high-tech, multi-media show chronicling the impact of the auto on our society. The museum store stocks a marvelous collection of auto memorabilia and the best book collection anywhere.

Excursions

Nevada Historical Society Museum in Reno

Wed.-Sun., 10am-5pm. Open all year.
In Reno at 1650 No. Virginia St. off I-80.
702-688-1190
After 12/15/98
775-688-1190

The museum has well-documented dioramas of Nevada history, including debris from the pioneer trails across the hot Nevada desert. There are wall-size maps of the emigrant routes across the state, and the bookstore sells books about Nevada's colorful history including pamphlets for rock hounds and lovers of ghost towns.

Tour Companies - South Lake Tahoe

Tahoe Tours

Reservations required.
Departures 10:30am daily from the casinos.
530-544-8687

In brand new minibuses, this company offers daily narrated tours around the rim of the lake, with plenty of stops at the best places for photographs. They also stop in Squaw Valley for a ride on the cable car to High Camp, or for shopping and lunch at the Boatworks Mall in Tahoe City, or they may stop to tour the Ehrman Mansion at Sugar Pine Point. This is any easy and relaxing way to see the best of Tahoe and let someone else do the driving.

Adventures Unlimited

Reservations required.
702-588-4772
After 12/15/98
775-588-4772

For twelve years Julie and Rick Wright have been taking people on narrated tours of many special places in the area. Their 30-passenger vans are specially equipped with televisions and headsets. There are gambling tours to the North Shore casinos, mansion tours or trips to Virginia City. In the fall you can go on an Apple Hill Winery Tour, a great way to have your own designated driver for a wine tasting adventure.

Excursions

Reservations required.
Zephyr Cove
702-588-6142
After 12/15/98
775-588-6142

Eco Adventures

Owner Bob Anderson loves to tell people about the natural and human history of the region. Scheduled tours typically include two to 13 people with an experienced guide, free transportation, lunch at one of his favorite restaurants and all admissions where applicable. One tour explores the natural history of Lake Tahoe with illuminating information about the geology, plants, animals and history. A Virginia City tour stops at Carson City's Capitol Building and the Nevada State Museum. Bob also leads rafting trips on the East Carson and Truckee Rivers, as well as guided hikes in Spooner State Park. You can even plan a private tour to any local destination.

1938 Packard 1607 Convertible Coupe featured on the 1930s period street scene in the National Automobile Museum.

Courtesy of the National Automobile Museum

Water Sports Rentals

Donner Lake

Donner Lake Village
*15695 Donner Pass Rd.
Donner Lake*
530-587-6081
Fishing Boats
Ski Doos
Pedalboats

Peddle Oar Paddle
*Donner Memorial State
Park Donner Lake*
530-747-1902
Ski Doos
Kayaks
Canoes
Pedalboats

Lake Tahoe North and West Shore

Tahoe Water Adventures
*120 Grove St.
Tahoe City*
530-583-3225
Jet Skis
Tandem Sports
Sea Doos
Ski Boats
Canoes

Lighthouse Watersports Center
*Pier behind Safeway
Tahoe City*
530-583-6000
Tandem Jet Skis
Zodiac Pro Jets
Waverunners
Fishing Boats

Tahoe Boat Company
*700 No. Lake Blvd.
Tahoe City*
530-583-5567
Ski Boats
Party Boats

Tahoe Paddle and Oar
*7860 No. Tahoe Blvd.,
Tahoe City*
530-581-3029
Canoes
Kayaks
Guided Tours

High Sierra Water Ski School
*1850 West Lake Blvd.
Tahoe City*
530-583-7417
*5190 West Lake Blvd.
Homewood*
530-525-1214
Water Skis
Power Boats
Jet Skis
Canoes
Sailboats

Kings Beach Aqua Sports
*Kings Beach Recreation Area
Kings Beach*
530-546-2782
Sailboats
Pedalboats
Kayaks
Canoes
Jet Skis

North Tahoe Marina
*7360 No. Lake Blvd.
Tahoe Vista*
530-546-4889
Power Boats
Water Skis

South Lake Tahoe, Echo Summit and Carson Pass

Fallen Leaf Marina
Fallen Leaf Lake
530-544-0787
Sailboats
Power Boats
Kayaks

Lake Tahoe Water Ski School
*Richardson's Resort
Camp Richardson*
530-544-7747
Water Skis
Power Boats
Lessons

Kayak Tahoe
*Richardson's Resort
Camp Richardson*
530-544-2011
Canoes
Kayaks

Anchorage Marina
*Camp Richardson
So. Lake Tahoe*
530-542-6570
Power Boats
Jet Skis

Water Sports Rentals

Ski Run Boat Company
Ski Run Marina
So. Lake Tahoe
530-544-0200
Fishing Boats
Jet Skis & Seadoos
Ski Boats
Pontoon Boats

Action Water Sports of Tahoe
Timber Cove Marina
So. Lake Tahoe
530-544-2942
Jet Skis
Waverunners

Tahoe Keys Rentals
Tahoe Keys Marina
So. Lake Tahoe
530-541-8405
Power Boats
Jet Skis
Windsurfers
Water Skis
Kneeboards
Innertubes

Sailboard Fantasies
Timber Cove Marina
So. Lake Tahoe
530-541-7245
Sailboats
Kayaks

Lakeside Marina
4041 Lakeshore Blvd.
So. Lake Tahoe
530-541-6626
Powerboats
Waverunners

Water Sports of Tahoe
Ski Run Marina
Ski Run Blvd.
So. Lake Tahoe
530-544-0200
Power Boats
Waverunners
Kayaks

Lakeview Sports
3131 U.S. 50
Across from El Dorado Campground
So. Lake Tahoe
530-544-7160
Jet Skis
Power Boats
Patio Boats
Windsurfers
Emerald Bay Tours

Timber Cove Marina
3411 U.S. 50
So. Lake Tahoe
530-544-2942
Jet Skis
Power Boats
Windsurfers
Sailboats
Kayaks
Catamarans

H₂O Sports
Round Hill Pines Beach
702-588-4155
After 12/15/98
775-588-4155
Sea Doos
Paddleboats
Kayaks

Zephyr Cove Marina
Zephyr Cove
702-588-3833
After 12/15/98
775-588-3833
Jet Skis
Water Skis
Power Boats
Kayaks and Canoes

Captain Kirk's Beach Club
Zephyr Cove
702-588-3530
After 12/15/98
775-588-3530
Jet Skis

Lake Tahoe Water Ski School
Camp Richardson
530-544-7747
Water Skis
Power Boats

Echo Lakes Chalet
Lower Echo Lake
530-659-7207
Fishing Boats
Canoes

Caples Lake Resort
4 miles west of Carson Pass on Hwy. 88.
209-258-8888
Power Boats
Kayaks and Canoes

Hope Valley Outdoor Center
Hwy. 88 just east of Sorensen's
530-694-2266
Kayaks with car rack

Beaches

More than thirty public beaches ring the shores of Lake Tahoe inviting you to loll on a blanket to soak up the sun, help the kids build sand castles or take long walks. Those along the North and East Shores are mostly sandy with shallow water, making them ideal choices for families. Along the West Shore most beaches tend to be rocky until you reach Meeks Bay. The beaches west of the South Tahoe *Y* are operated by the U.S. Forest Service, and some are free. These beaches can all be accessed via the bike path. The Nifty Fifty Trolley also stops at certain beaches, and the Lake Lapper stops at Camp Richardson, the U.S.F.S. Visitor Center, Emerald Bay, Meeks Bay and Sugar Pine Point, Sand Harbor, and Chimney Beach, all great beaches.

For those seeking warmer water and a more intimate view, Donner Lake west of Truckee has two beaches to offer.

Donner Lake

Donner Memorial State Park

Entrance fee per vehicle. On Donner Pass Rd. just west of the I-80 Donner State Park exit.

The beach at China Cove in the southwest corner of the park has a magnificent view of Donner Pass. Picnic tables and barbeque grills in a secluded forest setting make this an excellent choice for a day's outing that can include a visit to the museum and a walk in the woods. There is no lifeguard on duty, and this beach can be windy in the afternoon.

Beaches

Donner Lake West End Beach

Entrance fee per person.
At the west end of Donner Lake on South Shore Dr. and Donner Pass Rd.

Operated by the Truckee Donner Recreation and Parks District, the beach and lawn area has facilities for every member of the family. There is a volleyball net and one tennis court, picnic tables and barbeque grills, jungle gym and swings, horseshoe pits and pedalboats for rent. With a lifeguard on duty, this is probably one of the best choices for families with small children. An added attraction is the beautiful view of the Carson Range to the east. This is a favorite beach of locals and Nevadans, especially on weekends, so come early to find parking close to the beach.

North Shore - Tahoe City to Incline Village

Tahoe City Commons Beach

Located in the center of Tahoe City.

A playground and large grassy area complement this beach in the heart of town, a great place to spend the afternoon when you first arrive. The views are spectacular as well.

Tahoe State Recreation Area

Entrance fee per vehicle.
A half mile east of the Tahoe City Y.

The beach is open daybreak to sunset. Operated by California State Parks, it offers camping, picnic facilities, barbeques and restrooms as well as a beach with shallow water.

Beaches

Entrance fee per vehicle. Take Lake Forest Rd. off Hwy. 28 one mile east of the Tahoe City Y.

Lake Forest Beach, Skylandia Park and Beach, Pomin Beach and Lake Tahoe Public Access and Boat Launch

A wealth of beach and park possibilities are located in the Lake Forest area near Dollar Point. Some of the better-kept secrets are the trails through Skylandia Park woods. For those who want to mix boating with a day at the beach, this is a good choice.

On Hwy. 28 in Carnelian Bay.

Patton Beach

This small rocky beach has picnic facilities and barbeque grills and beautiful views of the blue waters of Carnelian and Agate Bays.

At the end of National Ave. in Tahoe Vista.

National Avenue Beach

A small grassy area for picnicking is close to the beach. It may look private, but it is open to the public free of charge.

Near Piño Grande Ave. in Tahoe Vista.

Moondunes Beach

This small sunbathing and swimming beach has shallow water suitable for small children, but there are no picnic facilities or restrooms.

Off Hwy. 28 across from Agatam St. in Tahoe Vista.

Agatam Beach

The beautiful sandy beach has shallow water that makes swimming enjoyable. With picnic tables, barbeques and restrooms, this is a great place to spend the day with a view down the lake toward South Shore. Best of all, it is free.

Beaches

End of Secline St. in Kings Beach.

Secline Beach

This small, undeveloped beach has fantastic views down the lake and it is free.

Free parking for beach access. Fees for facilities. Just west of Hwy. 267 on Hwy. 28 in Kings Beach.

North Tahoe Beach Center

The sandy beach next to the community center is open to the public free of charge. However, there are fees to use the clubhouse, sauna, showers or large hot tub and picnic facilities.

Entrance fee per vehicle. Near the intersection of Hwys. 28 and 267 in Kings Beach.

Kings Beach State Recreation Area

This state-operated, sandy beach has shallow water and views the length of the lake. There is a children's playground as well as picnic facilities, barbeques and restrooms.

At the end of Coon St., Kings Beach.

Coon Street Picnic Area and Park

A quiet beach at the end of Coon Street is next to the brand new park near the State Recreation Area parking lot. There are benches, grass and picnic facilities from which to enjoy the magnificent views down the lake while little ones play in the sand. There are restrooms.

Beaches

Incline Village Beaches

IVGID office: 893 Southwood Boulevard, Incline Village.

The beaches along Lakeshore Drive are not open to the public, but, if you are renting, you may obtain a permit from the Incline Village General Improvement District (IVGID) that operates all the recreational facilities in Incline Village. Renters must have a form signed by the owner or rental agent and pay a small fee. Passes are purchased at the IVGID office.

Lake Tahoe West Shore

William Kent Campground

On Hwy. 89 2 miles south of the Tahoe City Y.

This rocky beach is operated by the U.S. Forest Service and has picnic tables, barbeques and restrooms. It's a good sunbathing spot with expansive views across the lake to the Nevada mountains, although not necessarily a comfortable place to swim.

Sunnyside Beach

Located on the north side of Sunnyside Resort.

The pebbles on this beach are perfect for skimming across the lake. It is a good place to amuse the children before or after dining at Sunnyside Resort.

Sugar Pine Point State Park

Entrance fee per vehicle. On Hwy. 89 10 miles south of the Tahoe City Y.

The pier and boat launch are part of the original summer haven of the Ehrmans who donated their beautiful corner of Lake Tahoe to the State of California. The lawns sloping down to the water make a perfect picnic spot and it is a great destination for a boat trip or bike ride along the West Shore. After your picnic on the lawn or pier, be sure to tour the mansion.

Beaches

Meeks Bay Resort and Campground

Entrance fee per vehicle. *On Hwy. 89 11 miles south of the Tahoe City Y.*

The resort is located near a wide sandy beach with boat launching, picnic facilities and restrooms. It has been a favorite with campers for many years.

D. L. Bliss State Park

Fee per vehicle to enter park. *On Hwy. 89 10 miles north of the South Tahoe Y, 16.5 miles south of the Tahoe City Y.*

Beautiful beaches line the lakeshore just north of Rubicon Point. This is often a launching site for those with kayaks and canoes who wish to explore the coves and beaches south of the point on down to Emerald Bay. For those who tire of sitting in the sun, take the Rubicon Trail to Emerald Bay. (See page 138 in "Special Hikes" for a description.)

Emerald Bay Beach

Fee to tour Vikingsholm. *Hike one mile from the Emerald Bay Overlook parking, 9.2 miles north of South Tahoe Y.*

One mile down the trail from the overlook is a beautiful white beach. This a great place for a picnic, but don't feed the begging Canada geese or they will continue to pester you. The Vikingsholm is there to tour. With a car shuttle arranged you might want to consider hiking from Bliss Park on the Rubicon Trail to Emerald Bay, or you can come early and hike to Eagle Falls. (See page 140 in "Special Hikes.") Boaters can make an outing to Emerald Bay. The parking lots fill early here. You might want to try the Lake Lapper Bus for this outing.

Baldwin Beach

Fee per car. No dogs allowed, no lifeguard. *Off Hwy. 89 four miles north of the South Tahoe Y.*

The beach is managed by the U.S. Forest Service. With ample parking and views across the lake to Heavenly Ski Resort and a long wide beach, this is a good place to take the kids for the day. Restrooms and picnic facilities are available.

Summer

Beaches

Kiva Beach, Tallac Historic Site

No fee. No dogs allowed. *Off Hwy. 89 about 3 miles north of the South Tahoe Y.*

This long beach is seldom crowded and stretches from Richardson's Resort to the Kiva Beach Picnic Area. If you want to mix a little history with a day at the beach, park in the Kiva Beach parking lot and walk along the paths of the Tallac Historic Site before your picnic and day at the beach. This is good beach for those who prefer to bike in and stop at the Historic Site beforehand.

Camp Richardson's Resort Beach

Fee per vehicle. No dogs allowed at any time. *Located 2.6 miles north of the South Tahoe Y on Hwy. 89.*

The beach at Richardson's Resort is under concession from the U.S. Forest Service. All kinds of water-related activities are offered here, including kayak tours, parasailing, boat rentals and cruises to Emerald Bay. Guests at the resort and campground favor this beach, so it can be crowded on weekends.

Pope Beach

Fee per vehicle. No dogs allowed. *Two miles north of the South Tahoe Y off Hwy. 89.*

This is a very popular U.S. Forest Service beach. Beautiful views and a gently sloping swimming area create an ideal location for a day of sunning and swimming. Dogs are not allowed because the area is a wildlife sanctuary for nesting waterfowl. You can avoid the traffic by taking the trolley or riding bicycles here. See "Area Bus Service" on page 2 for information and phone numbers.

Thomas Reagan Memorial Beach

No dogs allowed. *Take Lakeview Dr. off U.S. 50 to Sacramento St. in So. Lake Tahoe.*

This South Lake Tahoe Recreation Department beach has a snack bar and a playground for the children. Views to the north are spectacular. The water is shallow and therefore often warm.

Beaches

No dogs allowed.
U.S. 50 between Rufus Ave. and Lakeview Dr. in So. Lake Tahoe.

El Dorado Beach

Operated by the South Lake Tahoe Recreation Department, this beach offers at least a mile of walking with views to the North Shore. This beach was affected by the drought and may be better for walking than swimming. There are picnic facilities with barbeques and restrooms.

Limited parking. No dogs allowed.
On U.S. 50 east of El Dorado Beach behind Timber Cove Lodge.

Connolly Beach

This small beach is operated by the South Lake Tahoe Recreation Department. This is a shallow beach, and due to the drought may have grass growing in the water. However, water temperatures are warm, making this a good place for toddlers. There are restrooms and picnic facilities.

Fee to park and fee per person.
About 1.5 miles north of Stateline on U.S. 50. Look for the sign.

Round Hill Pines Beach

This is a private concession beach on U.S. Forest Service land. It is great for families because of its protected location and the variety of activities available. A heated pool allows swimming even when the lake's water temperatures are cold. There are two volleyball courts as well as horseshoe pits and a tennis court that is not for a championship game but is fine for practicing. You can rent pedalboats and, for the more adventurous, a Sea Doo (jet ski for two).

A protected sun deck next to the snack bar has tables and barbeques for sandless picnics. The barbeque and beach facilities are rented to large groups throughout the summer, but the beach remains open to the public at all times.

Summer

Beaches

Nevada Beach

Fee per vehicle. Drive 1.5 miles north of Stateline on U.S. 50 to Elk Point Rd. then .8 mile west to parking.

This beautiful beach next to the campground is also for day visitors. There is a special boaters' area if you want to rent a boat at Zephyr Cove and cruise in. The views from this beach across to Mount Tallac are some of the best.

Zephyr Cove

Fee per vehicle. At Zephyr Cove 4 miles north of Stateline on U.S. 50.

There is a U.S. Forest Service beach at the cove as well as a commercial beach. Boat rentals and cruise lines that leave from the cove make this an excellent choice for families that want a variety of activities. There are restrooms, picnic facilities and barbeques along with a snack bar and a full restaurant at the Zephyr Cove Resort.

Important Note Regarding East Shore Beaches

As of the time of publication, plans are underway to restrict parking along Highway 28 between Sand Harbor and Spooner Lake. A beach shuttle service will be available to leave you at certain trailheads to the beaches described below. In order to protect the lake from erosion caused by people going cross country down to the beaches, you are requested to use designated trails.

Secret Harbor Beaches

Chemical toilets. Dogs allowed. A parking lot for the beaches is on Hwy. 28, 5 miles north of U.S. 50. Parking along the road is restricted.

Operated by the U.S. Forest Service, a series of secluded coves surrounded by shining granite boulders can be reached with a moderate hike along an access road that winds gently downhill. Take the first trail to the right to access the most northerly beach called Chimney Beach. Secret Harbor beach is in a cove is at the end of the road. Some of these beaches are preferred by nude bathers.

Beaches

Entrance fee per vehicle.
On Hwy. 28, five miles south of Incline Village or 8 miles north of U.S. 50.

Sand Harbor

This beach in the Lake Tahoe Nevada State Park has one of the most spectacular views anywhere in the Tahoe Basin. It is well worth the drive to spend a day on its long sandy beaches. There are walking paths onto rocky promontories and acres of shallow water for swimming. Facilities at the park include picnic areas, barbeques, restrooms and a boat launch at the northernmost entrance to the park. Sand Harbor is the site for Shakespeare performances in August. In midsummer the parking lots fill early.

Sand Harbor beach.

Summer

Boating

With its crystal-clear water and spectacular scenery, Lake Tahoe is a boater's paradise. Whether you want to paddle along the shore, try your hand at windsurfing, charter a boat for fishing, or explore the lakeshore with a powerboat, all is possible. There are lovely coves where you can put in to a beach for a picnic. However, storms with high winds can come up at any time and Lake Tahoe can froth up with ocean-size waves, so be sure to check the weather forecast with the launch facility before casting off on your own.

Several beaches are favorite destinations for boaters. There is a boaters' beach and campground on the north side of Emerald Bay, although many just cruise in to the sandy beaches at the west end to take a tour of Vikingsholm or have a picnic. Nevada Beach, Round Hill Pines Beach and Zephyr Cove attract boaters on the East Shore. North along the East Shore are Skunk Harbor, Secret Harbor and, of course, Sand Harbor.

Moored for the day at Skunk Harbor.

Boating

Water craft rentals of all kinds are available at many locations at Donner Lake and Lake Tahoe. See "Water Sports Rentals" on pages 46 and 47 for addresses and telephone numbers. Some public launch ramps charge only for parking. Marinas charge for use of their launch facilities. Marinas and public launch ramps at Lake Tahoe are at the following locations, listed in the following order: West Shore, Tahoe City, North Shore, along the East Shore, around the South Shore and north to Camp Richardson.

>Meeks Bay Resort: 530-525-7242
>Homewood Marina: 530-525-5966
>Obexer's in Homewood: 530-525-7962
>Sunnyside Marina at Sunnyside Resort: 530-583-7201
>Tahoe Boat Company in Tahoe City: 530-583-5567
>Lake Forest Beach Area public ramp: 530-581-4017
>Sierra Boat Company in Carnelian Bay: 530-546-2551
>North Tahoe Marina, Tahoe Vista: 530-546-8248, 546-4889
>Coon Street public launch ramp, Kings Beach: 530-546-7248
>Sand Harbor Boat Launch: 702-831-0494*
>Cave Rock on U. S. 50: 702-831-0494*
>Zephyr Cove Marina, Boat mooring only: 702-588-6644*
>Lakeside Marina, So. Lake Tahoe: 530-541-6626
>Ski Run Marina, So. Lake Tahoe: 530-544-0200
>El Dorado Boat Ramp, Hwy. 50, So. Lake Tahoe
>Timber Cove Marina, So. Lake Tahoe: 530-544-2942
>Tahoe Keys Marina, So. Lake Tahoe: 530-541-2155
>Anchorage Marina, Camp Richardson: 530-541-1777

Other locations for boating are Echo Lakes and Fallen Leaf Lake. Lower Echo Lake and Fallen Leaf Lake have boat rentals and a launch site for your own boat. Echo Lakes is particularly nice for canoes or kayaks as you can paddle from Lower Lake into Upper Echo Lake. In the Carson Pass area, boat rentals and a launch site are available at Caples Lake Resort. See Caples Lake under "Fishing" on page 74.

* **After 12/15/98 all 702 numbers will be 775.**

Boating

Donner Lake is on Donner Pass Rd. 3 miles west of Downtown Truckee.

Donner Lake

Donner Lake is a favorite place for all kinds of boating. Morning, when the lake is calm, is the perfect time to canoe or water-ski. Anglers will be found on the lake at all times of day and in all seasons. Most docks on the north shore are open to the public. See "Water Sports Rentals" on page 46 for kayaks, canoes and other craft to rent.

Fee. Open Memorial Day to Labor Day. Donner Pass Rd. at the west end of Donner Lake.

Truckee Donner Recreation and Parks Boat Launch

The Truckee Donner Recreation and Parks District operates a public boat launch on Donner Pass Road not far from the West End Beach. The lake is augmented by a dam and releases usually begin the day after Labor Day.

Take the Boca exit off I-80, drive north on Stampede Dam Rd. Prosser Creek Reservoir is on Prosser Dam Rd. off Hwy. 89 North.

Prosser Creek, Boca and Stampede Reservoirs

Water-skiing is permitted on Boca and Stampede Reservoirs. Prosser Creek Reservoir is open to sailing and fishing. Boat launching ramps are available at each lake. However, the water level drops during the summer so that some launching ramps become inaccessible.

Boating on Donner Lake.

Boating

Water Ski Schools - North Lake Tahoe

1850 West Lake Blvd., Sunnyside
530-583-7417
5190 West Lake Blvd., Homewood
530-525-1214

High Sierra Water Ski School and Sailing Center

For more than twenty years the school has been offering expert water ski instruction to all ages in their boats or your own. Satisfaction is guaranteed and some of their instructors specialize in teaching children. Their sailing school offers group or private lessons in Lasers, Hobie Cats and Coronados.

700 No. Lake Blvd. at Tahoe Boat Co. Marina.
530-583-3209

Captain Kelly's Water Ski School

You can rent your boat, skis and wet suit or take a lesson at Captain Kelly's. This ski school also offers sailing charters, guided tours for full or half-day. They even rent tubes, skurf boards and knee boards.

8194 No. Lake Blvd., Kings Beach
530-546-7412

Goldcrest Resort Water Ski School

Children as young as 4 years old have taken lessons from this school. The instructors will hold on to beginners to make sure that they get up and ski next to them if they wish. After your lessons, you can use the heated pool and jacuzzi at the resort the rest of the day, and they'll even serve you continental breakfast if you have an early lesson.

Water Ski Schools - South Lake Tahoe

Camp Richardson
530-544-7747

Lake Tahoe Water Ski School

This ski school gives lessons at two locations and will pick you up at any waterfront location upon request. They give lessons for skiers of all abilities and supply wet suits.

Summer

Boating

Tahoe Keys Marina, So. Lake Tahoe
530-544-5099

Werley's Water Ski School

Werley's offers lessons to children and beginners as well as experienced skiers who wish to learn slalom and tricks. Werley's has kneeboards and offers boat rides. All equipment is included with each lesson.

Kayaking

Kayaking has become a popular way to enjoy a quiet hour or day on the water. It is easy to learn, and once you've mastered the stroke, you can rent a kayak or get your own to glide along the shore and explore the coves and bays.

Reservations required.
Tours leave from the Regional Park just south of the Tahoe City Y in Tahoe City.
530-581-2441
800-581-2441

Tahoe Whitewater Tours

Tahoe Whitewater Tours takes up to 12 people on the tour of a lifetime. They transport you to their starting point at Eagle Point and lead you in one and two-person kayaks around Emerald Bay. You don't need to have kayaked before, as their experienced guides teach you how to paddle. Picnics are provided at the boat camp in Emerald Bay or on Fannette Island. The leaders also conduct trips for handicapped or wheelchair sports enthusiasts.

Reservations recommended.
Timber Cove Marina, So. Lake Tahoe
530-544-2011

Kayak Tahoe

No need for special experience to go out on the lake with Kayak Tahoe. The Llanoys offer special tours, give you lessons or rent kayaks. They offer Emerald Bay tours throughout the summer. In October their tours watch the kokanee salmon run at the mouth of Taylor Creek. From their Hope Valley Outdoor Center they offer kayak lessons on the East Fork of the Carson River and rent open deck kayaks for float trips on the West Fork of the Carson River.

Cruising Lake Tahoe

There is no better way to experience the beauty of the Lake Tahoe basin than to cruise to the middle of the lake or to the fabled Emerald Bay. You can pick a sailing yacht, catamaran, luxury yacht or one of three large paddlewheelers that operate from the North Shore or South Shore. All require reservations. In addition, a number of fishing charter boats offer cruises of Emerald Bay for small groups. See "Fishing Charters" on page 76 for details.

North Tahoe Cruises and Sailing Charters

Lighthouse Marina, behind Safeway, Tahoe City
530-583-0141

North Tahoe Cruises

The *Tahoe Gal*, a Mississippi paddlewheeler, cruises daily to Emerald Bay. With restaurant and bar service on board, you can sit on the deck or inside and see the beautiful homes, beaches and parks along the West Shore. The boat's captain provides commentary on Tahoe's human and natural history on the trip south. Weather permitting, they operate all year. There are daily dinner cruises, and private parties may hire the boat for a dinner-dance cruise.

May 15-Oct 15
Hyatt Regency Lake Tahoe, Incline Village.
Reservations through the Hyatt Regency Activities desk.
702-832-1234, ext. 51. After 12/15/98
775-832-1234

Tahoe Sailing Charters

Tahoe Sailing charters offers skippered sailing cruises, yacht charters, sailing lessons and even regatta racing on their 33-foot sloop *Avalanche*. Cruises last two hours and are for up to six people. If you wish you can plan a special sunset sail or Emerald Bay trip.

Cruising Lake Tahoe

Krinnit Yacht Charters

Summer only. *Hyatt Regency Lake Tahoe, Inlcine Village* Reservations through Hyatt Regency Activities Desk 702-832-1234, ext. 51. After 12/15/98 775-832-1234

You can sail on their 27-foot Catalina yacht with an experienced captain who will take up to six people for a two-hour cruise, or longer if you wish. He'll throw in private sailing instruction as well. Sailing from the Hyatt Regency Lake Tahoe pier, you'll have a chance to practice the fundamentals of sailing on the crystal blue waters of Lake Tahoe. If you are staying at the Hyatt you can charge it to your room. Light refreshments are included in the charter price.

Sierra Cloud Catamaran Cruises

Summer only. *Hyatt Regency Lake Tahoe, Incline Village* Reservations Hyatt Regency Activities Desk 702-832-1234, ext. 51. After 12/15/98 775-832-1234

Sail Lake Tahoe on a 55-foot Catamaran for up to 2 hours while the captain tells you tales of Tahoe. You'll leave the Hyatt Regency Pier either in the morning or at two times in the afternoon. You are more apt to use wind power in the afternoon. Snacks include cheese, crackers and fruit with beer, wine and sodas. If you're planning a special group party, you can order special snacks or catered meals from the Hyatt's Convention Services.

South Lake Tahoe Cruises

Tahoe Para-dice Private Charters

Summer, *Richardson's Resort.* Winter, *Tahoe Keys* 530-541-7499

The 70-foot *Tahoe Para-dice* takes up to 49 passengers every day on a cruise to Emerald Bay for a close-up view of Vikingsholm. They offer party cruises and weddings with live entertainment or a hot tub for a memorable event.

Cruising Lake Tahoe

*900 Ski Run Blvd.,
So. Lake Tahoe
530-541-3364*

Tahoe Queen

Hornblower Cruises-Lake Tahoe, operate the glass-bottomed paddlewheeler *Tahoe Queen* for year-round cruises to Emerald Bay. The crew and captain are happy to tell you tales of Tahoe legends while you watch the magnificent scenery. A richly appointed interior enhances the dining experience of a sunset dinner-dance cruise. The company operates the *Tahoe Queen* ski shuttle to Squaw Valley daily. With an all-you-can-eat breakfast in the morning and cocktails, dinner and dancing on the return trip, this is any easy way to ski the North Shore's biggest mountain and leave the driving to the ship's captain. The service starts in January, depending on snow conditions. Beginning in summer for 1998 Hornblower plans a high-speed taxi service between Ski Run Marina and Tahoe City. Now you can enjoy a water journey across the lake and take the Lake Lapper bus home for the best of both views of the magnificent scenery.

*At Zephyr Cove Marina, 4 miles north of Stateline on U.S. 50.
702-588-3508
After 12/15/98
775-588-3508*

M.S. Dixie

The original paddlewheeler company has been Cruisin' the Lake since 1949. The *M.S. Dixie II*, a newly commissioned Mississippi sternwheeler, sails to Emerald Bay year-round. With heated decks they can offer comfortable winter cruises. Their dinner-dance cruise to Emerald Bay is a favorite year-round, three and a half hours of dining with complimentary wine and dancing to tunes of Tahoe's "Phoenix." From April to November there is a champagne brunch on a 90-minute cruise to South Shore. A special two-hour dinner cruise that is just right for families and with special rates for seniors leaves daily in the summer at 5:00 p.m. Breakfast cruises to historic Glenbrook take place in the summer only.

Cruising Lake Tahoe

Woodwind Lake Tahoe

Reservations recommended. At Zephyr Cove Pier, 4 miles north of Stateline on U.S. 50 and Camp Richardson So. Lake Tahoe 702-588-3000 After 12/15/98 775-588-3000

Here is a special opportunity to feel the wind in your face sailing Lake Tahoe on a brand new 55-foot catamaran with glass-bottom views. Four times a day this sailing ship departs from Zephyr Cove with up to 50 passengers on board. A romantic sunset champagne cruise departs every evening, a special way to see the sun set behind the western mountains ringing the lake. Beverages are included in the ticket price. Special charters and weddings can be arranged. Their 30-passenger trimaran sails out of Camp Richardson on the South Shore.

The *M.S. Dixie II* in Emerald Bay.

© Ellie Huggins

Fishing

Boca, Stampede and Prosser Creek reservoirs near Truckee offer good fishing. Many streams off Highway 89 north of Truckee are also good places to cast a fly. Donner Lake's north shore docks are easily accessible and many good-sized trout have been landed from these locations. Near South Lake Tahoe you will find excellent fishing at Fallen Leaf Lake and the Echo Lakes. In the Carson Pass area, Caples Lake and the Blue Lakes are favorites. All lakes are regularly stocked with rainbow trout in summer.

Lake Tahoe is open to fishing all year. However, upstream to the first lake of any tributaries, and the banks of Lake Tahoe within 300 feet of the mouth of a tributary, are only open to anglers from July 1 to September 30. If you don't mind hiking, the lakes in Desolation Wilderness beckon with excellent fishing possibilities. Don't forget that along with your fishing license you will need a wilderness permit and your favorite mosquito repellant.

For those who want to catch one of Lake Tahoe's famous Mackinaw or kokanee salmon, there are numerous charter services and fly-fishing guides listed in the next section "Fishing Charters" on page 76.

Hardy anglers can try ice fishing at either Spooner Lake, Donner Lake, Caples Lakes or the reservoirs when they are frozen. It would be a good idea, however, to check on the condition of the ice with the local stores that sell fishing licenses.

Remember a fishing license is necessary for all anglers 16 years and older. These may be purchased at most sporting goods and hardware stores.

The daily limit for Lake Tahoe is 5 trout, but no more than 2 Mackinaw. Fishing in Lake Tahoe is legal one hour before sunrise to two hours after sunset. In all other bodies of water you may fish from one hour before sunrise to only one hour after sunset.

Fishing

Truckee Area

Donner Lake

Troll all year or ice fish for those famous Mackinaw trout when the lake is frozen. In the summer of 1991, a 29-pound Mackinaw was caught during the fishing derby held by Mountain Hardware and Sports. Bank fishing brings in rainbow and brown trout. The north shore docks and boat launch area are favorite spots for casting a line to catch the planted rainbows. Kokanee salmon are also found here.

Martis Creek Lake

Located southeast of Truckee off Hwy. 267.

This is a catch-and-release lake where the famous cutthroat trout are caught. Only barbless artificial lures or flies are allowed.

Prosser Creek Reservoir

Take Prosser Dam Rd. off Hwy. 89 North.

You can bank fish and troll for rainbow and brown trout in this local reservoir.

Waiting for the rainbows to bite.

Fishing

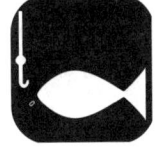

Drive 2 miles north from Boca exit off I-80 on Stampede Dam Rd.

Boca Reservoir

Both bank fishing and trolling for rainbow and brown trout are good on this local reservoir, and fly-fishing is worthwhile near the inlet of the Little Truckee River. A special wheelchair access ramp is located at the dam.

Drive north on Stampede Dam Rd. 7-8 miles from Boca exit off I-80.

Stampede Reservoir

Fish from the bank or troll here for rainbow and brown trout. This is one of the best spots for kokanee salmon. The water level is drawn down during the summer. Check with a local sporting goods store for the latest information about boat launching and fishing.

Little Truckee River between Stampede and Boca Reservoirs

Fly-fishing for both rainbow and brook trout is good in this stream below the Stampede Dam. Follow directions to Stampede Reservoir. The stream is below the dam. However, due to extremely high releases of water in 1994, the habitat in this part of the river has been changed. Check with local sporting goods stores about the status of this section of the Little Truckee.

Truckee River between Tahoe City and Truckee

In past years, the river was planted with rainbow trout below River Ranch at the entrance to Alpine Meadows. The January 1997 flood may have altered the habitat, so it is advisable to check with local sporting goods stores for current status.

Fishing

Truckee River between Truckee and Nevada State Line

Accessed from Glenshire Dr. and Hirschdale Rd. east of Truckee.

This is a wild trout river. No live bait or barbed hooks are allowed and there are size limits. A two-mile stretch of the river is marked private and is off-limits. A Truckee River Access Map is available at most stores that sell bait and equipment.

Sagehen Creek

Take Hwy. 89 North 7.5 mi. from the I-80 Sierraville exit.

Sagehen Creek is catch and release only and is a favorite for fly-fishing. The wildflowers are spectacular on the trails along the creek, which makes this an excellent place to take a companion who may not want to fish.

Lake Tahoe Area

Lake Tahoe Bank Fishing

You can find rainbow trout along the North Shore at Dollar Point, Crystal Bay Point, or along the West Shore south of Tahoe City. Sand Harbor and Cave Rock are listed separately below. The tributaries into the lake are closed to fishing except for certain months in the summer. Be sure to check with the stores that sell licenses to find out the dates and which streams are open.

Fallen Leaf Lake

Drive south on Fallen Leaf Rd. from Hwy. 89 to Fallen Leaf Lodge.

This beautiful alpine lake, created by a glacier that scooped out a long bowl, is deep enough for Mackinaw. You will need a boat and spinners to reel in this trophy fish. Otherwise, try using worms from the bank near the lodge for rainbow trout. The lodge has boats for rent and a launch ramp open to the public.

Fishing

Park at U.S. Forest Service Interpretive Center 3.2 miles from the South Tahoe Y or at Cathedral Rd.

Taylor Creek

Taylor Creek drains Fallen Leaf Lake and is a principal spawning stream for the kokanee salmon of Lake Tahoe. An autumn tour to the Stream Profile Chamber on the short nature trail from the Visitor Center allows you to see the kokanee salmon spawning. The rest of the year you will have a chance to view underwater life in the stream.

The fishing season starts July 1 here and you will need worms, eggs or flies to catch the resident brown and rainbow trout.

Hike along Trout Creek or the Upper Truckee River from U.S. 50 between Al Tahoe Blvd. and Tahoe Keys Blvd. in So. Lake Tahoe.

Trout Creek and the Upper Truckee River

Fishing season starts on July 1 on these tributaries into Lake Tahoe where only native fish are found. Hike along the stream and bring your fly rod or regular tackle with small spinners, salmon eggs or worms. However, when the runoff is flowing fast, you will need some skill to land these wary trout.

Fee per vehicle. Drive north from Stateline 6 miles on U.S. 50 to the Cave Rock Boat Launch parking area.

Cave Rock

The boat launch and small cove beach to the south are operated by the Nevada State Parks Department. The rocks along the shore are a favorite place for catching the lake's rainbow or brown trout. Bring spinners, worms, salmon eggs or even marshmallows for bait.

 _____ **Fishing**

On Lake Tahoe Blvd. 1 mile south of Hwy. 50 intersection. 530-573-2600

Sawmill Pond

The pond is operated by the U.S. Forest Service for anglers 15 years old and under, although adults may help children fish.

Fee per vehicle. In Lake Tahoe Nevada State Park on Hwy. 28 just north of the U.S. 50.

Spooner Lake

Spooner Lake is the only catch-and-release lake in Nevada. The lake was drawn down during the winter of 1996 and at the time of writing it was not yet restocked. Check with Nevada State Parks or local sporting goods stores about the status of fishing at the lake.

Fee per vehicle. On Hwy. 28, about 8 miles north of U.S. 50 and 5 miles south of Incline Village.

Sand Harbor

There is no more beautiful place at Lake Tahoe to sit on the shore and cast for the trout that inhabit the waters around the rocky shoreline here. You'll be able to catch rainbow and brown trout, and, if not all members of the family want to fish, the rest can enjoy the beach and swimming.

Drive 9 miles west on U.S. 50 from the South Tahoe Y to Echo Lake Rd. Drive north to the Sno-Park and turn left following signs to Echo Lake. Park only where allowed.

Echo Lakes

The Echo Lakes have long been favorite fishing lakes. The homeowners here help the California Fish and Game Department distribute the plants of catchable trout. Favorite shore fishing spots are near the dam and along the north shore of Lower Echo Lake. Rainbows, brook trout and an occasional kokanee salmon can be caught on lures, salmon eggs and power bait. Fly-fishing is also popular here. The Echo Chalet rents fishing boats and canoes. Since water-skiing is not allowed on Upper Echo Lake, trolling is especially good there.

Fishing

Memorial Day to Labor Day.
1023 Blue Lake Ave., So. Lake Tahoe
530-541-1491

Tahoe Trout Farm

Here's a chance for everyone in the family to catch the limit. However, you will need to have a large group over for dinner if you do. Admission, bait and tackle are free. You only pay for your catch.

Carson Pass Area

Anyone willing to hike several miles can reach scores of back country lakes from the Carson Pass area. All you need is one of the excellent hiking guidebooks of the region for descriptions of the trails to alpine lakes that are regularly stocked. A few easy ones are in the "Special Hikes" section starting on page 158. Suggestions follow for places that you can reach by car.

The Carson River

The Carson River meanders through Hope, Faith and Charity Valleys and can be reached easily at Picketts Junction or from Hope Valley Campground on Blue Lakes Road. Anglers have been known to catch cutthroats right off the bridge at Picketts Junction, or you can try your favorite fly or bait anywhere you can get to the bank. The river is stocked with rainbow. Below Picketts Junction the river runs swiftly downhill. The best access points are at the various U.S. Forest Service Campgrounds east of Sorensen's Resort. If you want to take lessons from the best, stop at Sorensen's and sign up with Horse Feathers Fly-Fishing School who will guide you into the back country or take you on foot to nearby lakes.

Fishing

Accessed off Hwy. 88 or Blue Lakes Rd. at Hope Valley. Drive south about 10 miles to Lower Blue Lake Campground.

Blue Lakes

The Upper and Lower Blue Lakes can be reached easily with any automobile. However, to reach other lakes in the region, you will want a four-wheel-drive vehicle. The lakes offer some of the best fishing in the region and are stocked with rainbow. Power bait, worms or your favorite fly will probably catch the daily limit.

Four miles west of Carson Pass on Hwy. 88. 209-258-8888

Caples Lake

Caples Lake is inhabited by six species of trout: Mackinaw, brown, rainbow, cutthroat, eastern brook and cutbow. Boat rentals are available at the Caples Resort Marina. You will want to take a boat onto the lake for those feisty Mackinaw, but casting a line from the bank can bring in many of the other species. The lodge offers boat rides to the far shores for those who want to hike into back country lakes or streams for rainbow or brown trout. Anglers may want to bring along a companion, for this is spectacular country for gazers, photographers or flower lovers to spend a quiet day while others are fishing.

North of Hwy. 88 below Caples Lake. Parking at Kirkwood Inn.

Caples Creek

Many branches of Caples Creek can be reached from the trail to Lake Margaret. Fly-fishing along the creek will bring in rainbow or brown trout while non-fishing companions can enjoy a day on the banks of this creek as it winds its way through forest and meadow.

Early morning on Donner Lake.

Summer

Fishing Charters

Trolling for Mackinaw trout and kokanee salmon that live deep in Lake Tahoe, casting for wild trout or learning techniques to fish in local creeks and alpine lakes are best done with a local guide. This section lists the Lake Tahoe and Donner Lake charter services and fly-fishing guides. Most boat trips start either before dawn or late in the afternoon. All charter companies supply tackle, and one-day licences, if necessary. Some also provide sightseeing tours as well. The fly-fishing guides offer half-day, all-day or longer trips to special lakes and streams. Two schools of fly-fishing are also listed. Reservations are necessary.

Fishing Lake Tahoe with Kingfish.

Fishing Charters

Truckee - North Lake Tahoe

Truckee
530-587-9302
800-354-0958

Clearwater Guides

Chris Turner will take you out on Donner Lake, Stampede Reservoir or Lake Tahoe to find trophy-size browns, kokanee or Mackinaw. Groups of one to six persons can choose between 4 and 7-hour trips on Donner Lake and Stampede Reservoir. He leaves from the North Shore for 4 and 5-hour trips on Lake Tahoe. The boat has state-of-the-art electronics and they provide all the tackle and one-day licenses.

Tahoma
530-525-6575

Johnson Tackle and Guide Service

This service offers fly-fishing lessons and guided trips to local lakes and streams including longer trips into the back country.

*Homewood
next to West
Shore Café.*
530-525-5360

Kingfish

The *Kingfish* is a 43-foot boat specially designed and built for Lake Tahoe. This charter service operates all year. Trips leave early in the morning with snacks, coffee and cold drinks provided, and they'll even clean the fish for you. Daily tours to Emerald Bay are offered in the afternoons.

Tahoe City
530-581-0924

Reel Deal Sportfishing and Lake Tours

Fish year-round with Captain Big Pete on his comfortable cabin cruiser with fully loaded galley. He supplies all tackle. You can also arrange a tour of the lake.

Fishing Charters

Sierra Boat Company, Carnelian Bay
530-546-5444

Mickey's Big Mack Charters

Mickey operates 48-foot and 32-foot boats out of Sierra Boat Company in Carnelian Bay. His 30 years of experience assures that he will find the fish. You can select a full trip and take four people for the price of three. All you need is a fishing license and your own food and drink.

Next to Roundhouse Mall, Tahoe City
530-587-6027

Reel Magic Sport Fishing

Early morning sportfishing trips leave daily. Bring your own food and drink.

North Tahoe Marina, Tahoe Vista
530-546-2500

Mac-A-Tac Fishing Charters

Mac-A-Tac specializes in groups of three to six people. Charters leave early in the morning or late afternoon. Sightseeing charters are also available. Bring your own food and drink.

South Lake Tahoe

Anchorage Marina at Camp Richardson.
530-577-6834

Dennis' Eagle Point Fishing Charter

Dennis Mitchell has a special offer to make. He'll take you out morning or afternoon and, if you catch the biggest fish for the week, he'll take you out free the next time. Charters go any month of the year, so bundle up and try fishing one day of your ski vacation.

Tahoe Paradise
530-577-2246

Captain Bruce Hernandez Guide Service

Bruce Hernandez offers his expert guide service to take you on the lake and catch the big ones. He supplies all tackle and bait aboard his 25-foot Taira Cutty.

Fishing Charters

Ski Run Marina, So. Lake Tahoe
530-541-5448
530-577-4147

Tahoe Sports Fishing

Captain Dean and Captain John have seven boats from 26-foot to 34-foot and over 29 years experience. They offer half-day or all-day trips and furnish all the gear.

Tahoe Keys Marina
530-541-1806

Blue Ribbon Fishing Charters

Owner John Hinson has been fishing the lake since 1969. He will take you out for Mackinaw and kokanee and supply all the tackle and your license.

Round Hill Pines Beach Marina.
702-588-4916
After 12/15/98
775-588-4916

Don's Fishing Charters

Catch your fish from the comfort of the 30-foot luxury sport fishing yacht *Cherie D* with all tackle and bait provided.

Zephyr Cove, 4 miles north of Stateline on Hwy. 50.
702-588-4102
After 12/15/98
775-588-4102

O'Malley's Fishing Charters

O'Malley offers private charters with all tackle provided. His 22-foot Radon craft has all the latest equipment to help you find the big ones.

Zephyr Cove Marina, 4 miles north of Stateline on Hwy. 50.
702-588-4665
530-577-5065
After 12/15/98
775-588-4665

First Strike Sport Fishing

You can take a charter for a day on the lake, or fish for kokanee, Mackinaw, rainbow or brown. All tackle is provided. They also offer vacation packages for several days of fishing.

Summer

Fly-Fishing Guides

If you want to learn more about fly-fishing from the experts or want a guide to help you find golden trout in an alpine lake, there are experienced guides to take you to their special places for wild trout or teach you new skills.

Truckee - North Lake Tahoe

Truckee
530-587-7333

Thy Rod and Staff

Frank Pisciotta, a licensed guide endorsed by Orvis, teaches catch and release with barbless hooks. He specializes in finding the rare wild trout in the area. He'll take you and the kids to those special creeks where you can try your new art and probably catch a few. Nothing comes home for dinner however. He teaches in the best tradition of Norman McClean from *A River Runs Through It*.

Truckee
530-587-7005

California School of Flyfishing

Ralph and Lisa Cutter's California School of Flyfishing has been honored by *Rod and Reel* magazine. Together they published *Sierra Trout Guide*, a best-selling guide to fishing in the Sierra. Operating since 1981 out of Truckee, Lisa takes novices and experienced alike to the Truckee River, Martis Lake and other North Sierra waters. Your day with her includes instruction in the skills of flycasting, mastering knots and reading the water.

Homewood
530-525-9101

Riffleworks

Tim O'Connor has 20 years of fly-fishing experience to share with anglers of all levels. He gives a special two-day beginner clinic in the Truckee-Tahoe area at Martis Creek Lake or the Truckee River. He also leads trips to the Central Valley.

Fly-Fishing Guides

Tahoma
530-525-6575

Johnson Guide Service

This service operating on the West Shore of Lake Tahoe offers fly-fishing lessons and guided trips to local lakes and streams. You can also arrange an overnight into the back country.

South Lake Tahoe

So. Lake Tahoe
530-541-3254

A-Action High Sierra Fishing Adventures

Captain George has over 30 years experience and will take you out for a five-hour guided fishing tour. All bait and tackle is provided.

So. Lake Tahoe
530-542-0759

Alpine Fly-Fishing Service

Jim guides to lakes in the Carson Pass or to alpine fishing country as far south as Mono County. He is experienced in finding the best places to cast your fly.

Fee per hour for lesson.

At Sorensen's Resort just east of the junction of Hwy. 88 and Hwy. 89.
530-694-2399

Horse Feathers Fly-Fishing School

Judy Warren will be your instructor for an "Introduction to Fly-Fishing." The class deals with casting, short line fly presentation, fly selection, reading water, knot tying, streamside entomology, equipment selection and stress reduction/relaxation. The hours are flexible, and tackle can be provided. She also conducts classes in fly tying. Try this and you may be hooked for life. Horse Feathers can also guide you to back country lakes in the Carson Pass region.

Fly-Fishing Guides

Reservations required.
Zephyr Cove
702-588-3310
After 12/15/98
775-588-3310

Trout Creek Flies and Tackle

With 20 years experience fly-fishing in the area, Geoff Beer has opened his shop Trout Creek Flies and Tackle where you can get advice and purchase everything needed to try your hand in local streams and lakes. Newly added are Sunday introductory classes and special guided trips to areas near Markleeville in Alpine County. He also offers clinics through Kirkwood Resort, so check the homeowners newsletters for dates.

Reservations required.
P.O. Box 7003, Stateline, NV 89449
702-588-3186
After 12/15/98
775-588-3186

Smiling Trout

Ralph Gooch will take one, two and three people out to local lakes and rivers for fly or spin-fishing. His trips go as far away as Pyramid Lake in Nevada, which he says is great during the winter. He teaches the art of fly-fishing as well as fly tying and prefers to do catch and release trips.

Lisa Cutter showing her catch before release.

Rafting

Rafting on the Truckee River

Mountain Air Sports
530-583-RAFT

Truckee River Raft Rentals
530-583-0123

Fanny Bridge Raft Rentals
530-583-3021

Three companies offer self-guided family raft trips on the Truckee River between Tahoe City and River Ranch at Alpine Meadows Rd. These trips are a safe, leisurely, float on the river for about four miles downstream. Bring bathing suit, hat and plenty of sun screen, and if you must stop along the way, please use the restrooms provided by the companies and respect the private property along the river. The companies provide return buses to Tahoe City after you disembark.

Tahoe Whitewater Tours

Information and reservations:
530-581-2441

Leaving in vans from Tahoe City at 8:00 a.m., this group takes you on one-day rafting trips on the South Fork of the American River or the East Fork of the Carson River. Both are considered beginner runs, but the American River will provide more thrills. New this season is a challenging ride on the Truckee River from Boca to Floristan. This group also offers Emerald Bay kayak tours. See "Boating" on page 62 for a complete description. The owner of Tahoe Whitewater Tours is an experienced guide for handicapped or wheelchair sports enthusiasts.

Tahoe Whitewater guide, Dan Zemple, with boy scouts on the Truckee River.

Bicycle Rentals

Truckee and North Lake Tahoe

Porter's Ski and Sport
Crossroads Shopping Center
Truckee
530-587-1500
Mountain Bikes
Roller Blades

Daves Summer Sports
10200 Donner Pass Rd.
Truckee
530-582-0900
Mountain Bikes
Roller Blades
Kids' Bikes

Paco's Truckee River Bicycle
Gateway Shopping Center
Truckee
530-587-5561
Mountain Bikes

Truckee Bike Works
11400 Donner Pass Road
Truckee
530-587-3933
Mountain Bikes
Kids' Bikes
Tandems

Squaw Valley Sport Shop
Squaw Valley
530-583-3356
Mountain Bikes

Porter's Tahoe City
501 No. Lake Blvd.
Tahoe City
530-583-2314
Mountain Bikes
Roller Blades

T.S.R. Bike Rentals
At Fanny Bridge
Tahoe City
530-583-0123
Mountain Bikes
Kids' Bikes

Cyclepaths Mountain Bike
1785 West Lake Blvd.
Tahoe City
530-581-1171
Mountain Bikes
Tandems
Tours

Tahoe Gear
5095 West Lake Blvd.
Homewood
530-525-5233
Mountain Bikes

West Side Sports
5395 West Lake Blvd.
Homewood
530-525-0310
Mountain Bikes
Kids' Bikes
Tandems
Roller Blades

Olympic Bike Shop
620 No. Lake Blvd.
Tahoe City
530-581-2500
Mountain Bikes
Tandems

Northstar Mountain Bike
Northstar-at-Tahoe Resort
530-562-2248
Mountain Bikes
Kids' Mountain Bikes

Tahoe Bike and Ski
8600 No. Lake Blvd.
Kings Beach
530-546-7437
Mountain Bikes
Road Bikes
Tandems

Mountain Cyclery
Behind the Naughty Dawg off No. Lake Blvd.
Tahoe City
530-581-5861
8299 No. Lake Blvd.
Kings Beach
530-546-3535
Mountain Bikes
Kiddie Carts
Helmets
Tours

Bicycle Rentals

South Lake Tahoe

Anderson's Bicycle Rental
645 Emerald Bay Rd. near the South Tahoe Y
530-541-0500
Mountain Bikes
Kids' Bikes
Tandems
Kiddie Carts

Richardson's Bicycle Rentals
*Richardson's Resort on Hwy. 89
Camp Richardson*
530-542-6584
Mountain Bikes
Kiddie Carts
Cycle Surreys
Tandems
Roller Blades

Don Cheepo's Adventures
*3349 Hwy. 50
So. Lake Tahoe*
530-544-0356
Mountain Bikes
Kids' Bikes
Tandems

Country Scooters
*800 Emerald Bay Rd.
So. Lake Tahoe*
530-544-3500
Mountain Bikes
Scooters
Tandems
Kids' Bikes
Roller Blades

Sierra Cycle Works
*3430 Hwy. 50
So. Lake Tahoe*
530-541-7505
Mountain Bikes

Tahoe Bike Shop
*2277 Lake Tahoe Blvd.
So. Lake Tahoe*
530-544-8060
Mountain Bikes

Tahoe Sports Ltd.
*South Y Center,
Crescent V Center
So. Lake Tahoe*
530-544-2284
Mountain Bikes

Lakeview Sports
*3131 Hwy. 50
"On the Beach"
So. Lake Tahoe*
530-544-7160
Mountain Bikes
Tandems
Kids' Bikes
Cycle Surreys
Beach Cruisers
Road Bikes
Roller Blades

Precision Bicycle and Rollerblade Rentals
*1111 Ski Run Blvd.
So. Lake Tahoe*
530-542-BIKE
Mountain Bikes
Kids' Bikes
Tandems
Roller Blades

Summer

Bicycling

North Tahoe and Truckee

U.S. Forest Service, Truckee area headquarters are at the northwest corner of I-80 and Hwy. 89 North.

There are marked bicycle paths in several locations in the North Tahoe-Truckee area, and the Tahoe National Forest is a mountain biker's dream. U.S. Forest Service roads abound in almost every wilderness area. A Tahoe National Forest map is for sale at the Truckee U.S. Forest Service headquarters. The map shows all the roads in the Tahoe National Forest. Mountain bikes are not allowed on the Pacific Crest Trail or into Desolation Wilderness. The area around Boca, Prosser Creek and Stampede Reservoirs offers challenging day-long rides on good dirt roads with many lovely spots for picnics.

Bicycle Paths

Donner Lake and Donner Memorial State Park

There are 3 miles of flat roads in Donner Memorial State Park. If you wish to extend your ride to circle the lake, a distance of 6 miles, ride west from the park entrance on Donner Pass Road to the west end of the lake. Turn south on South Shore Drive and continue to the end of the road. A trail enters the park here and joins park roads at the beach. Ride north along the road which will bring you back to the park entrance.

Truckee to Squaw Valley

Cyclists from Truckee will find a marked bicycle route on Highway 89 between Interstate 80 in Truckee and Squaw Valley, a distance of 8.4 miles. A bike path that parallels the Squaw Valley meadow and golf course begins one mile up Squaw Valley Road. Once there you can ride the cable

Bicycling

car to High Camp and zoom down one of the trails in the mountain bike park. The views are spectacular. See the description of the park on page 94.

Tahoe City to Alpine Meadows

This trail is easily accessed from the Truckee River Public Access Trailhead just south of the Tahoe City *Y*. A bridge over the Truckee River leads to an easy 4-mile ride to River Ranch where you can stop for lunch on the patio, or take a picnic for any good riverside spot along the way.

West Shore Bike Path from the Tahoe City *Y* to Sugar Pine Point State Park

This trail is also accessed from the Trailhead above and follows Highway 89 South along the West Shore. It is easily broken up into sections with picnicking or dining opportunities along the way. From the *Y* to Sunnyside makes an excellent lunch or brunch ride, or you can go farther south to Kaspian Picnic Area, where the beach or U.S. Forest Service Campground offers good picnic sites. From Tahoe City to Sugar Pine Point State Park and back is an all-day ride. If you start at Kilner Park partway down, this is excellent family ride. Note: The bicycle path crosses Highway 89 several times, and riders must stop and walk across each intersection with care.

Tahoe City to Dollar Point

The trail is along the south side of Highway 28 between Tahoe City and Dollar Point. It is not necessarily a good trail for an outing because of the traffic on the highway.

Bicycling

North Tahoe Regional Park in Tahoe Vista

A marked trail goes steeply up National Avenue to Pinedrop Street and into the park where there are miles of mountain biking trails to explore.

Lakeshore Boulevard in Incline Village

This trail runs from one end of Lakeshore Boulevard to the other, offering great views of the million-dollar real estate along the way. The trail is used by walkers and runners, so ride carefully.

Bicycle Paths and Routes - South Lake Tahoe

The city of South Lake Tahoe maintains a nearly flat 14.4-mile bike trail system. The trail starts in the Stateline area (see map) where it meanders through the town on separate paths and bike routes by the side of the road. One mile north of the South Tahoe *Y* next to Highway 89 (Emerald Bay Road) the Pope-Baldwin Bike Path will take you to Spring Creek Road with access to the beaches from Pope to Baldwin, as well as the Tallac Historic Site and the U.S. Forest Service Visitor Center. Another bike trail is on the south side of U.S. 50 between Meyers and Pioneer Trail which allows access to Upper Truckee Road in Lake Valley. Mountain bike enthusiasts will find much challenging terrain in the area, and expert riders who really want to be tested can try the Flume Trail from Spooner Lake. Wherever you ride, it's smart and safe always to wear a helmet.

Bicycling

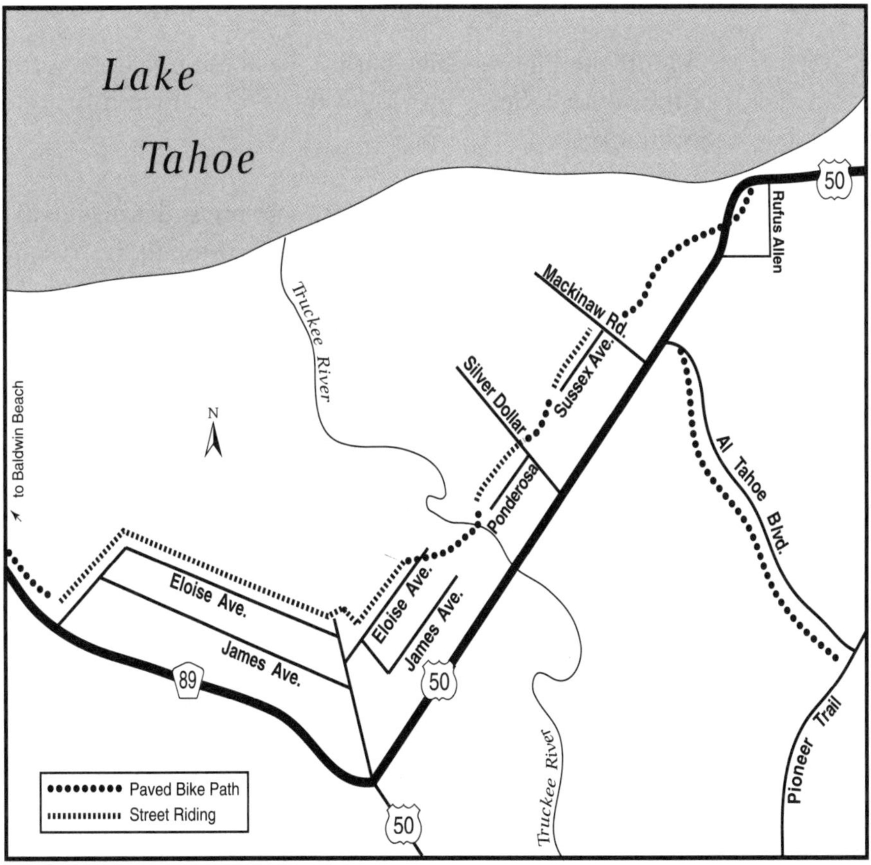

South Lake Tahoe bicycle paths and routes.

Bicycling

The following descriptions are for paved trails. All are suitable for families who want to rent bicycles and ride around town or to the beach.

Pope-Baldwin Bike Path

This off-the-highway bike path starts about one mile north of the South Tahoe *Y* on Highway 89. Easy. Four miles to Spring Creek.

The U.S. Forest Service maintains an almost flat bike path that is parallel to Highway 89. It winds through the forest to connect with roads or trails down to the beaches. You can also use your bike in the Tallac Historic Site to visit the various buildings. This is the perfect trail for families who want to bike to the beach for a day, or try a longer trip to the U.S. Forest Service Visitor Center.

Pioneer Trail to Highway 89

A paved trail on the east side of Highway 50 between Pioneer Trail and Highway 89. A bike lane is provided along Al Tahoe Boulevard and Pioneer Trail. It is possible to ride the several miles from Heavenly all the way to Highway 89 on either a bike lane or paved trail.

Upper Truckee Road

Upper Truckee Road intersects U.S. 50 one-half mile west of Highway 89. Easy. Three miles each way.

Upper Truckee Road wanders south through a quiet subdivision for two miles on a flat road, crossing the Upper Truckee River several times. This historical bike tour passes the Celio Ranch, located partway up the road.

Bicycling

The Celio family has been here since the 1860s. The property is marked with a bronze plaque on the right side of the road. The story of the family is recounted on page 269 in "Museums." If you park near the third crossing of the river, you can take a picnic and find a spot by the river to rest before returning to your car. A longer trip could include the bike trail from Pioneer Trail to Myers.

Father and child along the Pope-Baldwin bike path.

Bicycling

Mountain Bike Parks - Yuba Gap Highway 80

Eagle Mountain Bike Resort

One mile off I-80 at the Yuba Gap exit.
530-389-2254
800-391-2254

Eagle Mountain Cross-Country Ski Area is converted to a mountain bike park with 400 miles of bike trails. During the week they are mostly open for organized groups or private parties. Individuals may use the park weekends and holidays, but you may want to call ahead for a schedule of their many specialized races and events.

Mountain Bike Parks - North Lake Tahoe

Northstar-at-Tahoe

Fee for lifts. Off Hwy. 267 about 6 miles south of Truckee.
530-562-2248

This resort offers challenging mountain bike routes on Mount Pluto. You can ride two of the ski area lifts with your bike to access miles of trails of all levels. Clinics are offered each morning for those interested in perfecting their mountain climbing techniques. The resort also hosts races during the season.

Squaw Valley Mountain Bike Park

Fee for cable car. Squaw Valley 24-hour information
530-583-6955

An extensive park has single track and roads for an exciting biking experience and fabulous views of Lake Tahoe. You can start below and huff and puff to the top, or ride the cable car for a thrilling downhill adventure. There are trails for all abilities, with 15 percent that are suitable for beginners, and you can purchase a swim with your tram ticket and enjoy biking the upper mountain before plunging in the pool to cool off. When new ski lifts are under construction, some access roads may be closed to bikers.

Bicycling

Lakeview Mountain Bike Park

From the Tahoe City Y drive north on Hwy. 28 to Fabian Way. Turn left, follow signs via Village Rd. and Country Club Dr.

Most of the trail system of the Lakeview Cross-Country Ski Area is open and perfect for mountain bike experiences for all abilities. The Fiberboard Freeway, the route for the Great Cross-Country Ski Race allows a full day ride to Truckee and back. If you are not up to the return trip, arrange a car shuttle at either end. In Truckee the road takes off from Thelin Drive.

Mountain Bike Parks - Carson Pass

Kirkwood Resort

At Kirkwood Resort 6 miles west of Carson Pass on Hwy. 88. Rentals and tickets at the Kirkwood Adventure Center in the Red Cliffs Lodge. 209-258-7283

Two chair lifts access many trails for all abilities that lead to the top of the park. Trails then descend to the base facilities, with unsurpassed views of the mountain scenery and many places to stop for a picnic or looking at the wildflower display. Lessons and guided tours are available with advance reservations. For more adventurous riders the Adventure Center staff will supply you with maps to the many bike trails in the Carson Pass area.

Summer

Bicycling

Mountain Bike Roads

Prosser Creek, Stampede and Boca Reservoir Tour.
Moderate. Twenty-seven miles with minimal elevation gain.

Drive north on Highway 89 to Prosser Dam Road and turn right. Drive three miles across Prosser Dam and park at the intersection of Dog Valley Rd. and Boca Rd.

A good dirt road leads north to Stampede Reservoir with eight miles of good dirt road riding. The scenery alternates between deep woods and open sagebrush meadows. The generally rolling terrain is interrupted by only one climb of any consequence. Stampede Reservoir is about halfway through the ride and a good place to stop for lunch. There are picnic sites and a vista point alongside the roadway over Stampede's spillway. The road surface reverts to asphalt at Stampede, and once you've crossed the dam and climbed a short steep grade, the road turns to the south and heads for Boca. Nearing Boca, there is a final, relatively flat section which crosses through great open meadows and offers huge panoramic views of the surrounding peaks. At Boca Reservoir Dam, the route back to Prosser is clearly marked.

Commemorative Overland Emigrant Trail
For experienced, single track riders. Twelve miles each way.

At the I-80 Boca Exit drive 8 miles on Stampede Dam Rd. to Dog Valley Rd. across the dam. Parking is at the end of the pavement. Donner Camp is 3 miles north of I-80 on Hwy. 89 North.

A new single track trail traverses the meadows and forest between Stampede Reservoir and the Donner Camp on Highway 89 North. The well-marked trail begins just near the end of the pavement southwest of Logger campground. You will cross old logging roads many times and must ford Prosser Creek before reaching Donner Camp.

Bicycling

Mountain Bike Roads - South Lake Tahoe

It would be impossible to write about the plethora of places where dedicated mountain bikers can find thrills. However, we have chosen a ride at Spooner Lake and a ride in Hope Valley on moderately hilly terrain with spectacular scenery along the way. The locale is especially beautiful in autumn when the aspens paint the valley and hillsides gold. None of these rides are suitable for young children, but novice mountain bike riders will find the terrain suitable to test your new skills. Local bike shops will have maps and books to describe all other possibilities in the area.

Spooner Lake Park is one-half mile north of the intersection of Hwy. 28 and U.S. 50.

Marlette Lake in Spooner Lake Park. Moderate to strenuous with 1,140 feet elevation gain, 270 feet loss. 4.8 miles to the lake's edge, 6.2 miles to the dam.

Start in Spooner Lake State Park riding downhill out of the park toward the dam. The dirt road begins and heads along North Canyon Creek to road 15N04A that intersects to the right. Continue straight to Marlette Lake. The creek will be on your right during the last mile which is a strenuous climb. This is a spectacular ride in the fall when the aspens along Canyon Creek turn the hillsides gold. (This is not a suitable ride for young children.)

Experienced riders may continue on the famous Flume Trail that leaves from Marlette Lake and exits on Tunnel Creek Road in Incline Village. This trail is not for beginners. You will want a car shuttle for this one.

Bicycling

Riding the Flume Trail.

You can start this ride from Pickett's Junction (intersection of Hwy. 89 south and Hwy. 88) or at the beginning of Blue Lakes Rd. off Hwy. 88.

Blue Lakes and Beyond. Easy. Six miles one way with 100 ft. elevation gain. Bring fishing rod, camera and mosquito repellant.

This easy riding dirt road meanders through a valley with spectacular scenery, especially in the fall. Begin riding at Lower Blue Lake Campground. Turn left onto Blue Lakes Road. At 1.2 miles turn right towards Tamarack Lake. You will pass the road to Upper and Lower Sunset Lakes at 4.3 miles. Either detour to the lakes or continue straight. At 4.5 miles go right into Indian Valley. This is a small valley with a meandering creek. The road continues for 1.5 miles to the Wilderness Boundary. Mountain bikes are not allowed in wilderness areas. If you didn't detour into the lakes area riding in, do so on the way back.

Bicycling

Part of Sorensen's on Hwy. 88 just east of the main resort complex.
530-694-2266
530-694-2203

Hope Valley Outdoor Center

The folks who operated the Hope Valley Cross Country trail system in winter rent mountain bikes. They provide a map to the trails as well as expert advice about the best terrain in the area. For a pleasant day trip return to the junction of Highways 88 and 89, turn south and ride up Burnside Lake Road as far as you wish. When you have finished riding, the café and grocery store at the Outdoor Center have food and drink to revive you. This is an area that is ablaze with autumn color, so you might want to plan a trip here in the fall.

At the intersection of Hwy. 88 and Hwy. 89. Park off the highway.

Burnside Lake Moderate, 6.2 miles one way with 1100 ft. elevation gain.

The ride on Burnside Road starts in Hope Valley at Pickett's Junction, the intersection of Highway 89 and Highway 88. If you have rented your bikes at the Hope Valley Outdoor Center, you can ride up Highway 88 a mile or so to this point. A dirt road heads south and climbs gradually to Burnside Lake, with many views of Hope and Faith Valleys to the west. Traffic should be relatively light and the ride is suitable for children with some experience and novice riders.

# Horseback Riding

Truckee and North Lake Tahoe

Tahoe Donner Equestrian Center

Reservations recommended. Alder Creek Dr., Tahoe Donner 530-587-9470

Tahoe Donner Equestrian Center is in the Tahoe Donner development. This large stable has one and two-hour trail rides as well as all day and full moon rides at night. Half-hour pony rides and lessons are also available. Saturday nights at 5 p.m. there is a 90-minute ride followed by a barbeque. They also offer a Horsemanship Camp (See "Just for Kids" on page 162 for details) and boarding for your steed if you reserve early in the season.

Northstar Stables

Reservations recommended. Northstar-at-Tahoe Resort 530-562-1230

Northstar Stables offers year-round, family trail rides and barbeque rides on trails throughout the forest on the resort. There are pony rides for children and lessons.

Squaw Valley Stables

Squaw Valley 530-583-RIDE

Squaw Valley Stables offers one, two and three-hour rides that leave hourly on a route around the edge of the valley. Reservations are not needed. Six-year-olds may take the two-hour valley rides and pony rides are available for tots. Special breakfast and group rides can be arranged. Half-day rides climb from the valley to High Camp. Lessons are by reservation.

Alpine Meadows Stables

Alpine Meadows Rd., Alpine Meadows 530-583-3905

Alpine Meadows Stables offers one and two-hour rides across Bear Creek and through the forest. Children as young as five years old are allowed. Half-day rides require reservations.

Horseback Riding

Receiving instructions before a ride at Tahoe Donner.

South Lake Tahoe

Cascade Stables

Reservations recommended. Six miles north of the South Tahoe Y off Hwy. 89. 530-541-2055

This stable near Cascade Lake offers everything from one-hour scenic rides to all-day trips into Desolation Wilderness, plus fishing and extended pack trips. Breakfast and steak dinner rides go to Cascade Lake. Children must be at least 8 years old and there is a 200-pound weight limit.

Camp Richardson's Corral

Reservations required. On Hwy. 89 at Fallen Leaf Rd., 2.6 miles north of the South Tahoe Y. 530-541-3113

Ride along the Aspen, Meadow and Fallen Leaf Lake trails for a one-hour ride, or take a two-hour or half-day trail ride through mountain meadows and forest. Other offerings include a morning ride to a hearty cowboy breakfast or an easy evening ride that ends with a steak barbeque. There are wagon rides for families with little

Horseback Riding

ones. On overnight or extended pack trips into the wilderness with a guide, they provide you with everything but a fishing license.

Sunset Ranch

On U.S. 50 one-quarter mile west of the South Lake Tahoe airport.
530-541-9001

This stable will take small children and beginners. There is a petting zoo for the little ones while you wait to ride. You can also ride here without a guide. Their trails wind along the Upper Truckee River and across lovely meadows. They have hourly as well as half-day and all-day rides year-round. They offer a discount for early birds who ride before 9:00 a.m.

Zephyr Cove Stables

Reservations suggested, required for meal rides. At Zephyr Cove, 4 miles north of Stateline on U.S. 50.
702-588-5664
After 12/15/98
775-588-5664

Zephyr Cove Stables will take you into the High Sierra wilderness with fabulous views of Lake Tahoe. All rides are guided by courteous cowboys who will help you. One and two-hour rides, as well as breakfast, lunch and dinner rides are available. Reservations are required for these. Bus service from the casinos will bring you out to Zephyr Cove.

Carson Pass

Kirkwood Stables

Reservations recommended. Five miles west of Carson Pass on Hwy. 88 next to Kirkwood Inn.
209-258-RIDE

The Lazy K Pack Station operates the Kirkwood Stables offering guided trail rides around the resort as well as into the surrounding National Forest lands. Rides last from one hour to all day and pony rides are available for young children. Catered lunches can be arranged and groups can request horse-drawn wagon rides for special occasions.

Tennis

Many tennis courts are open to the public in various locations in Truckee and at Lake Tahoe. Most require reservations and have fees per person per hour. The free courts are in parks or at schools, although some are of dubious quality.

Fee to enter beach.
Corner So. Shore Dr. and Donner Pass Rd.

Donner Lake West End Beach

There is one court that is fine for a casual game or for practicing with the children.

Off Hwy. 267 just south of Truckee.

Truckee Regional Park

These two courts are not of the best quality.

Fee.
Granlibakken Rd., Tahoe City
530-583-4242

Granlibakken Resort

Six courts at this resort are open to the public.

Ward Ave. and Hwy. 89, Tahoe City

Kilner Park

Two tennis courts are nestled in the woods with a courtside reservation system and coin lighted at night. They are not available some hours due to tennis lessons. However, you can take a walk in the park or sit by the lake while you wait to play.

On Hwy. 89 10 miles south of the Tahoe City Y.
530-525-7982

Sugar Pine Point State Park

There is one court near the Ehrman mansion. Pack a picnic lunch, take your tennis racket, and spend the day in the park. There is a day use fee to enter park but it is free to bike riders.

Tennis

Tahoe Marina Lodge

*Fee to use.
270 No. Lake Blvd.,
Tahoe City
530-583-2365*

This lodge near the *Y* in Tahoe City has courts open to the public.

North Tahoe High School

*2945 Polaris Rd.,
Tahoe City*

The four courts at the school are open to the public free of charge.

North Tahoe Regional Park

*Fee to use lighted courts.
Donner Rd. and Estates Dr.,
Tahoe Vista*

Five courts in the park are open to the public and are lighted at night.

Kings Beach Elementary School

*Steelhead Ave. and Wolf St.,
Kings Beach*

The school has two courts that are open to the public.

Incline High School

*Incline Blvd.,
Incline Village*

Two newly-surfaced courts are open to the public free of charge.

Incline Village Tennis Complex

*Fee per person per hour.
Incline Way,
Incline Village
702-832-1235**

Seven new courts are open to the public. Lessons are also available.

*After 12/12/98 (702) changes to (775)

Summer

Tennis

Fee per person. *987 Tahoe Blvd., Incline Village* 702-831-5258*	### Lakeside Tennis Club The club has resurfaced its nine courts, three of which are lighted. You must call ahead to reserve a court.

South Lake Tahoe

2940 Lake Tahoe Blvd., So. Lake Tahoe 530-541-4611

South Tahoe Middle School

The courts here are free on a first-come first served basis. All four courts are operated by the South Lake Tahoe Parks and Recreation Department. The courts at this complex are lighted for night games.

1735 Lake Tahoe Blvd., So. Lake Tahoe 530-541-4611

South Tahoe High School

There are six courts that are free on a first-come, first served basis. Three of the courts have lights for night games.

Warrior Way off U.S. 50, Zephyr Cove 702-588-7230*

Zephyr Cove County Park

Four public courts, all with lights, are open 24 hours at this local park. Here's your chance to play a midnight game.

Warrior Way, Zephyr Cove 702-588-7230*

Whittel High School

Three courts have coin operated lights 24 hours. First come, first served.

*After 12/12/98 (702) changes to (775)

Summer

Golf

If you enjoy golf, you will find your skills tested on any of the 13 Lake Tahoe-Truckee links. Three are resort courses, with the newest, the Resort at Squaw Creek, rated by golfing magazines as one of the nation's top 10 resort links.

Because the golf season is relatively short—it usually runs from May to October—all of the courses are crowded with locals and vacationers alike and require reservations.

A note about high altitude golf: the ball flies straighter and longer in the thinner air of Lake Tahoe. Remember to adjust your club selection accordingly. That usually means playing one club less on many shots.

North Lake Tahoe and Truckee

The resort courses:

Reservations required.
Squaw Valley
530-583-6300
800-327-3353

Resort at Squaw Creek is a true test of target golf. A premium is placed on shot selection not length. Squaw Creek meanders throughout the course and comes into play on all but six holes. The course's signature hole is the par-5 13th that plays close to 500 yards and requires a 200-yard carry over marshland off the tee.
Driving range: yes; Course rating: 70.9
Length: 6,931 yards (gold tees).

Northstar-at-Tahoe Resort
530-562-2490

Northstar is really two courses. The front side is links-style golf where big hitters can let it rip. But from No. 10 on, finesse and shot selection to postage-stamp greens are a must. No. 16 is Northstar's signature hole. It is a par-4, 450-yard tester with water waiting for those with chronic fades.
Driving range: yes; Course rating: 70.5;
Length: 6,897 yards (gold tees).

Golf

955 Fairway Blvd., Incline Village
702-832-1144
After 12/12/98
775-832-1144

Incline Village Championship Course combines tree-lined fairways and water on 13 of the 18 holes. There isn't a flat green to be found and the key to sinking putts is to remember that every putt breaks toward Lake Tahoe. The monstrous 600-yard, par-5 No. 4 is Incline's signature hole. Not enough that the fairway is flanked on both sides by out-of-bounds markers, normal landing areas are bordered by bunkers.
Driving range: yes; Course rating: 72.6; Length: 6,910 yards.

11531 Northwoods Blvd., Tahoe Donner
530-587-9440

Tahoe Donner plays tight and long, period. Not surprisingly, it is the toughest of Lake Tahoe's golf courses, and one of the hardest to get on (it is a semi-public course owned and operated by a homeowners' association) and reservations are an absolute must. The signature hole is the par-4 18th that plays downhill with water in front of an extremely well-bunkered green. It is not the hardest hole on the course, but it certainly typifies high Sierra golf.
Driving range: yes; Course rating: 73.1; length: 6,914 yds.

Nine-holers and executive courses

Hwy. 267 at Reynold Way, Truckee
530-587-3501

Ponderosa Golf Course only has nine holes, but each offers a test to golfers. Ponderosa greens and fairways are always in tip-top condition. No. 9 is a dogleg right with tall pines blocking a direct second shot to the green.
Driving range: no; Course rating: 67; Length 3,018 yards.

Golf

Corner of Hwys. 267 and 28, Kings Beach 530-546-9922

Old Brockway touts itself as one of the region's oldest and receives the heaviest play throughout the summer. The par-5 7th is 553 yards long and demands a strong drive and a sound short game.
Driving range: yes; Course rating: 69.5;
Length 3,202 yards

Golfers Pass off Mt. Rose Hwy., Incline Village 702-832-1150 After 12/12/98 775-832-1150

Incline Executive has one of the lake's shortest holes, the 113-yard 3rd, yet is the longest course of the nine holers. It is a fun course to tune up the short game.
Driving range: yes; Course rating: 55; Length 3,513 yards.

Behind Lucky Market, Tahoe City 530-583-1516

Tahoe City is a favorite hangout for long-time locals, both on and off the course. The entrance is hidden behind commercial development, but well worth the search. It is the shortest course on the North Shore in total yardage.
Driving range: no; Course rating: 64.3;
Length: 2,696 yards.

South Lake Tahoe

The resort courses:

Behind the Horizon Casino Resort on Lake Tahoe Parkway, Stateline 702-588-3566 After 12/12/98 775-588-3566

Edgewood has long been considered Lake Tahoe's premier resort course, with the lake coming into play on several of the holes. Indeed, the par-3 17th is reminiscent of fabled Pebble Beach, for when the prevailing winds come off the lake, golfers are forced to hit the ball over the lake in order to hit the green. Certainly, the last four holes demand the most from the golfer, but the par-5 16th, at 545 yards from the blues, is the course's signature hole. Not only is it the most picturesque, but every one who plays it has to

Golf

decide whether they have the skills necessary to go for a minuscule green on the second shot.
Driving range: yes; Course rating: 75.1;
Length: 7,491 yards.

View from the 18th green at Edgewood.

Golf

Nine-holers and executive courses

Corner of Fairway and Johnson Blvd. off U.S. 50 in So. Lake Tahoe 530-542-6097

Bijou Municipal Course is a favorite local's course as well as being the lake's shortest in overall length. Golfers tee off on the par-4, 300-yard No. 1 with the Sierra Nevada as a backdrop. The sixth hole, a 342-yard par 4, is the course's lone water hole.
Driving range: yes; Course rating: NR;
Length: 2,016 yards.

*Off U.S. 50 about 8 miles north of Stateline and 3 miles south of Hwy. 28.
702-749-5201
After 12/12/98
775-749-5201*

Glenbrook has several distinctions: it is Nevada's oldest (at 70 odd years old), it is considered by golfing experts as one of the country's best nine hole courses, it has the lake's shortest hole, and people once paid $1.50 to watch golfing legend Ben Hogan play the course. What the course lacks in length is more than made up for with tough, tight, tree-lined fairways. The par 3, 101-yard third hole is the course's signature hole, with golfers who overshoot the tiny green facing a swim in Lake Tahoe.
Driving range: yes; Course rating: 66.3;
Length: 2,906 yards.

AS WE WENT TO REPRINT, GLENBROOK GOLF COURSE WAS CLOSED TO THE PUBLIC.

Golf

On U.S. 50 at Meyers.
530-577-2121

Tahoe Paradise Golf Course underwent a facelift in 1994, with bunkers added on many holes and greens getting a well-deserved re-working. The improvements, when coupled with the tight landing areas and tilted fairways, makes the course a golfing challenge. The 15th, a dogleg par 4 that measures 254 yards, is a good example of the changes in the course. Instead of hitting to a small green, players now face a two-tier green that demands pinpoint placement. The par-3 14th is the signature hole. A player has to carry the entire 130-yard length in order to avoid putting the ball in the water.
Driving range: yes; Course rating: 59.9;
Length: 4,021 yards.

On the north side of Hwy. 50 just west of the Lake Tahoe Airport.
530-577-0788

Lake Tahoe Golf Course is for players who like to live dangerously: the Upper Truckee River criss-crosses like a coiled snake and other water hazards lie in wait along many of the holes. That said, Lake Tahoe GC has its own version of Augusta's Amen Corner, with holes 10 through 14 serious challenges for any golfer. The 16th, a par-4 357-yard dogleg left, is the course's signature hole, with everything that Lake Tahoe offers coming into play: water, trees and spectacular scenery.
Driving range: yes; Course rating: 70.9
Length: 6,718 yards

Golf

Miniature Golf

Two miniature golf courses are on the North Shore offering hours of fun for the family. In South Lake Tahoe two miniature golf courses offer other games as well. Both stay open into the evening.

Magic Carpet Golf

5167 No. Lake Blvd., Carnelian Bay 530-546-4279

Two courses, a 19-hole Castle and 28-hole dinosaur course offer hours of fun for the whole family.

Boberg's Kings Beach Mini Golf

8693 No. Lake Blvd., Kings Beach 530-546-3196

This course creates several hours of fun for the whole family in the evening or when you have tired of the beach.

Magic Carpet Golf

2455 Lake Tahoe Blvd., So. Lake Tahoe 530-541-3787

There is a discount for those who want to try the 19-hole castle course and 28-hole dinosaur course together. A video arcade and kiddie rides add to the fun.

Fantasy Kingdom

4046 Highway 50, So. Lake Tahoe 530-544-3833

Located not far from the casinos, this 23-hole course is perfect for an afternoon or evening of outdoor fun for the family.

Historical Walks

Truckee Area

The Emigrant Trail at Big Bend

Take I-80 west 16 miles to the Rainbow Rd. exit. Drive west on Rainbow Rd. past the Rainbow Lodge to the U. S. Forest Service parking lot on the north side of the road.

Look north from the easternmost end of the parking lot and you will see a brown steel Emigrant Trail marker. Pick your way down to the marker which was placed here by Trails West and marks the route of the trail at this point.

For a sleuthing adventure start walking east from the marker keeping to the lowest and flattest places. Do not drop down toward the river. Round, green Emigrant Trail signs with white lettering are tacked on the east side of many lodgepole trees. The forest of the emigrant period had large old trees spaced quite far apart, and much of the brush you see today would not have been growing here then.

See if you can determine the route the emigrants would have picked. You will eventually come to the river about a quarter mile to the east. The bank is quite flat and you will see why wagon masters chose this place to cross the Yuba River.

Retrace your steps to the parking lot. It will be much simpler, for the signs will guide you. Back at the Trails West sign look northwest across the granite to find another trail marker. You will notice that the wagons had to wind north downhill across the granite to reach a good route along the river. If you have very sharp eyes, you will be able to find two places where the wagon wheels slid across the granite leaving telltale rust marks. Run your hand over the marks to notice how the wheels polished the granite as smooth as glass.

Summer   *113*

Historical Walks

After returning to your car, drive west another quarter mile to the U.S. Forest Service Museum and Ranger Station. Here are exhibits about the Lincoln Highway that passed this way and an Emigrant Trail exhibit.
For those who want a guided tour of the trail, the Forest Service leads hikes every Saturday between July 4 and Labor Day. Check at the Forest Service Ranger Station for exact times.

Donner Summit Emigrant Trail and First Highways

Take the Soda Springs exit off I-80. Drive east on Donner Pass Rd. to Donner Summit and turn south on the road at the Alpine Skills International Donner Spitz Hütte. Drive about 200 yards until you see the sign on the left for the Pacific Crest Trail. Park along the side of the road.

The route of the Emigrant Trail is to the left of the Pacific Crest Trail. The traces are buried in a roadbed that was excavated for the intercontinental fiber optics cable. Climb over the rocks and follow the path. In summer the cliff to your left will be filled with clumps of blue or scarlet trumpet-shaped flowers called penstemons. The scarlet one was named "mountain pride" by John Muir. After walking about one-quarter mile down the trail, look carefully to the right for a large rock with a bronze plaque. This monument marks the trail of the wagon train led by Elisha Stephens that passed this way in November of 1844. They found this route over the pass in two feet of snow. In some places they had been forced to unload their wagons and haul them piece by piece up the cliffs. These pioneers were the first to bring their wagons over the forbidding Sierra Nevada, thus opening the trail to California. "The Emigrant Trail at Big Bend" walk on page 113 traverses another portion of the journey taken by this group.

Continue through the willow corridor down the road until you've gone under the railroad. At this point you are standing on a portion of State Highway 37, built in

Historical Walks

1915 for the new automobile traffic. The roadbed was abandoned in 1928 when the current alignment of U.S. 40 was finished. After passing through the tunnel, look back at the wall supporting the railroad tracks. This mortarless wall of rocks was built by the Chinese workers who labored here in 1867 and 1868 to build the Central Pacific Railroad, the first transcontinental railroad in the United States.

The roadbed curves down over the granite and through a marshy overgrowth to join today's road. If you walk along the upper section, you may be able to make out a turn-of-the-century advertisement painted on the rock proclaiming "Whitney Hotel Truckee."

A section of old Highway 37 as it curves down the hill after passing through the Chinese wall.

# Historical Walks

Historic Downtown Truckee

Truckee is the oldest High Sierra town in California, and much of the original town, as well as its first building, has been preserved. You can walk around downtown in less than an hour and end your tour with a meal or a snack at one of the many eateries on Commercial Row. And, of course, there are many shops to tempt you with their interesting merchandise.

Start your walking tour at The Truckee Hotel at the corner of Highway 267 and Bridge Street. This hostelry began life as the American Hotel in 1868. Later it was known as Whitney House, New Whitney House, Alpine Riverside, and now, The Truckee Hotel. Currently it is a bed and breakfast inn that has been renovated and decorated to reflect its nineteenth-century past. One suite honors Charles F. McGlashan, a famous early resident of Truckee and its most faithful booster at the turn of the century. The Passage restaurant located on the first floor offers elegant dining. (See "Dining Out" on page 220 for complete information.)

Walk north to Church Street where Gray's Log Cabin, Truckee's first building, is on the left a few hundred feet from the intersection. Now return to Bridge Street and continue walking north to Sierra Mountaineer, the stone building on the site of Truckee's original Gray's Toll Station. Walk west along Jibboom Street to the Old Jail, the last building on the right. The jail was in use continuously from 1875 until 1964. It now houses some exhibits gathered by the Truckee Donner Historical Society. Volunteers open the jail many weekends in the summer.

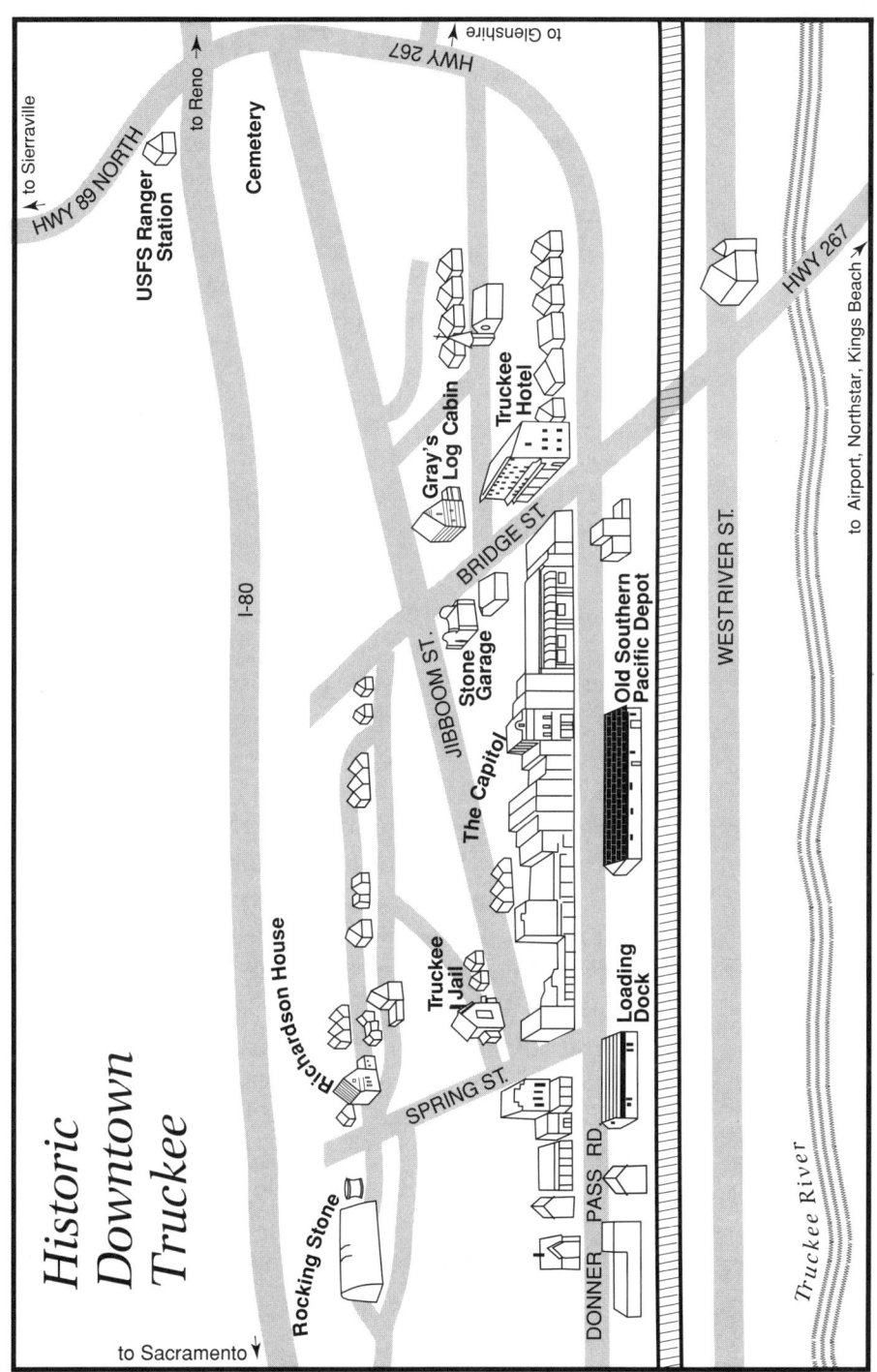

Summer 117

Historical Walks

Following the map on the previous page, complete your tour of Truckee's fine old buildings, all of which are now shops or restaurants. You might also wish to hike up to the rocking stone with its great vista of the town. To learn more about the legend of the rocking stone and Truckee's colorful past, see "History" on page 10.

Two books, available locally, recite detailed information about the area's history. *Truckee, an Illustrated History of the Town and its Surroundings* is by local author, Joanne Meschery. The other, *Fire and Ice, A Portrait of Truckee*, is published by the Truckee Donner Historical Society.

Boca Historic Town Site

Drive 6 miles east of Hwy. 89 North on I-80 to the Boca Reservoir and Hirschdale Rd. exit. Turn left, driving under the freeway and shortly after crossing the railroad tracks turn right up a gravel road to parking for the trail.

The United State Forest Service has recently opened this walk into Truckee's past with a quarter-mile walk on a hillside above the confluence of the Truckee River and the Little Truckee River as it exits the Boca Dam. Interpretive signs along the way point out the sites of the Boca Mill and Ice Company whose operations supported a town of more than two hundred during the latter decades of the 19th century. The lumber was cut to help build the Central Pacific Railroad and then the tunnels of the Comstock silver mines at Virginia City. The company dammed the river to create ponds which were harvested of their ice in winter, thus ensuring year-round employment for the men of the mill. The ice was used in railroad cars to preserve fruit shipments and to cool the tunnels of the mines. A prize-winning beer was made in the nearby Boca Brewery. However, the town's life was destined to be short. Having cut down all the trees in the area, the lumber mill closed.

Historical Walks

The closing of the silver mines and introduction of refrigerated railroad cars spelled doom for the ice industry. Then a fire destroyed the brewery and the town went into decline. The town was finally dismantled in 1927.

The base of the schoolhouse flagpole, old rusted iron gates and other metal detritus of civilization is everywhere along the path up the hill. The most poignant reminder of the past, however, is the tiny cemetery. A lonely iceland poppy planted by a grieving relative still blooms each spring, and three tiny headstones for deceased infants bear testimony to the harsh frontier life. When you return to your car, walk over to the site of the hotel where a lilac bush still blooms amid the trees.

Winter life was not all work. Ladies still enjoyed days on the slopes.

Historical Walks

South Lake Tahoe and Carson Pass

Although much of the evidence of the settlements in Lake Valley east of Meyers and the magnificent turn-of-the-century lakeside hotels is gone, there are a few places where you can walk around and imagine the opulent life-style of turn-of-the-century vacationers.

The Carson Pass area is filled with emigrant history. The Emigrant Trail was opened here by Mormons returning from California to Utah in 1848. Even though wagons had to negotiate two passes, the route became the most popular for groups on their way to the Hangtown (Placerville) diggings. Some diaries tell of those who stopped on the eastern slope to pan for gold along the Carson River. One easy walk, "Emigrant Trail over Carson Pass," will let you test the terrain the emigrants had to cross.

Tallac Historic Site

Fee and reservations for Pope Estate Tours. Museum daily, 10am-4pm through Labor Day.
From the South Tahoe Y, drive 3.1 miles north on Hwy. 89 to the Kiva Beach and Tallac Historic Site parking lot.
530-541-5227

The Tallac Historic Site is on 74 acres of the Pope, Heller and Baldwin/McGonagle family private estates that were transferred to the U.S. Forest Service in the 1960s and 1970s. Because it was necessary to restore many of the buildings on the site, the Tahoe Tallac Association, a bi-state non-profit organization, was formed to help raise money for restoration and to promote the area as a cultural center to increase community and visitor involvement.

Settlement of this beautiful part of the Lake Tahoe shoreline began when Yank Clement bought eight acres at Tallac Point in 1873. He foresaw the tourist potential of the area and built a hotel he named Tallac Point House. By 1875 his hotel was quite popular, but financial difficulties

Historical Walks

forced him to sell the property to E. J. "Lucky" Baldwin. This San Francisco Realtor and stock speculator turned the Tallac Point House into a first-class nineteenth-century destination resort of giant proportions, one that he claimed rivaled Saratoga Springs in New York. He piped water down from Fallen Leaf Lake, built bridle paths and promenade walks and installed electricity to light the paths at night. A steam plant supplied heat for the hotel rooms and dining room that seated 100. He constructed the first casino on the lake and added bowling alleys, sun parlors, ballroom, theatrical stage and more. This was surely the place in which to be seen and represented an era of high living at the lake.

When "Lucky" died in 1909, his daughter Anita took control and operated the resort into the 1920s. However, in 1927 she removed all the buildings because she wanted no more commercial activity on her property. The Tallac Hotel disappeared. When Anita Baldwin died, one-half of her considerable estate passed to her daughter, Dextra Baldwin McGonagle, who built a summer home on the shores of the lake. That home is now a museum operated by the U.S. Forest Service and is open to the public in summer. Here you can get a taste of the refined living of this prominent family, as well as learn about "Lucky" Baldwin's exploits as miner, financier and hotel proprietor. In one of the rooms you'll also find an excellent exhibit prepared by the Washo Tribal Council to acquaint visitors with the culture of these native tribes of the Tahoe Basin.

Neighboring land was the summer retreat for the Pope family, prominent in San Francisco Bay Area society. Next door to the Pope estate, Walter Heller, another prominent San Francisco financier, built a summer house on 200 feet

 # Historical Walks

of shoreline along with two small cottages with a common veranda and, finally, the main house called Valhalla, with 40-foot high ceilings and grand fireplace (now the site of Valhalla Concerts).

Start your walk heading east along the bike path. The first group of buildings houses art workshops and galleries operated by the Tahoe Tallac Association. The galleries and artists studios are open to the public from 11:00 a.m. to 3:00 p.m. every day except Thursday. Artists in residence have openings on Sunday afternoons from 1:00 p.m. to 3:00 p.m. The U.S. Forest Service leads tours of the Pope Estate daily during the summer.

Walk on the path to the Baldwin House Museum and then take the paved path to Valhalla and the Arts Store of the Tahoe Tallac Association. The store features work of local artists and many other interesting items. To return to your car, walk along the path that hugs the shore and be sure to visit the gazebo and pond with its carefully planted gardens.

Valhalla is the site of regular concerts and outdoor musical events as well as art workshops throughout the summer. Be sure to check the schedule posted on the boards near the grand hall. Regular concerts are listed in the "Special Events" section on pages 275 and 276.

Historical Walks

Take Hwy. 88 west toward Carson Pass. Just east of the Pass turn south on old Hwy. 88 and drive about one-quarter mile to the former vista point.

Emigrant Trail over Carson Pass

The route over Carson Pass was opened by Mormons returning to Salt Lake City from California in 1848. The next year, as thousands rushed to the California mines, this trail became a favorite for those seeking the most direct route to Hangtown (Placerville) and its nearby gold. It is estimated that at least 4,000 wagons passed this way in 1849, and by 1850 this became the preferred route to the California gold sites.

Start walking downhill on the former highway just east of the parking area. In about 100 feet take the easiest route down (left) off the road into a grove of large fir trees. You will see a metal arrow on one of the trees. Continue steeply downhill as far as you wish, guided by more trail markers on the trees. Notice how each tree has a groove near its base left by the chains emigrants used to winch their wagons up this hill. As you huff and puff back up toward the road, you will understand the task that the emigrants faced to haul their wagons up this first pass over the Sierra.

When you reach the road, look uphill and you will find another marker on a tree. Follow these markers uphill along the south side of the road until you reach a rock with what at first glance is modern graffiti. The plaque on the rock will explain that a group of Odd Fellows paused in their toil up this slope "to paint on this and adjacent boulders their names and links of the great order they so dearly loved."

# Historical Walks

In 1853, William Brown wrote in his diary about this portion of his trip: "Started early, traveled over good roads, came to Red Lake. Here we begin to see the Elephant, the High Mountain was before us to ascend. We got up a short distance and camped on a level on the mountain side. . . . Teams here had to double as there was a part of the road over a smooth steep rock and cattle could not stand on it. They had to haul the waggons to the rock, take the teams around and haul over by long ropes tied to the tongues of the waggons."

At this point cross the small creek and return to the road and your car.

Odd Fellows' nineteenth century graffiti. Whitewash has been used to enhance the emigrant carvings in the rock

Historical Walks

Take Hwy. 88 west from Pickett's Junction to Carson Pass.

Carson Pass

Carson Pass is the location of an Emigrant Museum that opened in 1994 and is staffed by volunteers in the summer. Here you can get information about trails in the area and buy books and maps as well as see the interpretive panels about the emigrants who passed this way.

After visiting the museum, be sure to check out the monument to Kit Carson. It memorializes the tree where Kit carved his name in 1844 when he and John Charles Frémont were trying to cross the Sierra Nevada to California after a year of mapping the Pacific Northwest and Nevada. On this expedition they stopped at Pyramid Lake northeast of Reno, giving the lake its name because of the pyramid-shaped rock near the southeastern shore. By the time they reached this spot, they were weary and practically snowbound. Carson and Frémont climbed Red Lake Peak to the north, and were the first Americans to see Lake Tahoe and note its location on maps. Frémont called the mountain lake he saw "Lake Bonpland" after a French botanist of the period.

If you would like to see Lake Tahoe as Frémont might have spied it, take the hike on page 160 that takes you up the Pacific Crest Trail to Meiss Pass.

Farther west in the parking lot is a monolith with a broken top. It was placed here by the Nevada chapter of E. Clampus Vitus to commemorate "Snowshoe" Thompson who carried the mail every winter over this pass between Hangtown (Placerville), California, and Genoa, Nevada.

Tom Fiene enjoying the view from the Rubicon Trail.

Special Hikes

We have selected special hikes that take several hours and are best planned to include a picnic along the way. Most have some elevation gain, and hiking boots are recommended but not required. Each hike is graded (easy, moderate, or strenuous) according to the total miles and elevation gain. Symbols describe the following:

suitable for children   has notable wildflowers   swimming   peak climb   dogs allowed

Hikes at Donner Summit are listed first and from west to east around Lake Tahoe. Carson Pass area hikes are listed in the last section. We have chosen only a few of many possible trails into Desolation Wilderness or along the Tahoe Rim Trail. We list some of the most popular and least difficult hikes, as well as one or two lesser known trails into lakes nestled in granite bowls, or across open ridges with spectacular views of the mountains surrounding Lake Tahoe. One of the treats awaiting hikers in the Tahoe Basin is the opportunity to view the "gem of the Sierra" from a variety of vantage points above the lake.

In recent years, the volunteer effort to establish and build a Tahoe Rim Trail, a 150-mile hiking and equestrian trail which follows the ridge tops of the Lake Tahoe Basin, has resulted in the completion of most of the segments. Distances between trailheads with parking will require a car shuttle to hike the entire distance. We have described two segments of the trail in the South Lake Tahoe area, one with a car shuttle for the complete trip and one with a loop possibility. For more information and a trail brochure, call 530-577-0676, or write The Tahoe Rim Trail, P.O. Box 11551, South Lake Tahoe, CA 96155.

 **Special Hikes**

For those who seek an overnight experience or who want to try more strenuous hiking, we suggest that you buy one or more of the following books available in the bookstores. Michael Scialfa has produced a small booklet with 13 hikes entitled *Trail Guide to the Lake Tahoe Basin*. Jeffrey P. Schaffer has compiled two trail guides to the area. *The Tahoe Sierra, A Natural History Guide to 100 Hikes in the Northern Sierra* has detailed descriptions of hikes off Highways 49, 80 and 50. The section on trails off Highway 50 applies to the South Tahoe region. His other title, *Desolation Wilderness and the South Lake Tahoe Region*, includes a map of the Fallen Leaf Lake quadrangle which can be most helpful for planning your own forays into the wilderness. For those interested in finding the best wildflower gardens in the entire area, *Lingering in Tahoe's Wild Gardens* by Julie Stauffer Carville is a wonderful guide, complete with drawings and descriptions of the flowers to be found.

A wilderness permit is required to hike in Desolation Wilderness. Day hikers can fill out a permit at the trailhead, but overnight campers must obtain a permit from the Eldorado National Forest, Camino Unit. The telephone number is 530-644-6048. Overnight reservations are limited to 1500 between Memorial Day and Labor Day and there is a maximum fee of $10.00 per person. Permits are 50% by reservation and 50% first-come-first-served.

More tips:

Mosquitoes abound in the first weeks after the snow melts, so pack the repellant.

Giardia, a tiny, microscopic organism, is in all the lakes and streams of the Sierra Nevada. Unless you own an approved filter, carry your own water. The intestinal disturbance from this bug is very unpleasant and can last a long time. Don't take chances.

Thieves, unfortunately, prey on cars in many parking lots. Take your valuables with you or leave them at home.

Special Hikes

Donner Summit

To hike north from Donner Pass Rd., take the Soda Springs exit off I-80 and drive east to the Alpine Skills International Donner Spitz Hütte. Park along the south side of the highway. The trail starts from the north side. To hike south from I-80, take the Castle Peak exit and follow signs to the Pacific Crest Trail on the south side of the freeway.

Pacific Crest Trail between Donner Pass and Castle Peak Trailhead. Moderate. Hike starts at 7,200 feet. Four miles one way with about 200 feet elevation gain.

This trail may be hiked in either direction. From Donner Pass Road, the trail starts on the north side of the highway. The hike features moderate ascents and descents through lodgepole forests and across granite ridges with magnificent vistas of Castle Peak to the north and Donner Lake and the Carson Range to the east. Wildflower gardens of red and blue penstemon, Indian paintbrush and many other species adorn either side of the trail in summer. This is an easy hike for children. Many fine picnic spots atop rocky promontories have magnificent views. Because the hike begins at 7,200 feet, you feel as though you are on top of the world.

Hiking south from the trailhead off I-80, the trail meanders through forests of white fir and Jeffrey pine, climbing gradually until you reach the crest with views toward Donner Lake and east. The mountain above you is the newly christened Mount Stephens, named for the leader of the first wagons to cross the Sierra Nevada in 1844. The group was known as the Stephens-Townsend-Murphy party. They had discovered and opened the Truckee route of the California Emigrant Trail. The scramble to the top of this peak affords expansive views of the region.

Special Hikes

Take the Soda Springs exit off I-80 and drive east to the Alpine Skills International Donner Spitz Hütte. Turn right for about 200 yards to the Pacific Crest Trail trailhead. Park along the side of the road.

Pacific Crest Trail from Donner Pass to Mount Lincoln and Anderson Peak. Moderate to strenuous. Five miles round trip to Mount Lincoln; 12 miles round trip to Anderson Peak, with 1,500 feet elevation gain.

The trail climbs the granite ridge south of Donner Pass with excellent vistas in all directions. Penstemon, tiger lilies, lupine and many other species abound, especially on the first mile of the trip over rocky ledges and under red firs. The trail crosses a road and continues in a moderate climb to the saddle between Mount Lincoln and Mount Judah. Be sure to go out to the ledge at Roller Pass near the sign for the Emigrant Trail. Those intrepid pioneers actually winched their wagons up this cliff from the Coldstream Valley below. It is only 2.5 miles to this point, and Roller Pass is an excellent picnic spot. Ambitious hikers can follow the trail across the ridge toward Anderson Peak. From this vantage point you can look south into the headwaters of the North Fork of the American River. The trail climbs around the shoulder to Anderson Peak before continuing to Tinker Knob. At this point you will want to return the way you came.

Special Hikes

Start at the Pacific Crest Trailhead at Donner Summit. Directions are on the previous page.

Mount Judah Loop Trail, across two Emigrant Trail passes. Moderate to strenuous. Six-mile loop with 2,000 feet elevation gain.

Take the Pacific Crest Trail described on the previous page to the saddle between Mount Lincoln and Mount Judah. This is the famous Roller Pass, used by emigrant wagon trains from 1846-1849. Walk over to the edge and imagine the work necessary to get the wagons up this fearsome cliff. This route was discovered in 1846 by Mr. Aram who had decided it took too long to get over Donner Pass up from the lake. He scouted the creek in Coldstream Valley and found a longer but easier route to the bottom of this cliff. The pass gets its name from the description in his diary, "We made a roller (log) and fastened chains together and pivoted the wagons up with 12 yoke of oxen on the top, and the same at the bottom." Later, other wagon trains found a way to zigzag up the slope to the north of the pass.

Retrace your steps around the first bend to the loop trail over the summit of Mt. Judah, where wildflower displays are spectacular in early summer. After descending from Mount Judah you arrive at a pass between Mt. Judah and Donner Peak. This old road is currently marked as an emigrant trail from Coldstream Valley. Recent research of diaries has been unable to substantiate that this historic road is a branch of the California Emigrant Trail. The diary accounts only mention the Roller Pass route. Follow the road west and downhill about a quarter mile to a trail connection back to the Pacific Crest Trail (PCT). Turn right on the PCT back to your car.

Summer

Special Hikes

Same directions as previous page.

Donner Peak. Easy. Three miles round trip with 1,000 feet elevation gain.

From the same Pacific Crest Trailhead at Donner Pass, take the Pacific Crest Trail for about a mile until it reaches the Mount Judah Loop Trail. Turn left up the trail until you come to a road that leads to a saddle just below Donner Peak to the left. The trail to the summit leads to a group of granite outcroppings a short scramble away. Views in all directions make this a superior picnic spot.

Take the Castle Peak exit off I-80 from east or west. Drive to the frontage road on the south side of the freeway, then east about one-quarter mile to the Pacific Crest Trailhead.

Summit Lake. Easy. Four miles round trip with 200 feet elevation gain.

The trail leads north to a tunnel under Interstate 80 then enters a forest and shortly after the underpass there is a sign to Summit Lake. The trail is clearly marked. This easy hike is a perfect family outing to picnic on the shores of a beautiful alpine lake.

Special Hikes

The park is on Donner Pass Rd. just west of the Donner State Park exit off I-80. The entrance to the park is marked with a state historic marker, and parking for the museum is to the left as you enter.

Around Donner Memorial State Park. Easy. About 1.5 miles with no elevation gain.

This is a perfect afternoon walk with ample opportunity to swim at the park's beach. After visiting the museum, take the road past the entrance kiosk and continue to the right. When you reach the outflow creek, there is a trail through the woods that is close to the water. Interpretive signs along this trail will increase your knowledge of history and ecology of the region. Near the beach in a cove at the southwest corner of the park, a trail leaves the main road and follows the perimeter of the park toward the campground. Keep bearing left on the road serving the campsites until you reach a *Y*. Turn right to return to your car. Bring your bathing suits and a picnic. The beach is an excellent place for children to play in the shallow water, and picnic tables are close by in the trees. The recent long drought has killed many of the lodgepole pines that have been cut down, leaving a very sparse forest in many areas.

There is also a short nature trail that leaves from the museum and crosses the outlet creek a few times.

Summer

Special Hikes

From I-80 drive 20 miles north on Highway 89N to Henness Pass Road. Drive west toward Jackson Meadow 1.5 miles. Turn left driving 0.8 mile toward Independence Lake crossing the Little Truckee River and turn right onto Old Henness Pass Road. The Mt. Lola Trailhead is 3.2 miles west. Park here to start the 4.5 mile hike. The trail is marked with white diamonds on trees as well as old T-shaped blazes.

Mt. Lola. Strenuous. Five to six hours for nine miles round trip with 2,600 feet elevation gain.

Mt. Lola, at 9,143 feet, affords unmatched 360° views of the Sierra and Carson Range. The hike up Mt. Lola offers an opportunity to study all the conifers of our region. The first part of the trail passes through colorful aspen and willow groves lining seasonal drainages. The forest here is predominantly white fir and Jeffrey pine. To identify a white fir, notice that the needles are 1 to 2 inches long arranged in two rows almost at right angles with the branch. The cones in summer are 3 to 5 inches high standing upright on the topmost branches. After one half hour of climbing you hear the sound of Cold Stream. At this point the trail passes into a forest of red fir and large Jeffrey pines. As you ascend the ridge, look back along the trail to see these upright red fir cones. The trail is close to some fine old specimens of Jeffrey pine. Its deeply furrowed, reddish bark smells of vanilla. Pick up a cone. The saying is, "Gentle Jeffrey, prickly Ponderosa." This is one way to determine if you are near a Jeffrey or Ponderosa pine.After about an hour of steady climbing the trail exits onto a logging road for a few hundred yards and crosses Cold Stream. Look for white arrows on a brown background indicating where the trail leaves the road. From this point you climb gently through the forest until entering a broad meadow with many old beaver ponds. An abandoned beaver house is clearly visible in one pond. If more climbing is not for you, coming this far makes a perfect outing.

Special Hikes

After the beaver ponds, one mile of climbing brings you to a ridge with your first views south and north. The trail crosses a plateau with bent and wind-sculpted hemlocks and western white pine. Notice the drooping form of hemlocks that John Muir called "the most graceful, pliant and sensitive" of Sierra trees. Western white pines have five needles in a bunch and the cones dangle three in a bunch from the highest branches. Also present are two-needle lodgepole pines. The last half mile of trail is very steep, but the 360° view from the top is well worth the effort. Just before the summit, there is a man-made rock shelter to the right. On the summit itself are square brick foundations of unknown origin. From this vantage point you can see Castle Peak and the peaks of Desolation Wilderness to the south as well as Northstar ski runs and the Carson Range. To the east is Independence Lake and Stampede Reservoir. In heavy snow years this trip cannot be taken until mid to late summer. Autumn is a great time for this hike when the aspens are in full color and the days cool.

The beautiful pink shooting star, found in moist meadows in early summer.

Special Hikes

Take Alpine Meadows Rd. off Hwy. 89. The trailhead is 2.1 miles west on the right-hand side across from Deer Park entrance.

Five Lakes Basin. Five miles round trip. Moderate with 980 feet elevation gain.

This well-marked popular trail climbs, sometimes steeply, for 2 miles then flattens before descending through red fir forest to the most northern of the five lakes. The lakes are clustered within a square-mile area, making this a great place to explore. The first mile of the hike is exposed as you climb along a south-facing slope, so be sure to bring plenty of water.

Drive 4 miles south from the Tahoe City Y on Hwy. 89 to the Kaspian Sno Park on Blackwood Canyon Rd. or 4.5 miles to a small parking area on the west side of the road.

Eagle Rock. Easy. One and a half miles round trip with 240 feet elevation gain.

This is a perfect late afternoon or early evening photo hike to one of the high points above the lake. There are two trails up Eagle Rock. The easiest in summer and fall is to take Blackwood Canyon Road about a quarter of a mile to a trail that ascends a ridge along a power line to the south. At the top, near a power line pole, an unofficial trail turns east up to the volcanic promontory that is Eagle Rock. Head out across the rocks to several tall Jeffrey pines. Be sure to bring your camera to record the expanse of the "Lake of the Sky" before you.

The other approach is from the parking area half a mile south of the Kaspian Recreation Parking. A broad trail

Special Hikes

follows Blackwood Creek for about a quarter mile. Take the first unofficial trail that heads uphill steeply through the brush. You will intersect the power line and find the trail heading east from the power line trail. This is a steep but quick way to reach the peak. You can return by following the power line trail down to Blackwood Canyon Road then out to Highway 89, returning south to your car along the bike path.

From the Tahoe City Y, drive 11 miles south on Hwy. 89 to the trailhead parking at Meeks Bay. From the South Tahoe Y drive 16 miles north on Hwy. 89.

Crag Lake. Moderately strenuous. Ten miles round trip with 2,000 feet elevation gain.

You will need to fill out a day use permit for this hike. The first mile of the trip is along a dirt road on the north side of Meeks Creek. There are many wildflower gardens to admire here. Look for tiger lilies and columbine. The trail into Desolation Wilderness begins at the far end of the valley and climbs quickly through the forest. Suddenly you will emerge onto the shining granite terrain that symbolizes the Desolation Wilderness. After a few miles climbing through the open forest of giant Jeffrey pine, you will come upon Lake Genevieve. You may be tempted to stop here, but it is only a short hike to Crag Lake, much larger and more scenic. Here the many rocky ledges beckon you to sunbathe, picnic and swim to cool off after the climb. This part of the hike is a perfect all-day family outing. Adventurous hikers may want to continue at least as far as Stony Ridge Lake which will give you a good workout, climbing another 1,000 feet.

Special Hikes

Fee per vehicle at Bliss Park.

Fee for guided Vikingsholm tours, June-Labor Day.

On Hwy. 89 10 miles north of the South Tahoe Y and 16 miles south of the Tahoe City Y. Drive into the park to the Calawee Cove parking lot at the edge of the lake.

Rubicon Trail from D.L. Bliss State Park to Emerald Bay. Easy. Nine miles round trip with 200 feet elevation gain.

The Rubicon Trail is easiest from D. L. Bliss State Park to Vikingsholm in Emerald Bay and back. You can shorten the walk and stop anywhere up to Emerald Point for a picnic on the beach before returning to your car, or you can arrange a car shuttle and hike just one way.

The trail starts at the south end of Calawee Cove parking lot and climbs up the ridge to the site of the Old Lighthouse. From there it is a gentle downhill trek to Emerald Point where the trail hugs the beach all the way to Vikingsholm. The views from this trail are the most spectacular anywhere in the area, each curve bringing into view another cove or another rock formation. In early summer, ospreys may be seen nesting on the top of trees, some at eye level from the trail.

Fee for the tour. Tours daily June-Labor Day.

The overlook is on Hwy. 89 about 8 miles north of the South Tahoe Y and 18 miles south of the Tahoe City Y.

Vikingsholm from Emerald Bay Overlook. Easy. One mile downhill to the beach.

The trail winds down an old road to Vikingsholm and the Emerald Bay Beach where you can watch the sternwheelers circle the bay. Canada geese may try to beg for food. They have become so tame that some consider them pests.

Special Hikes

Vikingsholm was built by Mrs. Lora J. Knight in 1929. She planned an exact reproduction of a Norse fortress from A.D. 800. Since many of the furnishings she tried to buy in Scandinavia were so valuable that they could not be exported, she had the designs meticulously copied to complete her Viking castle. She was rowed daily to her small house on the island in the middle of the bay where she had her afternoon tea.

Emerald Bay and Fannette Island from the overlook.

Summer

Special Hikes

On Hwy. 89 drive south 18 miles from the Tahoe City Y or 8 miles north of the South Tahoe Y.

Eagle Lake. Easy. Two miles round trip with 400 feet elevation gain.

You will need a wilderness permit for this hike. This is one of the easiest yet most spectacular hikes in the area. Start up the trail to Eagle Falls, a simple one-eighth mile climb to cross above the falls. Proceed through a red fir forest as you climb toward Eagle Lake. Before reaching the lake you will cross expanses of granite rock with beautiful specimens of old Jeffrey pines. It is only one mile to Eagle Lake in its granite bowl. The first shoreline you reach offers many wonderful picnic spots. If you wish to continue, the trail climbs the ridge on the east side of the lake and continues for several miles toward the three Velma Lakes. The views at the top of the first ridge are worth the climb, and the photo opportunities of Emerald Bay and Lake Tahoe from this elevation are superb. This is one of the most popular hikes in the Tahoe Basin and parking is very limited. During July and August, therefore, we suggest that you take the Lake Lapper bus to avoid the parking problem.

Special Hikes

On Hwy. 89 drive 18 miles south from the Tahoe City Y or 10 miles north of the South Tahoe Y to the Bayview Campground and Trailhead, opposite Emerald Bay Inspiration Point.

Cascade Falls. Easy. One and a half miles round trip, some up and down, but little elevation gain. No wilderness permit required. **Granite Lake.** Moderate. Two miles round trip with 800 feet elevation gain. Wilderness permit required.

The trail starts behind the wilderness permit sign-up board. Take the left fork which climbs gently until you are on a beautiful granite ledge above Cascade Lake. The trail dips then climbs again until Lake Tahoe and Cascade Lake are both visible. The top of the falls is best viewed early in the summer when snowmelt fills the creek. Be careful with small children when descending across the granite slabs to look at the top of the falls.

It's possible to follow the creek upstream where you will find wonderful picnic sites beside deep pools. Because it is so easy, this is a perfect hike for young children while parents will enjoy the views and photo opportunities.

More ambitious hikers may elect to take the trail into Desolation Wilderness to Granite Lake. You will need a permit for this one. It is a steep climb of about 800 feet in one mile. However, the views of Emerald Bay reward the effort, and a swim in this relatively warm lake will help cool you off before the return hike.

Special Hikes

Drive 3.9 miles north from the So. Tahoe Y on Hwy. 89 to Road 1306A. The trailhead is one mile up the road.

Mount Tallac. Strenuous. Ten miles round trip with 3,300 feet elevation gain. Wilderness permit required.

Climbing Mount Tallac to 9,735 feet is the experience of a lifetime, for not only have you achieved a true peak climb, but the view is unmatched anywhere. For those that aren't sure about their ability to make it to the top, you can stop at Floating Island Lake in 1.5 miles up a fairly shaded trail. Three quarters of a mile farther on is Cathedral Lake, another stopping place with excellent views of Fallen Leaf Lake. For those who wish to see spectacular wildflower gardens, the climb to the base of the bowl that hides Tallac's real peak from view affords another stopping place.

Hardy hikers can keep going up the bowl and across the several false tops to the north. This is a popular hike, and you might even find someone playing a musical instrument or drinking champagne to celebrate. It will all be worth the work when you take in the view. Lake Tahoe, Fallen Leaf and Cascade Lakes are to the east, while the granite bowls, peaks and lakes of Desolation Wilderness fill the western horizon. This is one hike where we recommend you wear hiking boots and carry plenty of water.

Special Hikes

Drive north on Hwy. 89 from the South Tahoe Y 3.2 miles to the U.S. Forest Service Visitor Center.

Rainbow Trail. Easy. One and a half mile loop trail. Paved with wheelchair access.

This nature trail leaves from the Visitor Center. Signs along the way explain the importance of Taylor Creek and the stream ecosystem that helps maintain a healthy forest and Lake Tahoe's water quality. This creek and its riparian zone are nesting and feeding habitats for a myriad of birds. Early in the summer, meadows burst into bloom with buttercups, phlox, wallflower and Indian paintbrush, to name just a few. The renovated Stream Profile Chamber is now open. In the chamber you will have an underwater view of swimming fish and, in October, when the kokanee salmon spawn, you can see hundreds of these fish with their red humped backs and strange beak-like jaws making their way up the creek to spawn before they die.

Drive south 4.6 miles from Hwy. 89 on Fallen Leaf Road. Park at the Marina parking lot. Walk along the shore and frontage road until you come to the church. See directions in the text for Angora Lakes parking lot.

Fallen Leaf Lake to Angora Lakes Resort Easy. One half mile from Angora Lakes parking lot with 160 feet elevation gain. Moderate. One and a half miles from Fallen Leaf to Angora Lakes with 1,120 feet elevation gain.

This is a great hike for those staying at Fallen Leaf Lake. The trail leaves from the church. The hike has many rewards, including unsurpassed views of Fallen Leaf and Lake Tahoe. The first quarter mile is on a rocky trail that goes in and out of the lake-level forest of cedar, white fir

Summer

Special Hikes

and Jeffrey pine. Thimbleberry and dogwood line the trail. After crossing a rocky ridge, the trail ascends via a set of easier switchbacks through a forest of beautiful red fir and western white pine. After reaching the parking lot, you join others who drove to this point to climb gradually on a wide sandy thoroughfare past the first Angora lake until you reach the resort, established in 1917. Children of friends who have long vacationed at Fallen Leaf dubbed this the "Lemonade Lake," because of the famous lemonade the resort serves. Bring your bathing suit for this one. The beach at the resort is open to all and lies along the northwest shore. Dogs can accompany you, but must remain on a leash at all times and may not swim. Dogs can swim at the lower lake, however. If you're looking for the shorter hike, we suggest that South Shore visitors take Lake Tahoe Boulevard 3 miles from the South Tahoe *Y* then turn right on Tahoe Mountain Road until it intersects Angora Ridge Road and drive 3.5 miles to the parking lot.

A wildflower garden along the Pacific Crest Trail.

Special Hikes

Take U.S. 50 west 5.3 miles from the South Tahoe Y to Upper Truckee Rd. Turn south and drive 3.6 miles to the sign for Hawley Grade National Recreation Trail. Take the single lane road into a small summer home development. Park at the end of the road.

The Hawley Grade Trail. Easy. Three and a half miles round trip with 700 feet elevation gain.

This is as much a historical adventure as a hike, for the Hawley Grade is the first wagon road built over this portion of the Sierra. Westbound settlers wanted an easier, more direct route than Carson Pass to drive directly to the Hangtown (Placerville) mines. After the Luther Pass road was surveyed in 1854, Asa Hawley set up a trading post in Lake Valley and built an easy ascent to Johnson Pass (Echo Pass). With money from private sources, he constructed a one-lane wagon road that significantly improved the journey to Hangtown. When the road was completed in 1857, El Dorado and Sacramento counties put up money to improve the western portions of the road, and an official route from the Carson Valley to Hangtown was established. But, not for long. When the Nevada Comstock mines lured eastbound traffic east across the Sierra Nevada, miners and their suppliers immediately sought a more direct route over the mountains. By 1860 a new road (old Meyers Grade) below today's U.S. 50 and north of Hawley Grade was constructed. It crossed the southern edge of the lake and over Daggett Pass (Kingsbury Grade) down to Genoa. This "Bonanza Road", as it was called, became the preferred route to Virginia City. Poor Hawley's westbound road became unprofitable and fell into disuse. Today, thanks to the U.S. Forest Service, we are able to hike this road (now a trail) and marvel at the engineering skill of Asa Hawley.

 **Special Hikes**

The trail begins past the last of the houses in a small development. You can hear the Upper Truckee River nearby as you climb past thickets of currant and willow.

As soon as the trail turns north, a gradual ascent to the summit begins. The first mile is through deep forest and an area with natural springs that ooze onto the trail, even in late summer. Notice how nature is managing to bring the contours of this slope into alignment, narrowing the size of the trail as you climb. Marvel at the ancient stands of Jeffrey pine and white fir that have been spared the lumberman's axe. After about a mile you cross a rock slide and emerge from the forest to glimpses of Lake Tahoe far to the north beyond Lake Valley. Later, you can look south to see the volcanic palisades under Stevens Peak and beyond it, Red Lake Peak. It was from this peak that John Charles Frémont first saw Lake Tahoe. Here you are looking toward the Upper Truckee River's headwaters.

This hike is best in the afternoon when the sun has begun to fall behind Echo Summit. It is also a great autumn hike when the aspens paint golden ribbons along the Upper Truckee River.

Special Hikes

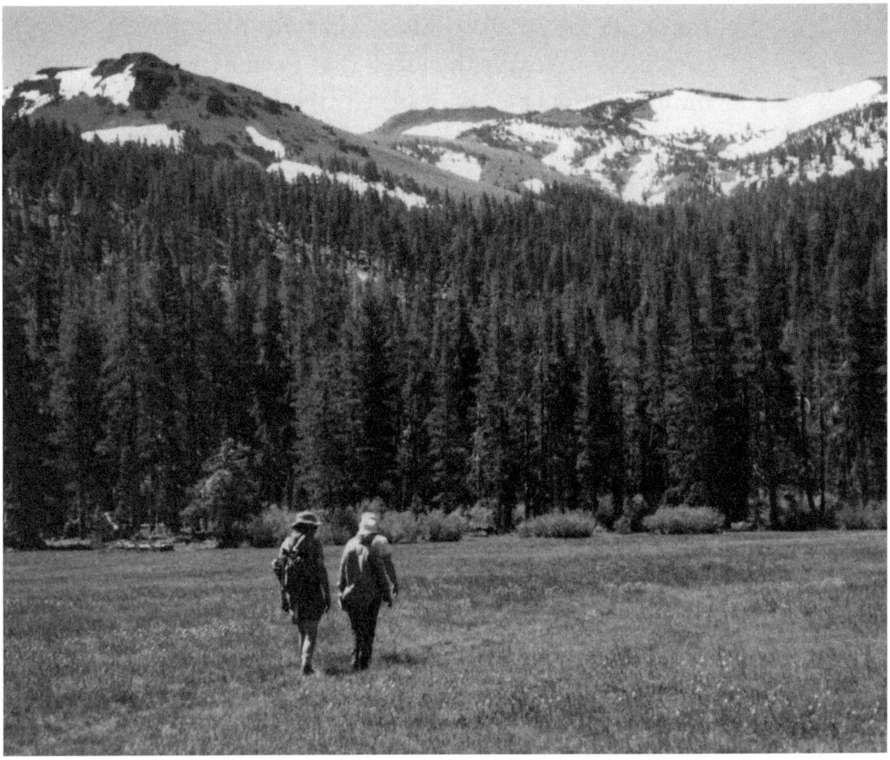

Hiking across Big Meadow.

Big Meadow Trailhead parking is 5 miles south of Meyers on Hwy. 89. Turn left off the road about 100 yards past the old roadside parking to a developed trailhead with restrooms and display board.

Big Meadow and Round Lake. Moderate. Six miles round trip with 800 feet elevation gain.

Walk to Highway 89. Cross the highway to find the trail to Big Meadow. The trail begins with a climb of several hundred feet through a forest of Jeffrey pine and white fir until you emerge onto the flat Big Meadow.

Special Hikes

Families with small children will find this a perfect beginners' hike, for the creek that meanders through the meadow offers plenty of places to safely wade or splash in cool waters. Early in the season you will need mosquito repellant.

To reach Round Lake, continue through the meadow and climb another few hundred feet through wildflower gardens adorning sandy slopes to the crest of the ridge separating Big Meadow Creek and Upper Truckee River drainages. From the ridge you will see Red Lake and Stevens Peaks. The trail now descends gradually a mile and a half to Round Lake. The west shore has many desirable picnic spots high above the lake. Notice the interesting rock formation that guards the eastern shore. These are volcanic palisades, and debris from these give the water of Round Lake a brownish hue. Bring a fishing rod to cast for the lake's cutthroat trout.

Sugar Pine

Round Lake can also be reached via a wildflower wonderland from Carson Pass over Meiss Pass and through Meiss Meadow. Round Lake is about equidistant from Highway 88 and Highway 89 and affords a good car shuttle opportunity. A description of the hike from Carson Pass can be found on page 160.

Closeup view of a Mariposa lily.

© Ellie Huggins

 _____ **Special Hikes**

Fee per person for tram ride. Reduced price after 5pm.

Take Ski Run Blvd. south to Needle Peak and follow signs to Heavenly Ski Resort parking. The tram is at the north end of the parking lot.

Heavenly Tahoe Vista Trail. First half mile easy, then moderate to strenuous. Two miles round trip with 1,000 feet elevation gain.

This is a "must do" hike for anyone who has never seen the views from Heavenly's ski slopes. The trail follows the west-facing slope north from the top of the tram. The first quarter mile to Neumann Point allows all levels of hikers to enjoy breathtaking views of Lake Tahoe nestled in its alpine bowl. However, if you plan to hike farther to Snowshoe Ridge, there are steep pitches to be negotiated over sandy, rocky terrain. Hiking boots or sport shoes will make this a much more pleasant hike, and you will want to bring water. The trail to Fremont Camp and on to the peak is very steep, rising to 9,200 feet. If you are not used to the altitude, take it easy and hike only as far as you feel comfortable.

During the first part of the trail, conveniently placed benches allow a rest stop to enjoy the incomparable views while your heart pounds. The trail passes through a forest of magnificent, old growth red fir, Jeffrey pine and western white pine. Your first vista point is at Neumann Point, named for a Heavenly ski instructor who perished in an avalanche below this point. Beneath you is the expanse of the South Shore, its beaches and beyond them the distinctive dark form of Mount Tallac. From this altitude the granite peaks of Desolation Wilderness shine on the

Special Hikes

horizon. As you continue along the trail, it climbs, sometimes steeply, to Snowshoe Ridge, named for the intrepid Norwegian who skied across the Sierra carrying the mail from 1856 to 1876. This vista point looks north to another broad view of the lake. If you decide to make the worthwhile climb to the peak above Fremont Camp, it will become very steep in places and you should be very careful on your return downhill.

When you return, you can either picnic on the deck or lunch in the Monument Peak Restaurant.

lupine

scarlet gilia

Special Hikes

Drive north 12 miles on U.S. 50 to Spooner Summit. Parking for the trailhead is on the north side of the highway in a signed area off the road just east of the summit.

Tahoe Rim Trail from Spooner Summit. Easy. 800 feet elevation gain, as far as you want to hike. Or moderate 8-mile hike returning to Spooner Lake (with car shuttle).

Hiking the first miles of this 13-mile segment of the Tahoe Rim Trail allows you to get some spectacular views of Lake Tahoe as well as the Carson Valley in Nevada. The trail starts at 7,150 feet and climbs gradually into the Carson Range of the Sierra Nevada. As you round the first bend you will catch glimpses of Spooner Lake and Lake Tahoe in the distance. The trail toward the first vista point passes through stands of second growth Jeffrey pine. From a group of granite boulders you will get your first view of the Carson Valley and the ranges of mountains to the south and east. At the top of the first long climb, in about 2 miles, is John's Rock. From these rocks opens a magnificent panorama of Lake Tahoe and the granite peaks of Desolation Wilderness. If snow still lies on the high peaks, look for the cross of snow on the southeast bowl of Mount Tallac. After John's Rock the trail flattens out and crosses an open plateau where giant red firs reign supreme. These beautiful trees were spared in the logging frenzy of the late 1800s. Leave the trail and go to a group of boulders to the west. From this vantage point you will be able to see Lake Tahoe, Emerald Bay and even Fallen Leaf Lake in its bowl under Mount Tallac. At mile 4 there is a connector trail down to the North Canyon Road of Spooner Lake Park where you can pick up a trail south to Spooner Summit and your car. If there are two cars in

Special Hikes

your group, you can arrange a car shuttle leaving one car at the park. There is a fee to park here.

For those who want a more strenuous hike, take the Rim Trail across the western slope of Snow Valley Peak until it intersects with an old road and bike trail that descends to North Canyon Road. From these trails you will get your most expansive views of Lake Tahoe and peaks of the western shore. During the height of summer, this can be a hot hike, so bring plenty of water.

Fee per vehicle. *On Hwy. 28 about one half mile north of the U.S. 50 intersection.*

Spooner Lake Nature Trail. Easy. One and a half miles around the lake.

Spooner Lake is part of the Lake Tahoe Nevada State Park and is a favorite starting place for experienced, mountain bike enthusiasts to climb to Marlette Lake and the famous Flume Trail. The trail around Spooner Lake is a natural to include with a family picnic in the park. It is particularly beautiful in autumn when the many aspens surrounding the lake are in full color. Several trails leave the picnic area and descend to the trailhead near the dam. Cross the dam and take the trail in a clockwise direction. Halfway around the lake you walk through aspen groves. These are quaking aspen, whose leaves tremble with the slightest breeze, giving rise to the Latin name *populus tremuloides*. Look closely at a leaf with its flattened stalk. This is what causes the leaf to move in the wind.

Special Hikes

Drive 2.5 miles north on Hwy. 28 from the intersection with U.S. 50. Park immediately in front of the gated road on the west side of Hwy. 28 or a few hundred yards north in a larger paved parking area.

Skunk Harbor. Moderate. Three miles round trip, 600 feet below the highway.

This could be classified as a beach, hike or historical walk. Although it is only 1.5 miles downhill to the beach, the climb back on a hot summer afternoon will negate the cooling affect of a swim. However, the view from this lovely cove is worth the effort and the sandy beach is among the nicest in the area.

The trail winds down on an old roadbed with interesting views over Prey Meadows. Unfortunately, it is surrounded by dead and dying white fir, stressed from the 1988-1994 drought. Below the trail after about one-half mile you will notice the roadbed of the former railroad that zigzagged its way up Slaughterhouse Canyon from the Glenbrook mills to Spooner Summit. When logging ceased at the end of the century, the Bliss family moved the track and stock to Tahoe City and built the Truckee to Tahoe City narrow gauge railroad. When you reach the end of the trail, you will be surprised to find a large stone house. This was built by George and Caroline Newhall in the 1920s as a secluded picnic site. They came by boat from their home on Rubicon Bay across the lake. George Whittell bought the home in 1937 and used it as a guest house. The U.S. Forest Service acquired the land in 1972 and is putting it on the National Register of Historic Places, a reminder of former gilded times on the lake. The beach is often visited by boaters as well as hikers. If you don't want to hike uphill in the hot afternoon sun, try a supper hike and a swim.

Special Hikes

Drive 6.7 miles east on Hwy. 431 to the paved parking area for the trail.

Tahoe Rim Trail Whole Access Loop at Tahoe Meadows. Easy. One mile loop.

Families with babies in strollers or those in wheelchairs can enjoy this newest trail of the Tahoe Rim Trail system. This loop around the high meadows allows you to enjoy a meadow and streamside environment filled with wildflowers and a section of lodgepole pine forest. Among the flowers to be enjoyed up close are bush lupine, asters, alpine daisies, yellow mimulus (monkey flowers), so-called because the face of a monkey to be seen on the flower's petals.

Moored at Skunk Harbor.

Summer

Special Hikes

Drive 6.9 miles on Hwy. 431 to a trailhead on the north side of the road. A pink cement block building is visible above the road. Park parallel to the north side of the highway.

Mount Rose. Moderate. Six miles round trip to start of peak climb with 600 feet elevation gain. Strenuous. Ten miles round trip with 1,978 feet elevation gain.

Like the Mount Tallac climb on the South Shore of Lake Tahoe, one does not have to make the whole trip to enjoy spectacular scenery and views. The first 3 miles of this hike to the top of 10,778-foot Mount Rose is on an old road with an easy grade and expansive views of Lake Tahoe around every curve. Trailside displays of delphinium, pink mimulus and lupine appear for the first two miles of hiking. When the delphinium are in bloom you may be treated to a sight of many hummingbirds zooming in for drinks of nectar. Deer are also often seen in meadows near the road. In about 2 miles you come to a pond in a lovely meadow. For those who do not wish to climb the peak, this pond is a perfect picnic spot. Look carefully at this point for cross-country ski trail markers high in the trees. These will lead you back downhill to intersect the main road about a half a mile below. Mount Rose is hidden from view at this point as the road curves to the left. Near this point a trail leaves the road on the right dipping into the headwaters of Galena Creek. The trail crosses the creek drainage and climbs north to the final one-mile climb east to the summit. It is a steep ascent and can be windy, but the views are worth the effort.

Special Hikes

Fee for water taxi.
Drive 8.9 miles west on U.S. 50 from the South Tahoe Y to Echo Lakes Rd. Drive north about one mile then turn left and follow signs to Echo Lakes. Park only where allowed.

Pacific Crest Trail at Echo Lakes. Easy. Two and three-quarter miles to Upper Echo Lake. Less than 100 ft. elevation gain.

This is a perfect hike for a family with young children. The trail starts across the dam and goes along the north side of the lake. After a short climb high above the summer homes, the trail contours along the north shore before descending to the forested slopes above Upper Echo Lake. Here you will find a signed trail that leads to the dock and water taxi back to your starting point. This is a seldom used trail that offers an opportunity to hike these beautiful granite slopes for a short distance and return across the water. Use the phone at the dock to call the water taxi.

From Upper Echo Lake there are numerous trails to beautiful lakes nestled in the granite landscape of Desolation Wilderness. The hike to Aloha Lake is a favorite. We suggest that you consult the appropriate U.S.G.S. quadrangle or one of the books listed on page 128 for descriptions of these hikes.

Special Hikes

Special Hikes at Carson Pass

The Carson Pass area offers hikes of every description through beautiful wildflower gardens, along creeks and rivers to lakes nestled in cirques under towering peaks. A few of the easiest are mentioned here. Carson Pass is an area as yet untouched by much development, and it is a place where you can hike into the wilderness with relative ease. Unlike Desolation Wilderness, no permit is needed and your dog is welcome. Since most of the hikes are above 8,500 feet, you may encounter snow well into July, and the wildflower season will be later than in the Tahoe Basin.

The new U.S. Forest Service information center at Carson Pass is staffed by knowledgeable volunteers of the Eldorado National Forest Interpretive Association from June to Labor Day. Here you can buy books and maps about the natural and human history of the region. There is a small display about the emigrant history of this region.

On Hwy. 88 at Carson Pass, 13 miles west of the junction with Hwy. 89. Park in the lot on the south side of the highway.

Winnemucca Lake and Beyond. Easy to moderate. Three miles round trip with 500 feet elevation gain.

The trail is marked by both blue diamonds high on the trees for cross-country skiers and the Pacific Crest Trail markers. Early in the summer wildflowers of every hue will thrill you along the open slopes. The trail starts uphill gradually through red fir until you reach the junction to Frog Lake in about a mile. Walk over and take in the view.

Special Hikes

Families with small children may want to stop here for a picnic and swim. The hike to Lake Winnemucca is an easy grade of only another 1.5 miles across an open plateau with views of Round Top Peak and Caples Lake. At the next trail junction, take the right hand fork to Winnemucca, which will come into view from a bluff. Surrounded by the steep cliffs under Round Top Peak (10,300 feet), the lake is a perfect stopping place and creates a day's outing that will give every member of the family a feeling of accomplishment. More ambitious hikers can continue climbing steeply to Round Top Lake (1 mile) and Fourth of July Lake (2 miles).

Winnemucca Lake in early summer.

 _____ **Special Hikes**

Park on the north side of Hwy. 88 a few hundred yards west of Carson Pass.

Meiss Pass, Meiss Meadow to Round Lake or Showers Lake. Easy to moderate. Two miles to Meiss Pass, 3.5 miles to Round Lake with 300 feet elevation gain to the pass, 400 feet down to Meiss Meadow or 4 miles to Showers Lake with 400 feet elevation gain from Meiss Meadow to Showers Lake.

This section of the Pacific Crest Trail north of Carson Pass offers some of the most expansive views of Lake Tahoe and the Desolation Wilderness peaks anywhere in the region and also has spectacular wildflower gardens. You only have to hike 1.5 miles for the opportunity to see Lake Tahoe as Kit Carson and John Charles Frémont did in 1844. The trail starts gently uphill through a forest of 500-year-old Sierra juniper that are still young enough to keep their form and bark. More gnarled specimens seen on lofty granite slabs can live for more than a thousand years. In the forest, columbine, lupine and scarlet gilia vie for attention, and memorable photographs of these gardens are possible. After crossing a small creek, the trail takes a couple of easy switchbacks past a small glacial tarn (pond) to the crest at Meiss Pass. Hike far enough to take in the view of Lake Tahoe. Red Lake Peak, where Carson and Frémont stood, is to the east. Looking back southwest you can see where the emigrants crossed just south of Thimble Peak above Kirkwood Ski Resort.

The pass area is filled with fields of Douglas iris in midsummer where the trail continues downhill to the Meiss cabins and meadow, named for Louis Meiss, whose

Special Hikes

son Benjamin bought these acres in 1901. Cattle have grazed here ever since. Take the right-hand fork at the next junction to hike to Round Lake. You will climb gently uphill through an old growth red fir forest with some of the finest specimens of this stately giant in the Tahoe area. The trail reaches Round Lake in another 1.5 miles, which beckons swimmers on a summer day into its surprisingly temperate water. You will want to hike to the northeast shore for a good swimming and picnic spot.

To reach Showers Lake, continue straight in Meiss Meadow another mile before a climb of 400 feet brings you over a ridge to a lovely lake nestled among granite boulders. The near shore of the lake has many camping spots, and the lake can be very crowded on summer weekends.

View of Lake Tahoe from Meiss Pass.

Just For Kids

Families coming to the region can choose from a variety of free or paid services that can make your kids' vacation like going away to camp. Some ski resorts now have year-round child care as well as special programs for small children and even teenagers. The U.S. Forest Service has interpretive activities that are geared for children and many campgrounds have evening campfire programs for the whole family. We have listed those that are ongoing, but check with the U.S. Forest Service Visitor Center and California State Parks for weekly offerings of hikes and nature programs. The Sierra Nevada Children's Museum in Truckee can provide hours of experiential learning for young people. See page 264 in "Museums" for the description.

Truckee and North Lake Tahoe

Donner Memorial State Park

Summer only.
Donner Memorial State Park, Donner Pass Rd., Truckee
530-582-7892

The Junior Ranger program at the state park is offered every day at 8:30 a.m. during the summer months. Nature walks and activities last for an hour. Whether staying at the park or in the Truckee area, your youngsters will enjoy one of the programs.

Tahoe Donner Equestrian Center Horsemanship Camps

Fee per week. Enrollment limited.
End of June through August.
Tahoe Donner
530-587-9470

The Equestrian Center holds weekly camps Monday through Friday from 9:00 a.m. to 3:00 p.m. Classes are for all levels of Western and English styles and feature basic horsemanship as well as how to care for your horse. Campers receive special instruction and practice for a show or games on the last day.

Just For Kids

Northstar-at-Tahoe Minors' Camp

Reservations required.
Northstar-at-Tahoe
530-562-2278

If you are staying at Northstar, or just planning to mountain bike, play golf or horseback ride at the resort, you can enroll your 2 to 10-year-olds in Minors' Camp. Children must be completely potty trained, and you must stay at the resort while your child is at camp. The fully licensed child care facility offers a wide variety of activities from off-site field trips to swimming, arts and crafts, creek walks and pony rides.

Squaw Valley

Resort at Squaw Creek

Reservations required.
Resort at Squaw Creek, Squaw Valley
530-583-6300

The resort hosts children in their Mountain Buddies™ program geared to interest, exercise and educate children between the ages of 3 and 13 years. With such activities as "wacky olympics" to test their mettle, rollerblading, ice skating and building snowmen in the winter, there are sports or arts and crafts for children every day all year. There are three sessions daily, and an evening session from 6:00 to 9:00 p.m.

Ten Little Indians

Reservations required. Summer and Winter.
Squaw Valley
530-583-0236

Squaw Valley Ski Corporation operates year-round child care for infants and children to 6 years old. In summer the kids enjoy swimming in the High Camp pool, nature walks, ice skating and arts and crafts. In the winter snowplay and early ski instruction help kids enjoy the snow and learn to ski in a helpful, caring environment. The day care center is fully licensed.

Summer

Just For Kids

Tahoe Trips and Trails

Reservations required.
800-581-4453

The company that leads adults on hikes of all abilities has added a new set of trips this summer. An August Family Sampler Tour is designed for families with kids six and up. Activites include a hayride breakfast at the Ponderosa Ranch and one evening of kid's activities so the parents can have the night off. Lodging and meals are incuded in this planned trip.

Little Peoples' Adventures

Reservaions recommended. Drop-ins at Tahoe Lake School.
375 Grove St., Tahoe City
530-581-4572

Tim Critz, with many years of experience coaching children, offers all kinds of outdoor adventures for kids between 6 and 13 years old, from canoeing and swimming to a climbing wall, horseback riding and biking. You can sign up your child for a day, week or an ultra 10-day fun pass. Drop-ins are based upon space availability.

West Shore and South Lake Tahoe

California State Parks

July 1 through Labor Day.
D.L. Bliss:
530-525-7277
Sugar Pine Point:
530-525-7982

Junior Ranger Programs are held at D.L. Bliss and Sugar Pine Point State Parks. Times vary at each park, so check at the entrance stations for information about family oriented hikes and campfire programs.

Just For Kids

U.S. Forest Service Programs

At the Fallen Leaf Campground Site 4A off Fallen Leaf Rd.

Woodsey Rangers meets at the Fallen Leaf Campground Monday through Friday at 10:00 a.m. Kids between 6 and 12 years old will be treated to games, treasure hunts and storytelling, with different programs each day. Learn about nature's magical environment from knowledgeable Forest Service rangers.

Camp Tadaka

Fee per day. 1180 Rufus Blvd., So. Lake Tahoe 530-542-6093

The South Lake Tahoe Parks and Recreation Department operates a summer day camp for first through sixth graders that is open to any child, whether visitor or resident. The camp features field trips, outdoor activities, games plus arts and crafts. Hours are from 7:30 a.m. to 6:00 p.m. There is no need to preregister, just show up before 7:30 a.m. in the morning. If you wish to enroll for a week, drop by the office at 1180 Rufus Allen Boulevard in South Lake Tahoe.

Carson Pass

Kirkwood Explorers

Fridays, Saturdays and Sundays. Summer only. Reservations recommended. Kirkwood Resort is 5 miles west of Carson Pass off Hwy. 88 and 18.5 miles from the junction with Hwy. 89. 209-258-6000

Kids between 5 and 14 years old can attend this day camp that features everything from fly-fishing instruction to nature crafts. Trained naturalists will keep the children happy between 9:00 a.m. and 3:00 p.m. doing a myriad of outdoor activities. On Saturdays there is a family recreation program with dinner followed by a campfire with storytelling and marshmallow roasting. Here's an opportunity to give the kids a day at camp while you hike, fish or relax, then relive your own camp memories with your children in the evening.

Ranger Programs

The United States Forest Service conducts many different ranger programs suitable for the whole family. The walks and tours take place at the Visitor Center, at the Tallac Historic Site and at Echo Lakes. The schedule is published in *Lake of the Sky Journal* available at many locations in South Lake Tahoe, at the Myers Visitor Information Kiosk and at the U. S. Forest Service Visitor Center.

U.S. Forest Service Visitor Center

The U.S. Forest Service Visitor Center is 3.2 miles north of the South Tahoe Y on Hwy. 89. 530-573-2674

Daily Programs.

A Patio Talk is given daily at the Visitor Center. Subjects of the talks are posted 24 hours in advance.

Weekly Programs

Wonders of Wildflowers walks take you out into the meadows near the Visitor Center. This is a wonderful way to be introduced to the local wildflowers so that you can recognize them on your own walks elsewhere in the basin.

The Creek Walk is a naturalist-led walk <u>in</u> Taylor Creek for two hours of fun. It is not recommended for kids under age 5. Wear old tennis shoes and shorts for this one.

Tallac Historic Site

Tallac Historic Site parking is 3.1 miles north of the South Lake Tahoe Y on Hwy. 89.

You can reach the Tallac Historic Site via the Trolley and on the paved bike trail that leaves South Lake Tahoe off Emerald Bay Road. So why not leave the car at home for your day here. The beaches here are described on page 54, the bike trail on page 92, and bus information on page 2.

Ranger Programs

Fee.
530-541-5227

Guided tours of the Pope Main House are offered Fridays through Mondays. Reservations are required.

The Boats of Tahoe tour at the Pope Boathouse offer a glimpse at the historic working and pleasure boats on Lake Tahoe at the turn-of-the-century.

Washoe Garden Plants tour will introduce you to the plants that the Washoe (sometimes "Washo") used for food and for fashioning into tools and baskets. Following this once-a-week tour, visit the Tallac Museum to learn more about Washoe history.

Echo Lakes

Drive 9 miles west on U.S. 50 from the South Tahoe Y to Echo Lake Rd. Drive north to the Sno-Park and turn left, following signs to Echo Lakes.

The Echo Lakes Boat Cruise takes place a couple of days a week. A naturalist will describe the glaciated landscape that surrounds the two lakes. This is a great way to become acquainted with this beautiful wilderness above Lake Tahoe. You may want to return for some of the hikes.

California State Parks

The California State Parks' rangers lead regular walks and campfire programs at each park during the summer. The schedules are posted at each park unit one week in advance. The park rangers also lead snowshoe and cross-country tours to different places in the Sierra District. The descriptions and dates are published each fall in *The Sierra District Fall - Winter Activities Schedule*. There are tours for all levels and some include cross-country ski instruction.

Summer

Winter Activities

With mountain peaks reaching 10,000 feet and snowstorms that can dump up to five feet of snow in a few days, the region is well-known for its downhill ski areas.

Before skiing was fashionable, hardy members of the Sierra Skiing Club could be seen schussing down the slopes above Truckee on their 10-foot "Norwegian skis". By 1909 Truckee was hosting a Winter Carnival complete with skiing and jumping exhibitions, sleigh rides, toboggan runs, and a "fantastical" Ice Palace constructed in the middle of town. Soda Springs Ski Area began with a rope tow in 1935. During the 1930s the Lake Tahoe Skii Club (the Scandinavian spelling of ski was used) hosted USSA and state championships at its ski jump. Sugar Bowl opened its Austrian-style resort with the first chairlift in the West in December 1939.

Ski hills were concentrated at Echo Summit before 1955. Chris Kuraisa turned a small ski hill into Heavenly Valley and opened with one chairlift in 1955. After the 1960 Winter Olympic Games at Squaw Valley, new downhill ski areas were developed throughout the Lake Tahoe region. Fourteen ski areas now welcome skiers and snowboarders with more than a hundred lifts on thousands of acres of skiable terrain from Donner Summit to Carson Pass.

Winter visitors to Lake Tahoe need not be dedicated skiers to enjoy a sojourn here. There is something for every taste and every member of the family. You might consider cross-country skiing, ice skating, a snowmobile tour through the forest, or a saucer ride down a snowy hill with the kids. Almost anyone can snowshoe and most rental shops now rent the new lightweight models. On certain weekends throughout the winter, the Sierra District of California State Parks offers guided cross-country and snowshoe trips.

If the weather does not cooperate, try sitting by a cozy fire in one of the area's great restaurants. With museums to visit and casinos for gambling, you might not even find time to shop.

Winter Activities

Winter Driving

Winter travel in the Sierra can be delayed by snowstorms or accidents on the freeway. When driving to the mountains, you are well-advised to do the following:

- √ Check your antifreeze and windshield washer reservoir.

- √ Always carry chains, chain repair links, a flashlight, tarp or other cloth to lie on while putting on chains, a shovel and ice scraper or broom for cleaning off snow.

- √ It is a good idea to have a blanket and extra clothing along in case you are stopped on the road for a long time. Carry some nibbles and a thermos of hot liquid.

Chain Controls

When a storm is in progress, CalTrans requires that drivers use chains or have a four-wheel-drive vehicle with snow tires for portions of mountain roads. Chain installers charge a fee to install your chains. Weather and road conditions change rapidly, so the chain control points change also.

The posted speed limit when chain controls are in effect is 25-30 miles per hour, and that applies to all vehicles, including four-wheel drives. Most spinouts and accidents involve four-wheel drive vehicles going at speeds greater than the limit.

The telephone number for road conditions is 800-427-7623.

Downhill Ski Areas

The Lake Tahoe region offers the full range of downhill skiing and snowboarding possibilities at 14 ski areas. There are terrain parks for boarders, and some areas have snow tubing, complete with lifts for the uphill ride. See page 208 in "Snowplay." The areas are listed from Donner Summit and Truckee, south on Highway 89 to Lake Tahoe areas then Echo Summit and Carson Pass. The descriptions include information about snowboard parks and special programs for children and first-time skiers, along with some of the special ticket rates. Since most areas have two-for-one tickets on certain days as well as women's days and discount tickets through retail outlets, check the Ski Tahoe free tab for this information or call the ski area. All ski areas have a rental shop on the premises. See page 310 for a description of *Mountain Dreamers*, a beautiful book about the pioneers who brought downhill skiing to the Sierra.

Donner Summit and Truckee

Boreal

At Castle Peak exit off I-80 west of Truckee.
530-426-3666
Snow phone:
530-426-3663

Boreal is usually the first area to open each season. With 100 acres of snowmaking, Boreal offers a snow condition guarantee. If you aren't satisfied, turn in your ticket within a half hour and get a full refund. Boreal devotes 30 percent of its 380 acres to novice slopes with access to novice terrain from the top of the Accelerator quad chairlift. Animal Crackers, the children's ski school, teaches kids 4 to 10 years old and a "Ski-With-Me" Parent/Child Ski School is available as well. Boreal advertises great snowboarding with lessons for all abilities. Their Jidassic Park and half-pipe are for more experienced snowboarders. In 1998 a family terrain park was created with dips and bumps that skiers and boarders can use.

Downhill Ski Areas

Lights keep the slopes open until 9:00 p.m. Seniors age 60 to 69 years old can get discounted tickets. Skiers 70 and over and 4 years old and under ski free. A new program of "EasySki" lessons, guarantees that you will attain the goal of top to bottom skiing or snowboarding or you may return for free lessons until you can. Perhaps the best deal in the area is the free Nugget chair where beginning skiers can practice all day.

Soda Springs Ski Area

One mile east of Soda Springs/Norden exit off I-80.
530-426-3663

Soda Springs is the area's oldest, having opened in 1935. It is operated by Boreal and offers uncrowded skiing at a modest price. Ski teams frequent the resort for training. The "Ski-With-Me" lessons are part of a parent participation program. And if you haven't skied enough during the day, your Soda Springs lift ticket will get you several more hours of skiing under the lights at Boreal. Senior discounts start at 60 years old. Children 7 and under and seniors 70 and over ski free. See "Snowplay" on page 208 for information about snow tubing.

Riding the tubing lift at Soda Springs.

Downhill Ski Areas

Sugar Bowl Ski Resort

On Donner Pass Rd. one half mile west of Donner Pass and 3 miles east of I-80 from the Soda Springs/Norden exit. Use the Magic Carpet Gondola to reach the Lodge. Mt. Judah parking entrance is across from Donner Ski Ranch.
530-426-9000
Snow phone: 530-426-3847

In 1939, Walt Disney and a group of Bay Area investors backed the plans of Hannes Schroll, a famous Austrian skier, to open an Austrian-style resort. Located on the west side of the range, Sugar Bowl benefits from the most snowfall in the region. Voted one of the best expert ski areas in the west, the famed Silver Belt chute under the Silver Belt Quad thrills skiers and observers alike. However the Lakeview Run from the top of Silver Belt quad on Mt. Lincoln has great intermediate cruising. Good beginner slopes are directly in front of the Lodge, while intermediates and experts can find good runs off Mt. Disney and Crow's Nest and from the lifts at the Mt. Judah parking area. A terrain park for snowboarders is accessed from the Mt. Judah Express Quad. The Jerome Hill

Spring lunch break on the deck of Sugar Bowl Lodge.

Downhill Ski Areas

Express accesses smooth, wide intermediate terrain and connecting runs go to the bottom of the novice Christmas Tree lift or to the Silver Belt Quad and the Lodge base area. You'll never need your car if you stay at the Sugar Bowl Lodge, where special ski week packages include room, breakfast and dinner, two classes a day and fun races complete with video shows and awards ceremonies. (See page 280 in "Historic Inns and B&B's" for a description.)

Sugar Bears Child Care Center is a state licensed facility for 3 to 6-year-olds that offers ski instruction. PowderKids is a special ski school for children 6 to 12 years old. Senior discounts start at 60 years old, and there are major discounts for children 12 years old and under. A large base lodge is slated to be ready for the 1999-2000 season, when Sugar Bowl will celebrate its 60th anniversary . The Magic Carpet Gondola and garage still service the Lodge and base facilities for most of the lifts.

Donner Ski Ranch

At Donner Summit 3.5 miles east of I-80 from the Soda Springs/ Norden exit, or one quarter mile west of Donner Pass on Donner Pass Rd.
530-426-3635

Donner Ski Ranch is one of the most affordable family ski areas, offering acres of open slopes in view of the lodge. If you are looking for the best deal in town for a day of great fun for both skiers and boarders with a few snow play tots in the crowd, this is the place for you. The snowplay area is across the highway to the east. Five lifts service 75 percent beginner and intermediate terrain with 750 feet of vertical. The longest run is one mile down the South Bowl. This is a favorite with groups and ski teams. There is night skiing on weekends. Senior discounts start at 60 years old.

Winter

Downhill Ski Areas

Ski Tahoe Donner

On Northwoods Blvd. in the Tahoe Donner development, 4.5 miles from the Donner Pass Rd. intersection. 530-587-9400 Snow phone: 530-587-9494

Tahoe Donner is known as a friendly family area and features wide-open slopes that are perfect for learning. The ski school teaches small classes with lots of individual attention. Snowflakes Ski School for children 3 to 6 years old includes indoor and outdoor instruction, equipment rental, lift ticket and snack in the price of a half or all-day session. If you are renting in the Tahoe Donner development, this is an excellent choice for that first day on the slopes. You could even run home for lunch.

Highway 89 South and West Shore

Squaw Valley USA

Two miles off Hwy. 89, eight and a half miles south of I-80 and 5.2 miles north of Tahoe City. 530-583-6985 Snow phone: 530-583-6955

The king of North Tahoe resorts has 31 lifts serving 4,000 acres of skiable terrain and a 2,850-foot vertical drop from the top of Granite Chief to the valley floor. Some of the most challenging expert slopes in the area are found here, but there are good, wide-open beginner slopes around the Gold Coast and High Camp areas. Beginners are well-advised to take the gondola or cable car down the mountain, as the mountain run to the valley is difficult in spots and gets crowded at the end of the day.

Intermediate skiers will find Shirley Lake and Siberia bowls fun for the whole day. New runs between Red Dog and the Resort at Squaw Creek open up magnificent terrain on the south side of the valley. Snowboarders will delight in the groomed halfpipe and those who haven't skied enough for the day can ski down the Mountain Run under lights after sunset. In 1999 Squaw Valley will replace the Squaw Peak gondola with a Funitel, a high-speed tram resistant to

Downhill Ski Areas

high winds, and the High Camp Pulse, a non-detachable conveyance connecting Gold Coast and High Camp. Not to be outdone by Colorado resorts, Intrawest Corporation from Canada is planning an Alpine Village at the base of the mountain.

The "Fun-in-the-Sun" program offers free first-time skiing Mondays through Fridays. Ten Little Indians Day Care has supervised activities for children six months through 2 years old while Papoose Snow School youngsters can learn to ski at their own pace in group activities that introduce children to the world of skiing. Skiers 12 years and under pay only $5 for a lift ticket. Seniors 65 to 75 years old and 13 to 15 year-olds pay a reduced price and Super Seniors 76 and over ski free. Non-skiing members of the group can keep occupied with ice skating or dining at High Camp Bath and Tennis Club. For the ultimate day and night experience, relax in the hot tub after a day on the slopes followed by dinner at Alexander's restaurant, and if you still have energy, skate under the stars or enjoy snow tubing at High Camp. See "Snowplay" on page 209 for a description of snow tubing and page 225 in "Dining Out" for a description of Alexander's.

Alpine Meadows Ski Area

Two miles off Hwy. 89 on Alpine Meadows Rd., 4 miles north of Tahoe City.
530-581-8225
Snow phone:
530-581-8374

Alpine Meadows, known as a great family resort, was developed by skiers, for skiers, offering service with a smile. It has one of the longest season in the basin, often staying open until after Memorial Day. For two years, *Snow Country* magazine readers rated Alpine Meadows first in the West. The base elevation is 6,835 feet with 12 lifts on 2,000 acres of terrain, including the new six-person Summit Chair. Ski runs for all abilities funnel down to the Day Lodge, making it easy to have a meeting place for

Winter

Downhill Ski Areas

lunch or at the end of the day. Alpine Bowl is a favorite place for intermediate skiers, while experts find plenty of challenge off Summit Chair. Powder hounds and expert skiers have acres of open bowls for exploration after one of the Sierra's famous storms. On a sunny spring skiing day, try a picnic lunch at the top of Scott's Peak with its beautiful view of Lake Tahoe. However, if the day is warm and sunny, start your day at Sherwood Forest and work your way around to the north-facing slopes off the Roundhouse and Summit chairs. Special lesson packages include a "New Skiers and Boarders Club" with a 3-hour lesson, all-day lift ticket for beginner/novice lifts and all-day equipment rental. The ski school holds classes for kids age 4 to 6 years old. Children 6 years old and under ski for $5. The senior discount ticket is for those 65 and over and $6 for 70+ skiers.

Alpine Meadows is home of the Tahoe Adaptive Ski School. Volunteers and instructors give lessons for people with all disabilities. They rent the appropriate equipment and give instruction on a special hill at the area.

Granlibakken Resort Ski Hill

Open wknds. and holidays only.
Granlibakken Rd. off Hwy. 89 about one-half mile south of the Tahoe City Y.
530-583-6203

Families and first-time skiers who stay at the resort will enjoy the poma lift outside their doors that serves 100 percent novice terrain. With a snowplay area where the littlest can slide down the hill on saucers or sleds while older kids ski, this is a great choice for people who want to ski with their families and avoid the crowds. Cross-country skiers will find wonderful back country terrain from the top of the lift.

Downhill Ski Areas

Six miles south of the Tahoe City Y on Hwy. 89.
530-525-2992
Snow phone:
530-525-2900

Homewood Ski Area

Homewood Ski Area has combined terrain with the former Tahoe Ski Bowl and is a friendly ski area with excellent runs for beginners and intermediates. It is a favorite with many West Shore families because of the moderately priced lift tickets. From the top of the mountain, skiers can take in the spectacular view of Lake Tahoe from the Rainbow Ridge run. Families with both skiers and snowboarders find a variety of terrain for skiers of all abilities and a Terrain Park just for snowboarders. The Children's Center Day Care takes care of kids 2 to 5 while the pre-school ski program is for 5 and 6-year-olds. Senior discounts start at 65 years old and children 8 years old and younger ski free.

Highway 267 and North Shore Lake Tahoe

Six miles south of Truckee off Hwy. 267.
530-562-1010
Snow phone:
530-562-1330

Northstar-at-Tahoe Resort

A great mountain beckons with long runs on superbly groomed slopes from the top of Mount Pluto. Beginners can take the pleasant, wide run from the day lodge down to the village. When the snow is fresh, the backside runs plunge down almost 2,000 feet to the bottom of the Backside Express quad chair lift. The Vista Express Quad opens up the excellent terrain on the south side of the upper mountain. Most runs are beautifully groomed for superb intermediate skiing. Snowmaking covers many of the best runs from the top of the mountain, making this a great early season choice.

The resort offers all kinds of special ski instruction, including special clinics for women and seniors. Free lessons for intermediate and advanced skiers start at the

# Downhill Ski Areas

top of the mountain every half hour between 10:00 and 2:00. Minors' Camp child care is available for children 2 to 6 years old (provided they are potty trained) with ski lessons in a special area near the base facility. The snow tubing facility nearby is described on page 209 in "Snowplay." Senior discounts start at 60 and 70+ skiers pay $5. Club Vertical offers skiers a chance to log vertical feet for prizes while enjoying discounted ticket prices and shorter lift lines. Free shuttle service transports guests from the condominiums and houses to the base facilities and free buses also pick up on the North Shore and in Truckee.

Mount Rose Ski Area

Drive 10 miles east on Hwy. 431 (the Mt. Rose Hwy.) at Incline Village. 702-849-0704 Snow phone: 702-849-0706 After 12/15/98 775-849-0704 and 775-849-0706

Because of its 9,700-foot elevation, skiers will find some of the lightest powder in the basin here, a variety of terrain for skiers of every ability and some of the best views in the region. Intermediate skiers will love the 2.5-mile Around the World run as well as the wide-open slopes of the East Bowl, the former Slide Mountain, with 1,440 vertical feet of skiing. The Mount Rose side has most of the expert terrain and a snowboard park. The area offers several first-time workshops as well as teen tickets that include a group workshop for boarders of all abilities. Special women's day ticket prices are a favorite of locals. Ski school for children starts at 3 years old. Seniors 60 and over ski for half price.

Downhill Ski Areas

At the top of Ski Way in Incline Village off Country Club Dr.
702 832-1177
Snow phone:
702 831-3211
After 12/15/98
775-832-1177
and
775-831-3211

Diamond Peak Ski Resort

This ski area offers a special family rate for a family of four that doesn't break the bank, and the gentle beginner terrain near the Day Lodge is perfect for first-time skiers and toddlers. Almost 50 percent of the terrain is for intermediate skiers. The 1.5-mile-long Crystal Ridge run is smooth and wide with magnificent views of Lake Tahoe. Snowmaking on 80 percent of the terrain ensures a long season. Snowboarders love this resort with its special halfpipe and terrain park. The new Launch Pad feeds skiers effortlessly onto the Lakeview and Crystal Peak Quad Express Chairs to whisk skiers to the top of the mountain. For lunch with a view, try the Snowflake Lodge at the top of Lakeview Quad. Seniors 60 to 69 years old receive discounts seven days a week. Starting at 70 years old, you can ski free.

Skiing off the summit at Diamond Peak.

Courtesy of Diamond Peak Ski Resort

Downhill Ski Areas

South Lake Tahoe and Carson Pass

Heavenly Ski Resort

Heavenly runs ski buses all day from all major hotels and casinos. California side: Take Ski Run Blvd. to parking. Nevada Side: From Kingsbury Grade drive 3 miles east to Tramway. Boulder Base Lodge is the first right turn. Stay straight on Aspen for Stagecoach Base Lodge.
702-586-7000
After 12/15/98
775-586-7000
Snow phone:
530-541-7544

With 4,500 skiable acres in two states and rising from 6,540 to 10,040 feet on the California side, this is a big mountain. Don't let the famous Gunbarrel run scare you as you arrive to take the tram, for there is plenty of moderate terrain just beyond your view. No other ski area offers such a spectacular backdrop of snow-covered peaks rising above Lake Tahoe on one side and the expansive Nevada basin and range on the other. Bring your camera and try the Ridge Run for smooth skiing accompanied by photo "ops" at every turn. Intermediate skiers will want to sample both sides of the mountain. The interesting terrain on the Nevada side is easily reached by connector trails. Intermediate skiers looking for a long run from the top of the Dipper chair may ski several thousand feet down on the Big Dipper and Galaxy trails to the bottom of Galaxy lift or even farther to the bottom of the Stagecoach chair. When the wind is blowing on the California side, this is an excellent choice. Expert skiers and powder hounds can now access acres of fresh snow in the Milky Way Bowl and Mott Canyon, served by their own chair. There is so much skiable terrain at this premier resort that it would take several days to ski the whole mountain.

The middle mountain at the top of the tram has beginner terrain, but families with children are well advised to take the bus to the Nevada side Boulder base lodge. Ski lessons and beginner terrain is accessed from this lodge. Beginners are encouraged to ride the tram or take the Gunbarrel chair downhill on the California side. An excellent ski school will take care of 3 to 12-year-olds from the California Base Lodge. Seniors 65 years and older ski for

Downhill Ski Areas

half price. Heavenly offers an interesting option for those who don't want a full ski lesson, a one-run mini-lesson from the top of several chairs on the California side. Heavenly is planning a major expansion that will add seven new lifts, new terrain, a gondola directly to a new mid-mountain lodge from the Park Avenue redevelopment area near the casinos plus extensive remodelling of the base facilities.

Sierra-at-Tahoe

Five shuttle buses make pickups at the casinos and all major motels in So. Lake Tahoe. Take U.S. 50 west 11.5 miles to turnoff. Ski area is 2.1 miles up the access road. 530-659-7453 Snow phone: 530-659-7475

Sierra-at-Tahoe, formerly Sierra Ski Ranch and sister resort to Northstar-at-Tahoe, offers 2,000 acres of skiable terrain with a vertical rise of 2,212 feet and a top elevation of 8,852 feet. The longest run from the top of the Sensation lift to the base of the recently developed west side of the mountain is over three miles of glorious cruising on wide slopes that are groomed daily. Two long runs, Sugar N' Spice and Wagon Wheel, wind gradually down the mountain giving novice skiers wonderful opportunities to perfect their turning techniques. A bonus for families is the Super-Stars ski school for 4 to 6-year-olds that will have your youngsters on the XTC quad in no time. The Broadway area for beginners is a wide meadow in full view of the base lodge. The "Magic Carpet" people mover helps beginners up the slopes. Experts who hunt powder among the trees will find plenty of runs alongside the groomed slopes. Club Vertical that is interchangeable with Northstar-at-Tahoe offers $5 discounts off tickets and special lift lines. Seniors 60 to 69 years old pay the same discounted rate as children and those 70 or older ski for only $5. The area has been voted by *Snow Country* readers the best in the west for on-mountain dining possibilities. Of particular note is the Grand View Grill at the top of Tahoe King and Grandview Express chairs.

# Downhill Ski Areas

Kirkwood Ski Resort

A bus takes skiers from any point in So. Lake Tahoe and returns at the end of the ski day. Reservations are required. Drive 30 miles south of Lake Tahoe via Hwy. 89 over Luther Pass to Hwy. 88. The ski area is 6 miles west of Carson Pass.
209-258-6000
Snow phone:
209-258-3000

If you want to ski from your front door onto a big mountain that has the best snow in the region, consider staying at Kirkwood Ski Resort, now under new management with big plans to make Kirkwood into a premier destination resort. A four-story lodge with 19 condominium units, retail shops and an immense lobby with world class views opened in 1997. Plans call for more ski-in, ski-out condominiums near the base of many lifts. The buildings will contain new dining and retail shops. Upgrade of the old double chairs servicing the Sunrise bowls under Thimble peak are planned for 1999 and beyond. A Chondola (combined gondola/chair lift) will replace the existing awkward Chair 2 access from the Village area to the top of Caples Crest.

Kirkwood offers runs for all abilities including a completely separate beginner area served by two lifts and its own Timbercreek Day Lodge and parking lot. This mountain is famous for its expert chutes off Thimble and Thunder Peaks and the Sisters. With 2,000 acres of skiable terrain, four triple lifts and six double chairs rising to 9,800 feet, there are runs for everyone, some of the best snow in the region, and seldom any lift lines. Intermediate skiers can ski wide runs off Solitude, The Ruet or Flying Carpet. Iron Horse and Sunrise chairlifts serve runs on the backside of the mountain off Thimble Peak. Try your spring skiing in the morning here. The new snowboard park provides thrills off Solitude or Cornice Chairs. The Kirkwood Ski School offers a new three-day beginner's package with the Elan SCX ski that guarantees you will be on a chair lift knowing how to stop and make a turn at the end of your first day. Instruction is for four-and-a-half hours, allowing for a more relaxed learning environment.

At the main Day Lodge there is licensed infant care hourly, half-day or all-day. Seniors over 60 ski at the children's discounted rate, and there is a special discount for young adults (ages 12-24).

Snowboarder shreds some deep powder.

Skating up the trail at Royal Gorge.

X-Country Skiing

If you have never tried cross-country skiing, you may wish to start at an official ski area. Here you can rent equipment, take a lesson and practice on groomed trails. Once you have learned the basic striding techniques and tried a few downhill portions of a trail, your enjoyment of the sport will increase. Then you may want to venture out onto some back country trails. Snowshoes have increased in popularity since the introduction of smaller lightweight models. You can rent them at most rental shops and venture anywhere, especially in the areas mentioned in the back country skiing descriptions. Some of the ski areas also rent snowshoes for use on their trails.

Cross-country (sometimes called nordic) ski areas are listed below from the Truckee area south to Lake Tahoe and Carson Pass. Distances are measured in kilometers (km=.6 mile) at cross-country areas.

Yuba Gap

Eagle Mountain

One mile south of I-80 at the Yuba Gap exit.
530-389-2254
800-391-2254

Eagle Mountain is just off I-80 less than a half hour from Truckee. It makes a great place to ski on your way up to the area, or on your way home. You will find more than 22 km of trials through forests and meadows. The trails near the lodge offer more than a mile of novice skiing with another couple of miles of more difficult terrain to the north. Experienced skiers and snowshoers will want to climb Eagle Mountain or take the six-mile Cisco Trail out to Cisco Butte. The comfortable lodge and the roaring fire beckon for a cup of coffee before you depart, or or even a gourmet meal prepared by chef, Dylan Gradhandt. Eagle Mountain Resort also operates a bicycle park and camp in the summer. See page 94 in "Bicycling" for details.

X-Country Skiing

Donner Summit and Truckee

Royal Gorge Cross Country Ski Resort

Take I-80 to the Soda Springs/Norden Exit. Drive east to Soda Springs Rd. Lake Van Norden Meadow parking is on the left after crossing the RR tracks. Follow signs to the Summit Station parking.
530-426-3871
800-634-3086

Royal Gorge is the largest nordic ski area in the country with 321 km of groomed track. The network of 83 trails includes the gently rolling terrain of Palisade Trail or the steep challenge of Devil's Peak. New lifts make the uphill portions of some trails easy. Ten warming huts and four trailside cafes make this a unique cross-country skiing adventure. For the ultimate experience, consider two nights at the Wilderness Lodge complete with a sleigh ride in on Sunday, Wednesday or Friday evening, two days of instruction and French country gourmet dinners at the lodge. Add to this hot mulled wine and the promise of a hot tub or sauna for tired muscles at the end of the day, and you have a ski vacation you won't soon forget. Experienced skiers in good condition looking for a special adventure can try the Rainbow Interconnect. Snow conditions permitting, this 22 km downhill run goes to Rainbow Lodge at Big Bend, also owned by Royal Gorge. Here you can enjoy a gourmet meal before returning to Summit Station on a free shuttle that operates on weekends. If you wish to stay at Rainbow Lodge during your ski holiday, see page 279 in "Historic Inns and B&B's." Seniors 65 and over can ski for half price on weekdays.

Clair Tappaan Lodge

On Donner Pass Rd. 2 miles east of the Soda Springs exit off I-80.
530-426-3632

There are 12 km of novice and intermediate trails operated by the Sierra Club's Clair Tappaan Lodge. They are open to the public as well as guests of the lodge. Parking is limited on weekends when the lodge is full.

X-Country Skiing

Tahoe Donner Cross Country

Take Northwoods Blvd. off Donner Pass Rd. in Truckee to Fjord, turn right to Alder Creek Dr. and left one-half mile to the parking lot.
530-587-9484

This area has 75 km of trails on 5,000 acres with extensive beginner terrain. Tiny Tracks Snow School is open for children on weekends and holidays. The Meadow Loop is an excellent place for your first experience. Children can join parents on the North Fork or Pony Express Loops. Skiers with some skill will find a ski to Euer Valley exhilarating, while experts and skaters can enjoy the climb to Donner Ridge at 7,800 feet where the Sunrise Bowl offers telemark opportunities. A limited choice of food and beverage is available at the Cookhouse in Euer Valley, while the Donner Party Café in the day lodge serves both breakfast and lunch. Try one of their delicious soups. Senior discounts are given any day for skiers 60 and over. If you are 70 years or older you ski for free.

Euer Valley overlook at Tahoe Donner Cross-Country Ski Area.

 # X-Country Skiing

View of Squaw Valley from Squaw Creek Cross Country.

Hwy. 89 and North Lake Tahoe

Squaw Creek Cross-Country Ski Center

Drive west of Hwy. 89 on Squaw Valley Rd. The entrance to the Resort at Squaw Creek is the first left. Valet parking is free if you eat at any restaurant.
530-581-6637

The 30 km of trails around the meadow in Squaw Valley are designed with the beginner in mind. It is also a great place to spend an afternoon, even if it's snowing. For families with very small children, or kids who don't want to ski all day, you can leave children 3 years and older at the Mountain Buddies day camp while you ski around the meadow. After skiing, try lunch on the deck at the resort or at the Ristorante Montagna. Seniors 65 and older ski for half price.

X-Country Skiing

From the Tahoe City Y drive east 2.5 mi. to Fabian Way and follow signs to the ski center via Village Rd. and Country Club Dr. in Tahoe City.
530-583-9358

Lakeview Cross-Country Ski Area

The ski area has 65 km of groomed trails on 3,600 acres. Beginners will find gentle hills on trails that wander through lovely red fir and pine forest. This area is the starting point for the Great Race between Tahoe City and Truckee, an annual ski race with hundreds of participants. The center has lessons for all ages and abilities and holds clinics and ski equipment demo days, as well as offering snowshoe tours.

At Northstar-at-Tahoe Resort 6 miles south of Truckee via Hwy. 267.
530-562-2475

Northstar Cross-Country and Telemark Ski Center

The trails leave from the mid-mountain Day Lodge. A trail pass includes the ride up on the gondola. A total of 65 km of trails fan out from mid-mountain. On the east side of the Day Lodge, 25 km of trails thread through the forest. Several steep hills make this area unsuitable for beginners. The other 45 km of trails leave from the Nordic Center west of the Day Lodge. Only 20 percent of the trails are for beginners. Intermediate skiers will find the Schaffer's Camp Trail perfect for a picnic outing. For those wishing to learn or practice telemark techniques, the close proximity to the downhill area makes this the telemark capital of the Tahoe area. Seniors 60 and over can buy discounted tickets.

In Tahoe Vista off National Ave.
530-546-5043

North Tahoe Regional Park

This is good place to take the whole family. Five kilometers of novice trails are near a snowplay hill where non-skiers can frolic with their sleds and saucers which can be rented here.

# X-Country Skiing

Granlibakken Resort

*At the end of Granlibakken Rd. off Hwy. 89 a half mile south of the Tahoe City Y.
530-583-6203*

Granlibakken has 3 km of beginner trails and an access trail to Paige Meadows for intermediate skiers who want to venture into the back country. You can also reach the Paige Meadows trail from the top of the lift at the ski hill. For families with small children, the snowplay area is next to the ski hill.

Incline Village

Diamond Peak Cross Country

*On Mt. Rose Hwy. (Hwy. 431) 5 miles from the intersection with Hwy. 28.
702-832-1177
After 12/15/98
775-832-1177*

The trails through magnificent forests of red fir and western white pine are on terrain that is not for rank beginners. However, those with some skill will find superior snow at the 8,200-foot elevation. The Knock Your Socks Off Lookout will do just that, with its expansive view of Lake Tahoe. On a sunny day, take a picnic and plan to stop here for one of the best views in the basin. If you have come from a lower elevation, take it easy on the first climb from the entrance station lodge. Senior tickets start at 60 years old. Buses to the cross country center leave from Diamond Peak Ski Area three times a day on weekends.

South Lake Tahoe

Lake Tahoe Winter Sports Center

*At the Lake Tahoe Golf Course 1.5 miles south of the airport on U.S. 50.
530-577-2940*

Beginner and intermediate skiers will find groomed trails that wander around the golf course ideal for that first time. Lessons as well as complete rental packages are available. If someone in your group prefers to drive a snowmobile, a groomed track is at the same location.

X-Country Skiing

South Lake Tahoe Parks and Recreation

At Bijou Park off Al Tahoe Blvd., So. Lake Tahoe.
530-541-4611

The South Lake Tahoe Park and Recreation Department maintains 10 km of groomed trails for practicing your striding or skating techniques. A minimal fee makes this an excellent choice for a few hours of skiing, and you can drop by the recreation department pool for a swim after your workout.

Spooner Lake Cross Country Ski Area

South of Incline Village 12.5 miles on Hwy. 28. The park is east of Hwy. 28 a half mile north of Hwy. 50.
702-749-5349
After 12/15/98
775-749-5349

Lovely flat trails around Spooner Lake are perfect for beginners. More ambitious skiers can climb toward some spectacular views of Lake Tahoe on Shepherd's Trail. These trails wind through aspen groves, making this one of the more interesting scenic spots. With 101 km on 23 trails in this extensive area, plan to take a picnic, particularly in the spring when you can stop at one of the Lake Tahoe overlooks. Moonlight tours are held on full moon nights. Call for dates.

Cross Country Ski Center at Camp Richardson

On Hwy. 89 two miles north of the South Tahoe Y.
530-542-6584

Camp Richardson Resort has created the perfect family cross-country ski center across the road from the resort. There are 15 km of easy groomed trails through the woods plus 35 km of more difficult skier-packed trails. On Friday nights there is a moonlight ski from the Beacon Bar and Grill weather permitting.

 X-Country Skiing

Carson Pass

Hope Valley Cross Country

The ski trails start at the junction of Hwy. 89 and Hwy. 88. Hope Valley Outdoor Center: 530-694-2266

The Hope Valley Cross Country trails are marked and skier groomed. Best of all, they are free. Beginners can take the Sawmill trail to the Burnside Lake trail, returning when the climb becomes too steep. Intermediate skiers will enjoy the climb to Burnside Lake, a perfect day's outing. This is truly wilderness skiing. Advance skiers can take the Indian Head trail that leaves directly behind Sorensen's Resort. Rentals and other gear and a map to the trails in Hope Valley are at the Hope Valley Outdoor Center east of Sorensen's on Highway 88.

Kirkwood Cross Country

On north side of Hwy. 88 just east of the entrance to Kirkwood Ski Resort. The Schneider trailhead is on Schneider Cow Camp Rd. 2 miles east of the Day Lodge. 209-258-6000

Kirkwood Cross Country has 80 km of trails on 4,200 acres in three trail networks. There is a special children's area near the Cross Country Day Lodge. Beginners and families will find the miles of trails around Kirkwood meadow perfect for that first experience. The summit trails accessed from the Schneider trailhead take you up onto the high crest with magnificent views in all directions. There are 9 km of easy trails and about 30 km of more difficult terrain in this location. Advanced skiers can also access these trails from the main loop near the lodge via the Agony and Ecstasy trails. The Caples Creek loop offers skiing where the silence is broken only by the sound of water in Caples Creek or wind in the pines. If you don't want to pack a lunch, or if the weather is not conducive to a picnic in the snow, try the lunch special or one of the delectable burgers at the historic Kirkwood Inn.

X-Country Skiing

Back Country Skiing

If you are looking for a back country experience, or only want to ski a few hours, there are many locations in the area where you can ski free. Some trails are accessed from California Sno-Park trailheads (see next page). Most of the trails listed here are groomed only by skiers who preceded you, but you will be able to have a quiet day in the woods where the only sounds will be the swish of your skis accompanied by the cheery chirp of chickadees. Each trail description indicates the degree of difficulty.

Father and son enjoy a Spring day touring.

X-Country Skiing

Sno-Park Ski Trails

The California Department of Transportation maintains a number of Sno-Park areas at certain trailheads. You must buy a permit for these from November through May. One-day or season Sno-Park permits are available at:

Truckee and North Lake Tahoe

Donner Memorial State Park: *at the east end of Donner Lake.* 530-582-7892
Mountain Hardware: *11320 Donner Pass Rd., Truckee.* 530-587-4844
Sierra Mountaineer: *Jibboom and Bridge Sts., Truckee.* 530-587-2025
Homewood Hardware: *5405 West Lake Blvd., Homewood.* 530-525-6367
CSAA office: *7717 North Lake Blvd., Kings Beach.* 530-546-4245

South Lake Tahoe and Carson Pass

Meyers Shell and Food Mart: *2950 Hwy. 50, Tahoe Paradise.* 530-577-4533
Old MacDonald's Enterprise: *1060 Ski Run Blvd., South Lake Tahoe.* 530-544-3663
Pow Wow Ski and Sport: *Sierra Ski Ranch Rd., Little Norway.* 530-659-7558
South Lake Tahoe Chamber of Commerce: *3066 Hwy. 50, South Lake Tahoe.* 530-541-5255
U.S. Forest Service/Lake Tahoe Basin: *870 Emerald Bay Rd., South Lake Tahoe.* 530-573-2600
Kirkwood Cross Country Center: *Highway 88, Kirkwood.* 209-258-7248

X-Country Skiing

Donner Summit and Truckee

Castle Peak

Take I-80 to the Castle Peak exit. Drive east on the frontage road to the Sno-Park. (Intermediate to Advanced)

You will need to walk to the trailhead on the north side of the freeway. This trail begins at 7,000 feet and leads to the Sierra Club Peter Grubb Hut over the 7,800-foot shoulder of Castle Peak. The trip is only recommended for those with good downhill skills.

Donner Memorial State Park

On Donner Pass Rd. just west of the Donner State Park I-80 exit. (Beginner)

The park is an excellent choice for families and beginners. An easy, marked trail follows the road to the beach at China Cove and through the forest around the perimeter of the park. From the beach you can also ski along the lakeshore returning to the road near your starting point. A winter visit to the Donner Museum to see the slide show about the Donner Party ordeals in 1846 reminds us all of the courage needed to emigrate to California in those days.

Kaspian Recreation Area to Blackwood Canyon

The Sno-Park is on the west side of Hwy. 89 four miles south of the Tahoe City Y. (Beginner and Intermediate)

The trail follows the road into Blackwood Canyon on gentle terrain. This is a perfect place for a sunny spring outing with lunch in the snow or a place to escape cabin fever during a storm. More ambitious skiers may want to climb toward Barker Pass but are warned to avoid steeper terrain in the canyon as it is prone to avalanches.

X-Country Skiing

South Lake Tahoe and Carson Pass

Taylor Creek

Capacity 30 cars. Snowmobiles permitted on the south side of Hwy. 89 toward Fallen Leaf Lake only. West side of Hwy. 89, about 3 miles north of the South Tahoe Y. (Beginner to Intermediate)

There are two major ski trails that leave from the south side of the parking lot. Blue diamonds or blue signs with a skier mark the trails. These are not groomed, and you must follow trails where other skiers have gone. One trail follows an old road to the spillway of Fallen Leaf Lake. Here you can choose to cross the spillway for an easy tour around Fallen Leaf Campground. The other trail skirts the west shore of the lake until you reach an old log cabin and picnic site. The return part of this loop passes the cabin uphill and returns through the woods until it intersects the unplowed Cathedral Road taking you back to the parking lot. Another trail on the north side of Highway 89, about 200 yards east, leads to the Tallac Historic Site and the shore of Lake Tahoe. This is an excellent trail for beginners. Maps of the trails are usually available from a display at the Sno-Park.

Echo Summit

Capacity 100 cars. No snowmobiles. The Sno-Park is 8 miles west of the South Tahoe Y on the south side of U.S. 50. (Beginner to Intermediate)

The trails in this area are laid out near the former Echo Summit Ski Area. From the parking lot follow the marked trail around the former ski lodge then south toward Benwood Meadow. Bring your camera as there are vistas toward Christmas Valley along the way. The Benwood Meadow tour is 4 miles round trip. The Echo Summit to Kirkwood race starts here, and advanced skiers might wish to continue the climb to Upper Benwood Meadow. This trail follows the Pacific Crest Trail and traverses avalanche prone terrain, so check the weather and snow conditions before embarking on this tour. Beginners may try the trail

X-Country Skiing

to Lake Audrain. This trail heads northwest from the entrance to the parking lot then turns south toward the lake. It is about 2 miles round trip. This is also an excellent snowplay area.

Echo Lake

Capacity 100 cars. No snowmobiles. Off U.S. 50 on the road to Echo Lake, one mile west of Echo Summit. (Beginner to Intermediate)

This is a very popular cross-country ski excursion. The trail to Lower and Upper Echo Lakes climbs gradually until you are overlooking Lower Echo Lake. There is a fairly steep descent to the lake. Once you have negotiated this, when conditions permit, you can ski across the lake toward Upper Echo Lake, which is usually frozen from January through March. Be sure to assess the conditions before skiing on the lake. In spring, skiing along the south shore is safest. There are many private cabins surrounding both lakes. Please respect this private property, and do not picnic on cabin porches. There is also great sledding on the hill down to Lower Echo Lake, so haul the saucer along for the kids to enjoy.

Carson Pass

Capacity 100 cars. No snowmobiles. A Sno-Park is at Carson Pass on Hwy. 88, 25 miles south of Lake Tahoe via Hwy. 89 and Luther Pass. (Intermediate to Advanced)

The most popular trail in the region is to Winnemucca Lake. Marked by blue diamond signs, it climbs steeply to Frog Lake then more gradually along a great open ridge toward Winnemucca Lake. If you want to make a loop, descend to Woods Lake campground, then follow an unplowed road in gentle grades back to the parking lot. This tour is only for intermediate to advanced skiers. Beginners might consider the route to Woods Lake and back.

Winter

X-Country Skiing

Other Back Country Trails

Truckee Area

Old Henness Pass Road East

From I-80 drive 19.7 miles on Hwy. 89 North. A few parking spaces are plowed on the right at the beginning of the Kyburz Flat Rd. (Beginner)

Park in the space that is plowed. The road up to Kyburz Flat is skier groomed and affords an easy uphill ski to a U.S. Forest Service interpretive area. The road turns gently downhill to Kyburz Flat and a bridge across a creek. Follow the road as far as you wish as it passes through a forest over gentle hills and vales. This is an excellent trail after a snowstorm, for it is little used and you can make your own tracks through the powder.

Martis Peak

Drive on Hwy. 267 to parking on the east side of the road about one half mile north of Brockway Summit. (Intermediate)

The trail leaves the parking area for a steady climb on old logging roads. There are signs on the trees to guide you in a generally northwesterly direction around the shoulder of Martis Peak to the overlook. When the snow is fresh this is a spectacular trip to lunch on the porch of the fire lookout with its expansive views of Martis Valley, Truckee and the peaks of Donner Summit and Castle Peak in the distance. The descent back to your car is only steep at the end and, unless the tracks are icy, can be maneuvered by novices.

X-Country Skiing

Tahoe City

Tahoe City to Alpine Meadows Bike Trail

Access at River Ranch on Hwy. 89 or from the 64-Acre Park just south of the Tahoe City Y. (Beginner)

This summertime bike trail is perfect for beginning skiers. If you start in Tahoe City, you can ski the 4 miles to River Ranch and back. The trail can also be accessed from River Ranch. However, it is sometimes covered with dirty snow thrown up by the snowplows.

Paige Meadows

Take Hwy. 89 south for 2.3 miles to Pine Ave. Turn right, then right on Tahoe Park Heights Dr., right on Big Pine Dr. and left on Silver Tip Dr. to the end of the road. (Intermediate)

The drive to the trailhead is up a very steep hill and may require chains or a 4WD. The trail leaves from the end of the road and descends through a forest. Take the first trail off to the right through the woods toward the meadow. Once in the meadow there is lovely flat terrain to explore. Rank beginners will find the first descent somewhat steep. The meadows may also be accessed from a trail that is marked from Granlibakken Ski Hill. See page 176 in "Downhill Ski Areas" for description.

Sugar Pine Point State Park

Fee per vehicle. Drive 9.3 miles south of the Tahoe City Y on Hwy. 89. The park entrance is on the west side of the road. (Beginner)

The state park maintains a groomed ski trail in the General Creek section west of the highway. The terrain is perfect for beginners. The California State Parks - Sierra District offers courses in cross-country skiing, so you might want to check with the nearest park headquarters to pick up the fall/winter schedule of ski classes and snowshoe trips

 # X-Country Skiing

Incline Village Area

Tahoe Meadows on Mount Rose Highway

There is parking along Hwy. 431 on both sides 6.7 miles from the intersection with Hwy. 28, about 14 miles north of Hwy. 50. (Beginner) Snowmobiles allowed. Snowplay areas.

Open meadows on both sides of the highway invite skiers and snowmobilers. Several hills on the north side of the highway are perfect for sledding. The meadows are at about 8,500 feet above sea level with excellent snow during a long season. The meadows and woods on the south side beckon skiers of all abilities, but are particularly good for families with small children just learning to walk on their skis and for beginners who wish to practice striding. More advanced skiers will want to climb the mountain through the trees to the south. The east end of this climb affords magnificent views of the Carson Valley.

Climb to Mount Rose

Ample parking is located on the south side of the road about .4 miles east of Tahoe Meadows. (Intermediate to Advanced.)

The trail ascends the ridge on the north side of the road. This is a ski for intermediate skiers who want to ski as high as they feel like and enjoy a wonderful long run downhill at the end of the day. Advanced skiers will find ample terrain off the road to test their skills.

X-Country Skiing

South Lake Tahoe

There are popular cross-country areas with unofficial parking, usually in a small turnout or at the side of the road. Be sure to assess whether there is enough room for your vehicle, and remember that during stormy weather you should not park along the road. Snowplows may bury your car, and you may have to dig to retrieve it, to say nothing of possible damage by the plow if the visibility is poor. We have included one area that is off Highway 89 near Luther Pass, since it has several excellent parking possibilities. However, good cross-country skiers who are confident of their abilities to handle a variety of terrain should buy a copy of Marcus Libkind's *Ski Tours in the Sierra Nevada*. Volume One includes all of Lake Tahoe while Volume Two describes tours in the Carson Pass, Bear Valley and Pinecrest areas.

Grass Lake Meadows on Highway 89

Take Hwy. 89 south from Meyers about 6.5 miles. There are several turnouts that offer access to the meadow on the west side of the road. (Beginner to Intermediate)

The endless meadow terrain just west of Luther Pass is the perfect place for a spring outing. Ski as far as you wish to find a picnic spot and return across the meadow using another route. You can't get lost here, as Highway 89 is always somewhere near the meadow. If you climb south toward Luther Pass, you will be in the Hope Valley watershed. Combine a morning here with an afternoon at Hope Valley and follow it with a trip to Grover Hot Springs (see page 39 in "Excursions") or Wally's Hot Springs (see page 42 in "Excursions") to ease tired muscles. To finish off the day in style, make a reservation for dinner at Sorensen's Resort (see page 245 in "Dining Out").

Skiers climb above Schneider Sheep Camp at Kirkwood Cross-Country.

Striding out at Kirkwood Cross-Country.

Ice Skating

Squaw Valley has two ice skating rinks, while South Lake Tahoe opened an all-year pavilion in 1996. Incline Village is planning a major facility for the near future.

Squaw Valley High Camp Bath and Tennis Club

Fee to ride cable car.
Squaw Valley Information:
530-583-7246

The Olympic-size ice rink at High Camp is a high-altitude skating experience with a view. There are two-hour sessions throughout the day and into the evening. You can rent both figure and hockey skates, or bring your own. If you buy a ski lift ticket, you can come up the mountain at night at no extra charge. You might even decide to spend the whole day at High Camp, with dinner followed by skating. Try this at full moon. The hot tubs are open in mid-March and the pool when the weather permits. The rink is covered for great summer season skating (June to September.) See page 38 in "Excursions" for information about all the High Camp Summer activities.

Resort at Squaw Creek

Reservations required.
Resort at Squaw Creek, Squaw Valley
530-583-6300

A small round rink is located above the swimming pools. The sessions generally last two hours. The fee is minimal if you bring your own skates.

South Lake Tahoe

South Lake Tahoe Recreation and Parks Ice Rink

The Department of Recreation and Parks and a private developer joined forces to build a year-round facility that opened in 1996. However, the facility closed in 1997 and a citizen's committee is working to fund it for the future.

Snowmobiling

If you just want to try your hand at driving a snowmobile, you can rent machines and drive a short distance on two golf courses and at the North Tahoe Regional Park. Three groups offer wilderness tours on U.S. Forest Service lands above Lake Tahoe. On the South Shore there are courses at the Lake Tahoe Golf Course and Sunset Ranch. There are longer rides through the woods or guided wilderness tours with local outfitters on both ends of the lake. All will rent the appropriate clothing and give instruction in driving single or double-rider machines.

North Lake Tahoe and Truckee

On National Ave. off Hwy. 28 in Tahoe Vista.
530-546-7248

North Tahoe Regional Park

The snowmobile track on a quarter-mile course makes a good place to learn or to determine if you are ready for an all-day trip. Rentals are available. The snowplay area and cross-country trails are adjacent, making this park a good choice for groups wishing to try different activities.

Tours start at Brockway Summit on Hwy. 267.
530-583-7192

Snowmobiling Unlimited

This group operates the track at the Regional Park, but their trips leave from Brockway Summit on Highway 267. Their groomed trails offer exceptional views of Lake Tahoe, so bring your camera and take a wilderness tour. There are both beginner and advanced trips.

Snowmobiling

At the corner of Hwy. 267 and Hwy 28, Kings Beach.
530-546-9909

High Sierra Snowmobile at Brockway Golf Course

A small track is operated on the golf course at the corner of Highway 267 and Highway 28. Here you can try your hand at driving before taking one of the longer tours. This is a great place to fill an hour or two with the whole family, then retire to a local restaurant for lunch or a snack.

*Reservations required.
8612 No. Lake Blvd.
Kings Beach*
530-583-9131

Mountain Lake Adventures

This outfit leads tours each day up onto Mount Watson where you can get magnificent views of Lake Tahoe. The tours leave at 11:30 a.m. and 2:00 p.m. and last two hours. Call for the meeting place.

251 No. Lake Blvd. behind Lucky's in Tahoe City.
530-581-3906

T C Sno Mo's at Tahoe City Golf Course

A snowmobile track is laid out on the golf course. This is a good place to practice driving before going on a longer ride. Rentals are available at the clubhouse. After you have gotten the knack of driving you may wish to try one of their wilderness tours.

*Reservations required.
The meeting point is 14.3 miles north of I-80 on Hwy. 89 North at the snowmobile staging area of the U.S. Forest Service.*
530-546-8667

Eagle Ridge Snowmobile Outfitters

Eagle Ridge leads guided wilderness tours on groomed trails. You can go for 2 hours, 3 hours, half day, all day or overnight. There are 175 miles of trails over 650 square miles of snowbound wilderness. With all new machines that are easy to drive, you will be provided with snacks and hot drinks along the way. They also offer overnights to Bassett's Station where three basic rooms are available, or you can upgrade to stay at the High Country Inn Bed and Breakfast nearby.

Snowmobiling

South Lake Tahoe

Lake Tahoe Winter Sports Center

Reservations required for wilderness tours. The snowmobile track is at the Lake Tahoe Golf Course 1.5 miles south of the airport on U.S. 50. Wilderness tours meet at the Sports Center at 3071 Hwy. 50 in Tahoe Paradise. 530-577-2940

Before taking this wilderness tour, you can try your hand driving a snowmobile at the Center's track course on the Lake Tahoe Golf Course. Rentals are by the half hour on a single or double-rider machine. For those in your group who would rather go under their own power, groomed cross-country trails leave from the golf course.

The special two-hour wilderness tours begin with a shuttle bus ride to Blue Lake in beautiful Hope Valley. Special overnight tours can be arranged as well. They rent clothes and provide you with the finest snowmobiles available that feature backrests and handlebar heaters.

Sunset Ranch

One-quarter mile west of the Lake Tahoe Airport on U.S. 50. 530-541-9001

Sunset Ranch has a snowmobile track for half-hour rides and guides tours around the 230-acre ranch. For those who might prefer to ride horseback, their stables are open in the winter.

Zephyr Cove Snowmobilin'

Reservations required. Free shuttle bus service from the casinos and hotels. Off U.S. 50 in Zephyr Cove, 4 miles north of the casinos. 702-588-3833 after 12/15/98 775-588-3833

Riders sign up at Zephyr Cove and are bused to Spooner Summit. The tours last two hours with several stops for photos. Groomed trails lead to a high point where on a good day you have spectacular views of Lake Tahoe, the Sierra and the Carson Valley. Single or double-rider machines and warm clothing are available for rent. First-time riders are welcomed and given instructions.

Getting ready to leave on a tour with Eagle Ridge.

Winter

Snowplay

Snowplay has taken on a whole new meaning with the advent of lift assisted tubing at three resorts in the Truckee/North Lake Tahoe area.

Official Snowplay Areas

Donner Summit and Truckee

Boreal

Wknds. and holidays only.
I-80 at Castle Peak.
530-426-3666

The snowplay area is at the west end of the ski area parking lot. The fee includes saucer rental. There is now a tubing area as well, but no lift. You must drag the tube up the hill.

Soda Springs Ski Area

All day ticket to the area also good on the lift.
One mile east of Soda Springs/Norden exit off I-80.
530-426-3663

Soda Springs has introduced family fun with tubing. Everyone in the family will want to try the three different runs from the top of the lift. Tubes are large enough so that small fry can go with an adult. The lift is almost as much fun as the ride.

Riding the lift at Soda Springs.

© Ellie Huggins

Snowplay

Northstar-at-Tahoe

Fee per hour. *Northstar-at-Tahoe Resort off Hwy. 267.* 530-562-1010

Northstar has added two tubing runs near the gondola building at the base of the mountain. A lift was added at the end of the 1998 season.

Squaw Valley

Fee to ride cable car. *Squaw Valley* 530-583-6985

The snow tubing area operates every day from 2:00 p.m. to 9:00 p.m. off Bailey's lift near High Camp. Here is fun for the whole family at the end of the day, or a place where non-skiing members of the group can play in the snow with the help of a lift to the top. This would be a great way to spend an afternoon, followed by skating and dinner at Alexander's. This just may be the highest place you've ever slid down the hill, and the view is spectacular.

Tahoe City and North Lake Tahoe

Tahoe Donner

Wknds. and holidays only. *Northwoods Blvd. near the clubhouse.* 530-587-9400

The broad hill with protective fences at the bottom is operated by the Tahoe Donner Association. This is a good place for a large group to play. The fee includes saucers.

Granlibakken Resort

Wknds. and holidays only. *Granlibakken Rd. in Tahoe City.* 530-583-6203

Granlibakken operates a snowplay area next to the ski hill. The hill is fenced for safe runouts. The fee includes saucer rental.

Winter

Snowplay

North Tahoe Regional Park

National Ave. in Tahoe Vista. 530-546-5043

The snowplay area has good protection for runouts. Because it is next to the cross-country ski area, families can engage in both activities. Equipment rentals are available, but no sleds with metal edges are allowed.

Incline Village

On Fairway Dr. off Northwoods Blvd. or Country Club Dr.

The snowplay hill is on the golf driving range next to The Chateau. Bring your own equipment. There is no supervision. The hill has different spots for short or long runs. Small children will be safe here.

South Lake Tahoe

Hansen's Resort

Fee to rent equipment. 1360 Ski Run Blvd., So. Lake Tahoe. 530-544-3361

Hansen's will loan you any equipment when you pay a fee to use their hill for three hours or more on weekends or one hour or more on weekdays at a lesser charge. For families with skiers at Heavenly, this is a wonderful choice for the little ones.

Unofficial Sledding Hills

These hills are located on private property, and listing them here does not mean that sledding is formally permitted. However, these hills are frequently used by locals.

Snowplay

Truckee-Downtown

On Donner Pass Road a quarter mile west of Downtown Truckee.

The hill falls from a forest to a meadow that used to be a dairy property. It is steep but there is plenty of runout. Bring your own equipment. There is ample parking across from the plumbing supply buildings.

Tahoe City

One eighth of a mile south of the Y.

Bring your own sleds or saucers. If parking is congested along the road, you can park in the regional 64-Acre Park on the west side of Highway 89.

Mount Rose Highway and Tahoe Meadows

On Hwy. 431 (Mt. Rose Hwy.) 6.7 mi above the intersection with Hwy. 28. Park on both sides of the highway or in the parking lot for the Tahoe Rim Trail.

The slopes across from Tahoe Meadows cross-country trails offer many possibilities for snowplay. At the 8,300-foot elevation this may be the first hill open in the winter. The slopes are generally steep, so you may want to ride with your children at first. This is a great location for a group with both snowplay and cross-country enthusiasts. On a fair day in spring, this is a wonderful place to spend the day, but bring the sunscreen.

South Lake Tahoe

Spooner Summit

At the intersection of Hwy. 28 and U.S. 50. Parking on the frontage road.

The high elevation and a north-facing slope offer snow conditions that are reliable late into spring. This hill is a favorite with teenagers and thrill seekers. It is very steep but has sufficient runout for safety. It is not recommended for small children.

Winter Adventures

Sleigh Rides

There are sleigh rides for your group alone or as part of regularly scheduled rides. You can even charter a wedding sleigh with one outfit. So dress warmly and take the family for a memorable experience.

Truckee Area

Northstar-at-Tahoe

Fee per person. At Northstar-at-Tahoe 6 miles south of Truckee. 530-562-1230

Northstar-at-Tahoe Resort offers daily sleigh rides from the Basque Restaurant, weather permitting. Dress warmly and bring the family out for this unique adventure.

Truckee Carriage and Coach Company

Fee per person. Resort at Squaw Creek, Squaw Valley 530-587-3867 Truckee 530-591-2248 Squaw Valley 530-591-3867 mobile phone

Here's a chance to ride in an authentic 100-year old sleigh that used to haul freight between Truckee and Tahoe City. Your party can have up to nine adults. Sleigh rides leave from behind the Resort at Squaw Creek daily in the afternoons, weather and snow conditions permitting. Evening rides are by reservation only.

South Lake Tahoe

Camp Richardson's Corral

Fee per person. Reservations required. On the west side of Hwy. 89 just north of the main entrance to Camp Richardson. 530-541-3113

The corral offers sleigh rides along the shores of Lake Tahoe or through mountain meadows. Dinner rides include a one-hour trip through the forest at sunset followed by a barbeque at the ranch house. Their special six-person, hand-painted sleigh rents out for weddings or other special occasions.

Winter Adventures

Romantic sleigh ride with Borges.

Borges Sleigh Rides

Fee per person. Reservations recommended. Lake Parkway East and U.S. 50 across from Caesars Tahoe in Stateline. 530-541-2953 Cellular 530-957-6338

Borges famous Belgian Blonds and Baskir Curleys from Russia are hitched to their sleighs and ready to take you for a one-hour tour over the meadow and through the woods to grandmother's house and to one of the most spectacular views of Lake Tahoe. Or you can schedule a private ride like the one shown above.

Winter Adventures

Fee per person.
On U.S. 50 one-quarter mile west of the Lake Tahoe Airport.
530-541-9001

Sunset Ranch

The Sunset Ranch and Riding Stables will take you on sleigh rides for 40 minutes around the meadows and along the Upper Truckee River. Their sleigh holds nine people. The stable is also open for winter horseback riding.

Fee per person. Reservations required.
Off Hwy. 88, west of Carson Pass 5 miles.
209-258-7433

Kirkwood Ski Resort

Kirkwood Stables will take groups by appointment, weather and snow conditions permitting. The sleigh is drawn around the meadow by two Clydesdale draft horses. Kids in the Mighty Mountain Ski School will often get a noon ride as part of the day's activities.

Special Ski Classes

Truckee Area

On Donner Pass Rd. at Donner Summit.
530-426-9108

Alpine Skills International

If you have ever dreamed of skiing the Haute Route from Chamonix, France, to Zermatt, Switzerland, or you want to hone your skills for skiing extreme slopes in the back country, this is the place to start. ASI teaches everything you need to know about ski touring, ski mountaineering, telemark and randonnée techniques as well as ice climbing. They lead back country tours around the Tahoe area and in the Eastern High Sierra and to exotic places like the French Alps and Equadorian Andes. Corporate team building classes and back country snowboarding are now available. Their instructors offer guide training in all the moutaineering skills. Courses take place at Donner Spitz Bunk and Breakfast Hut. See page 281 in "Historic Inns and B&B's" for a description.

Winter Adventures

Reservations, information
P.O. Box 9119, Truckee, CA 96162
530-582-4772
fax: 530-582-4515

North American Ski Training Center

Chris and Jenny Fellows have started an organization for intermediate and advanced skiers. Their ski improvement clinics will ingrain skills and techniques to last a lifetime. The courses offer intensive immersion into the world of skiing. The three-day clinics include room, board, all-day classes, on the snow video and drills and evening indoor clinics. Classes and their special clinics for all conditions, all terrain, adventure skiing and back country skills are held at Sugar Bowl, Kirkwood, and sites in Canada and Chile.

Reservations required.
702-588-4772
After 12/15/98
775-588-4772

South Lake Tahoe

Adventures Unlimited – Downhill and Cross-Country Ski Tours

This group will take you on a guided tour of local downhill ski areas with your own professional instructor. You are picked up at your hotel in a minivan to spend a day at Kirkwood, Sierra-at-Tahoe, Northstar-at-Tahoe, Squaw Valley or Alpine Meadows. Your day will include video-taped ski classes as well as tours of the resort. On your return trip at the end of the day, the van comes equipped with TV screens on each seat so you can see the video of your class. This is a wonderful way to learn about a ski area with a professional guide and instructor. Adventures Unlimited also leads cross-country ski tours to Spooner Lake Cross Country Ski Area or along the beach to the Tallac Historic Site, an easy ski outing with a history component. The guides tell stories about the people and times of Lucky Baldwin's Tallac Hotel. With both tours you can leave your car at home and leave the winter driving to others.

Winter Adventures

Sierra Ski Touring

*Reservations required.
702-782-3047
After 12/15/98
775-782-3047*

Dave Beck of the Husky Express leads special instructional telemark classes and avalanche training to Meiss Hut above Carson Pass. The Meiss Hut trips have a limit of eight people. He and Dottie Dennis also lead combined ski and mushing weekends to the same hut. They provide all the food in what they call hut cuisine. Adventurous back country skiers can also choose from three high country five-day trips. These trips are limited to six skiers.

Dog Sled Rides

The Husky Express Dog Sled Rides

*Fee per person. Reservations recommended. On the north side of Hwy. 88 a few miles west of the junction with Hwy. 89.
702-782-3047
after 12/15/98
775-782-3047*

Dottie Dennis and her team of huskies are waiting to take you on a sled ride across the Hope Valley. If you've ever watched the Iditarod sled dog race on television, here's your chance to experience the thrill of riding in a husky-drawn sled. Cross-Country skiers may enjoy the groomed trails laid out to make easier running for the dogs.

Looking across Caples Lake

Emigrant Pass above Kirkwood Resort.

Year-Round

Year-Round Activities

Winter and summer are high season for vacationers, but the Lake Tahoe region is special other times of the year. If you are looking for a quiet weekend with leisurely strolls in pine-scented forests, a chance to catch the wildflowers' first bloom or a glimpse of the golden aspen groves of Hope Valley, you should consider visiting the area in spring or fall.

In autumn, all summer hikes and bicycle rides are still possible. In spring, however, you will need to check the snow level to take any hikes above lake level. Spring skiing continues at some resorts until Memorial Day. Historical outings are popular any time of the year, and restaurants are far less crowded off-season. The "Historic Inns and B&B's" section starting on page 279 lists historic lodges and bed and breakfast inns from Soda Springs to Carson Pass. Each of the establishments offers a very special kind of experience on or near the lake or the wilderness beauty of the Carson Pass area.

In this section you can find information about entertainment for children at the casinos. We describe many restaurants where you can have a special dining experience, as well as museums and the area's best photo vista points. If you are interested in a show at the casinos or some music with diner or for dancing, the acts and locations of evening entertainment are listed in the free *North Tahoe Truckee Week* magazine or *Lake Tahoe Action* on the South Shore. The three North Shore papers, *The Sierra Sun, The Tahoe World* and *The Bonanza* have special entertainment sections as well. The last section of the book describes special events that occur in the region throughout the year.

Dining Out

The Lake Tahoe, Truckee and Carson Pass areas have innumerable eating establishments offering every kind of cuisine. Rather than list all the eateries, we have selected establishments where dining out can be a special experience, whether it is brunch at lakeside, dinner in a historic building or a fine restaurant on the top floor of a casino. We have also listed the Casino Hotel Buffets on page 247. Here you can get a good meal for a bargain price. Restaurants are listed geographically from Donner Summit to Truckee, Highway 89 south to Tahoe City, West Shore, North Shore and Incline Village to South Lake Tahoe and Carson Pass.

The average cost of dinner is rated according to the following formula:

$ Inexpensive, including soup or salad—under $15
$$ Moderate, including soup or salad—under $20
$$$ Moderately expensive, a la carte—entrees $16 to $22
$$$$ Expensive, a la carte—entrees over $22

These prices do not include alcohol, tax or tips.

It is always advisable to make a reservation for dinner at the height of the summer or winter season. During fall or spring, you can usually drop in and be seated with little or no wait.

A number of the historic dining establishments are also inns and are listed in "Historic Inns and B&B's" starting on page 279.

Dining Out

Donner Summit and Downtown Truckee

The Rainbow Lodge Engadine Café

$$ Dinner daily, Sun. brunch. Live music in the bar Fri. and Sat. nights. Not open Tues. and Wed. Spring and Fall. Rainbow Rd. exit off I-80 20 miles west of Truckee. 530-426-3661

The stone and wood tavern was built in the 1880s and expanded when automobile traffic along U.S. 40 began. It was first called Rainbow Tavern and Trout Farm. Diners caught trout from a stocked pond near the river and brought them to the cook. During the 1940s the Lodge offered guided ski tours to the Sugar Bowl Ski Area at Donner Summit to movie stars like Bing Crosby and Norma Shearer. Rainbow Lodge is now owned and operated by Royal Gorge Cross Country Ski Resort.

The European/Italian menu is varied. An all-you-can-eat pasta is served one night a week. Nightly specials are prepared by the talented chef. This is a perfect place for a delicious, leisurely dinner, and it is only 20 miles from Truckee via Interstate 80. For a description of the lodging here, see page 279 in "Historic Inns and B&B's."

The Passage Restaurant

$$ Lunch and dinner daily, brunch Sat. and Sun. Corner of Hwy. 267 and Bridge St., Truckee. 530-587-7619

The Passage is in the Truckee Hotel building. This historic hostelry started taking guests in 1868. The bar is a local gathering place that advertises the largest collection of single malt scotch in town. The restaurant features eclectic California cuisine complemented by an extensive wine list. The lunch menu includes interesting sandwiches and salads. In the summer there is dining on the terrace. After dinner you may wish to go next door and see the recently restored lobby of the Truckee Hotel which is described separately on page 282 in "Historic Inns and B&B's."

Dining Out

$$$ Dinner daily.
In old Hilltop Lodge off Hwy. 267 just south of the Truckee River bridge.
530-587-5711

Cottonwood Restaurant

Cottonwood Restaurant is at Hilltop across the Truckee River from downtown. The restaurant is near a turn-of-the-century winter sports area. In 1930 the ski hill offered a toboggan run, ski jump and glider landing strip. It is now the finish for skiers in The Great Race (Tahoe City to Truckee) during Snowfest. Photographs of these events through the ages are displayed on the walls of the bar and lounge. The restaurant serves a creative cuisine with a hint of Cajun. The Caesar salad appetizer, enough for two, is meant to be eaten with your fingers. Whole pieces of romaine are surrounded by cracker-size croutons drenched in garlic. The windows in the dining room afford a spectacular view of historic Downtown Truckee, especially when Christmas lights adorn the buildings. In summer try dining on the terrace overlooking the town.

$$ Lunch and dinner daily. Brunch, Sun.
Downtown Truckee
530-587-4164

O.B.'s Pub and Restaurant

O.B.'s has been a favorite of Truckee residents and visitors for 25 years. Step inside rustic "Old Truckee," with fine old photographs and antique implements decorating the plank walls. Formerly the home for a wholesale market, a retail baker, and, in the 1950s a grocery store, it finally opened in 1970 as a restaurant. It is the place for locals to stop in for a drink or hearty meal. The lunch menu is varied and downright tasty, offering delicious salads with a Mexican or Oriental touch as well as pasta and several kinds of hamburgers. Dinners run the gamut from steaks to chicken, as well as seafood and a house smoked seafood sampler appetizer. Portions are generous, making this an excellent choice after a day of mountain activities.

Year-Round

Dining Out

Pacific Crest Restaurant

$$$ Lunch, dinner daily. Reservations recommended. *Downtown Truckee* 530-587-2626

Ed Coleman has created an immediate hit with this recent addition to the Truckee dining scene, offering an interesting and novel Mediterranean cuisine. The lunch menu highlights wood-fired pizzas while dinner selections feature fish specialties including a delectable bouillabaisse and the pasta offerings that are always interesting. The elegant but casual atmosphere is very inviting and service is always attentive. The bar, one of Truckee's originals, was rescued from the back room of a store up the street.

Pianeta Cucina Italiana

$$$$ Dinner daily. Reservations recommended. *Downtown Truckee* 530-587-4694

Robyn Sills and Ed Coleman, owner of Pacific Crest have combined their considerable talents and experience to create an outstanding dining experience in the former Left Bank. The antipasti menu is a page long with tempting combinations such as spicy crab cakes over a bed of wilted spinach or a small plate of pasta of the day. Like any good Italian restaurant, the soup, salad and pasta menus are varied and include such specialties as mushroom and herb dumplings in a mushroom broth, and pasta in all configurations. You can't go wrong with anything on the menu, which can be complemented with a wine from their extensive list. If you're appetite won't let you order both pasta and an entreé, they will split either of these for a small surcharge. As locals will tell you, this is one restaurant you will want to try many times.

Dining Out

Jibbooms Wine Bar and Café

Dinner daily, lunch Wed. and Thurs.
Westgate Shopping Center.
530-550-1989

The wine bar and café serves Italian bistro food. Special offerings include flatbreads with interesting toppings. There are many pasta dishes, but the only meats are grilled salmon or a beef filet. Naturally, there is an extensive wine list and they also have microbrews. You may also order any menu item for take out, a great advantage after a busy day on the slopes.

Truckee Trattoria

$$ Dinner, Tue.-Sat. Reservations recommended.
Safeway Shopping Center, Truckee
530-582-1266

Ken and Liz Brown invite you into their modern Italian-style trattoria and treat you like family. Ken is the chef who prepares light Italian fare, with antipasti like bruscetta or mussels in wine sauce. All the pastas are prepared with light sauces using fresh ingredients. The place is small and a favorite with locals, so call ahead for reservations.

Timbercreek Restaurant at Northstar

$$$ Winter, breakfast, lunch and dinner daily. Summer, dinner daily. Reservations required for dinner.
Northstar Village, Northstar-at-Tahoe
530-562-2250

Located in the Northstar Village complex, the restaurant serves hearty entreés including cioppino and medallons of venison, or rack of lamb. Two vegetarian specialties of the house are medallons of roasted eggplant and a roasted roma tomato stuffed with spinach on a housemade foccacia. Appetizers and several salads that include a house-cured gravlax with shaved fennel and red onion complete the menu. Each entreé includes a suggested wine selection. The bar, located outside in a front room serves a café menu. If you are staying at Northstar, you needn't drive, for the dial-a-ride will pick you up and deliver you home.

Year-Round

Dining Out

Highway 89 South to Tahoe City

Graham's At Squaw Valley

$$$$ Dinner, Tue.-Sat. Fixed price mid-week. A la carte wknds. Reservations recommended. *Squaw Valley* 530-581-0454

Graham Rock is your convivial host at this special restaurant created from the oldest standing house in Squaw Valley, built by the Poulsen family. The menu changes every two weeks but a spread of roasted garlic eggplant and anchovies for the fresh baked, crusty bread starts every meal. There is a middle eastern touch to the cuisine, all beautifully presented and exquisite tasting. The extensive wine cellar features French, Italian and Spanish, as well as California wines. Graham Rock is also the owner of Chambers Landing Restaurant and Bar, a Lake Tahoe favorite (page 230) that is open during the summer.

Plumpjack Squaw Valley

$$$ Dinner daily. Reservations recommended. *In Plumpjack Squaw Valley Inn next to the Tram Bldg., Squaw Valley.* 530-583-1576

San Francisco's famous Plumpjack has opened a restaurant in Squaw Valley Inn to add luster to the culinary scene in Squaw Valley. The food is beautifully presented in a quiet, elegant dining room. The simple menu changes every two weeks offering a selection of interesting appetizers, salads and entreés, always with a pasta or risotto, a roasted fish and perhaps Grilled Beef Roulade or Roasted Duck Breast Confit. Plumpjack began life as a wine merchant who sought out lesser known vintners and promoted exciting young wineries. The restaurant reflects this history and features twenty or more wines by the glass at very reasonable prices.

Dining Out

Alexander's at High Camp Bath and Tennis Club

Fee to ride the cable car.
$$ Summer, 4pm-9pm.
Winter, 10am-9pm.
Reservations recommended.
High Camp, Squaw Valley
530-583-1742
530-583-2555

The view from High Camp at 8,200 feet is unmatched and adds to the experience of dinner at Alexander's. You can enjoy a sit-down dinner after a few night ski runs or ice skating or an evening hike around the plateau in summer. Alexander's features a café menu from 4:00 p.m. to 6:00 p.m. with burgers, salads and desserts. The dinner menu offers many house specials as well as broiled fish and steak with mushroom sauce.

Resort at Squaw Creek

$$$$ Glissandi
$$$ Cascades
$$$ Ristorante Montagna
Reservations required at Glissandi and Ristorante Montagna.
Resort at Squaw Creek, Squaw Valley
530-583-6300

This hotel and conference center is tucked under the slope of Snow King Mountain at the southeastern end of the valley. **Glissandi** offers elegant dining with a view of Squaw Peak and features continental cuisine. A less expensive alternative with almost the same view, **Cascades** serves an extensive, gourmet buffet with different themes. Friday night all you can eat fish buffet is a favorite. **Ristorante Montagna,** open for lunch and dinner, serves exceptional Italian cuisine. Their garlic bread can be a meal in itself. If you are looking for a ski-in unhurried lunch, this is a perfect line-free choice and the food is excellent.

River Ranch Lodging and Dining

$$$ Dinner daily all year.
Lunch, Summer only.
Hwy. 89 at Alpine Meadows Rd.
530-583-4264

One hundred years ago the Deer Park Inn occupied the site of River Ranch. It was a fashionable watering hole during the early part of the century when it was served by the narrow gauge railway between Truckee and Tahoe City. Abandoned in the 1930s, the old building was torn down to make way for the current structure. The bar is a local gathering place with tables that have a wonderful view of the Truckee River. You can sit here or in the quieter dining

Year-Round

Dining Out

room. The menu offers many meat dishes, with wild game specialties such as venison and elk. In summer the patio overlooking the river is a great place for lunch at the end of a pleasant bicycle ride from Tahoe City. A summer concert series is held on the patio. If you want to book a room in this fine old lodge, see page 285 in "Historic Inns and B&B's."

The Pfeifer House

$$$ Dinner daily except Tues.
On Hwy. 89, one-quarter mile north of Tahoe City Y.
530-583-3102

The Pfeifer House has been a restaurant for more than 55 years and has always been popular. Known as Lake Inn during its early years, it was a gambling house until 1947 when the courts decided to ban all gambling on the California side of the lake. Purchased by the Giannini family in 1950, it was renovated and, when Lois Pfeifer was appointed manager, they named it The Pfeifer House. Henry Obermuller and Franz Fassbender bought the business in 1972 and started serving award winning German/continental cuisine in the Alpine-style dining room.

Tahoe City

Tahoe House Restaurant and Bäckerei

$$$ Dinner, daily.
Reservations recommended.
On Hwy. 89 one half mile south of the Tahoe City Y.
530-583-1377

Traditional Swiss cuisine that is meticulously prepared by the chef/owners also includes fresh baked breads and delicious desserts made on the premises. Your hosts are the Vogt family who prepare German and Italian Swiss specialties including raclette and risotto as well as schnitzel and grilled bratwurst. The service is attentive and there is a children's menu. Save room for Chef Peter Vogt's creations such as homemade chocolate truffles.

Dining Out

$$$$
Reservations required.
Dinner, Tues.-Sun.
115 Grove,
Tahoe City
530-583-8551

Christy Hill

A magnificent view down the lake from this intimate restaurant complements a unique dining experience. The cuisine is a blend of California and continental and the food presentation equals the exquisite tastes. The appetizer menu offers tantalizing selections that run the gamut from quail to foie gras to Maryland soft shell crab. Entreés are equally diverse, and include two vegetarian specialties — eggplant parmesan or grilled portobello mushrooms and fettuccini. This is a great place for that special occasion.

$$$ Lunch, dinner daily.
Roundhouse Mall,
Tahoe City
530-583-0233

Grazie!

With excellent Italian cuisine and a view across the expanse of Lake Tahoe, you can't miss at this fine restaurant any time of year. You may never get past the mouth watering array of antipasti including a house carpaccio with the thinnest slices of beef, capers, olive oil and shaved parmesan. The pasta selections are many, including a create-your-own pasta. Pizzas and a complete menu of traditional grilled meats and a good selection of seafood complete the menu.

$$$ Dinner Wed.-Mon.
640 No. Lake Blvd.,
Tahoe City
530-583-5700

Wolfdale's

Wolfdale's, a North Shore gourmet tradition, features a unique cuisine combining a touch of the Orient with exquisite French cooking. The extensive menu offers special fish each night and there is always a sashimi appetizer as well as an Asian soup. The entreés usually include a risotto and a seared leg of venison with cherry sauce and, if you are a big eater, that turf is offered with a surf addition of king crab. This is our choice for a romantic dinner while watching the light of the setting sun over the lake.

Year-Round

Dining Out

$$$ Dinner
Thurs. thru
Tue.
*Upstairs at
550 N. Lake
Blvd., Tahoe
City*
530-581-3362

Truffula

In 1998, the former sous chef from Plumpjack who trained at the New England Culinary Academy opened this restaurant in the best gourmet tradition of North Lake Tahoe. Both the decor and the food presentation are inspired and each of the offerings are taste sensations. Appetizers are creative and soup offerings excellent. The house specialty is a three-course vegetarian sampler. The main dishes offer North African braised lamb or filet mignon with wild mushroom sauce with truffle scented mashed potatoes and a nightly fish special.

$$$ Dinner
daily.
Reservations
recommended.
*521 N. Lake
Blvd., Tahoe
City*
530-581-1416

Fiamma Cucina Rustica

Fiamma is in the best tradition of culinary excellence that visitors have come to expect at Lake Tahoe. A wide array of appetizers and inventive pasta and meat dishes make for an enjoyable dining experience. The wines are moderately priced and the service attentive. The restaurant is small, so reservations are important.

$$ Dinner
daily. Summer,
lunch only.
*Boatworks,
Tahoe City*
530-583-0188

Jake's on the Lake

A busy bar and dining with lake views from inside and on the deck make this a favorite of locals and visitors alike. The food is California fresh, with plenty of fish and pasta as well as pizza and hamburgers.

$$ Summer,
lunch and
dinner daily.
Winter, dinner.
*Boatworks,
Tahoe City*
530-583-0358

Hacienda del Lago

There is excellent Mexican fare in this upstairs restaurant with a spectacular view of the lake. This is a great place to satisfy your craving for fajitas or a taco salad while on a summer shopping spree at the mall.

Dining Out

West Shore

Sunnyside Restaurant and Lodge

$$ May to Sept., lunch and dinner daily, Oct.-Apr., dinner daily, apres ski from 4pm.
1850 West Lake Blvd., 2 miles south of Tahoe City.
530-583-7200

The restaurant in the Sunnyside resort offers summer lunch and dinner on the deck overlooking their busy harbor. The view from the dining room is almost as good. The cuisine is California fresh with many fish specials. The Seafood Bar Menu and Café Menu offer delectable dishes at a moderate cost. A light meal on the deck watching boats sail by is a great way to end a day of bicycling along the lake. The deep-fried zucchini appetizers are some of the best in town. The beach, within eyeshot of the deck, is a perfect spot for restless children to play while parents relax.

Swiss Lakewood Restaurant and Bar

$$$$ Dinner daily except Mon. Lunch in Summer only.
On Hwy. 89 6 miles south of Tahoe City in Homewood.
530-525-5211

Swiss Lakewood is one of Lake Tahoe's oldest restaurants, in continuous operation since 1919 when the English Village starting taking guests. Its doors have remained open through several owners and renovations. The current owners remodeled the building in 1971 and brought a little bit of Switzerland to the West Shore. The Swiss decor and hospitality are evident from the moment you enter, with attentive hosts and an extensive wine list to go with a menu of Swiss and Continental dishes. A special appetizer and crunchy, hot rolls arrive as soon as you have been seated. The menu includes veal in the Zurich tradition, Viennese-style Wiener schnitzel, tournedos and daily specials. Dinner here is expensive, so you might want to opt for a summer lunch on the patio under the pines, surrounded by their beautiful garden.

Year-Round

Dining Out

West Shore Café

$$$ Summer only, lunch and dinner daily.
5180 West Lake Blvd., Homewood
530-525-5200

This restaurant directly on the waterfront has tables on the dock as well as the lawn. The food is superb California fresh with a continental flair, beautifully presented to match the timeless view. Although expensive, it presents an opportunity for an unforgettable summer dining experience.

Chambers Landing

$$$ Summer only, lunch and dinner daily.
Sun. brunch.
Off Hwy. 89 in Tahoma.
530-525-7262

Come by bicycle, boat or car to dine in an "Old Tahoe" historic lakeside dining establishment overlooking McKinney Bay. Graham Rock of Graham's at Squaw Valley prepares a Mediterranean cuisine with a full menu of vegetarian, fish and meat dishes. Lunch offerings include hamburgers and salads. This is a great bicycling destination on a summer day.

Norfolk Woods Inn

$$$$ Breakfast, lunch daily.
Dinner, Thurs.-Mon.
6941 West Lake Blvd., Tahoma
530-525-5000

Another quaint "Old Tahoe" building projects a homey atmosphere, but with gourmet fare all the way. Chef Michael Schwerdtfeger has won Best Taste for Quality Food and Best Marriage of Food and Wine at the Autumn Food and Wine Jubilee. Winning dishes were Pasta Pillows and Emerald Bay Lamb. If you have room at the end of your meal, the selection of deserts will surely tempt you. The restaurant is part of the Inn, so breakfast is served daily and includes Eggs Benedict, Corned Beef Hash or Mountain Omelettes. The dining experience here is unrushed and the food exceptional. The lodging at Norfolk Woods Inn is described on page 290 in "Historic Inns and B&B's."

Dining Out

North Shore Lake Tahoe

Gar Woods Grill and Pier

$$ Lunch and dinner daily, Sun. brunch.
5000 No. Lake Blvd., Carnelian Bay
530-546-3366

In summer sit on the deck or in winter enjoy the notable views from any table. Tahoe's classic wood boating era is remembered with photos, and the mahogany beams and tables add to the nautical theme. The lunch menu features soups, sandwiches and specials. Try the beer batter prawns for an appetizer before choosing from pork tenderloin, house pastas or seafood specialties for your dinner entreé.

Boulevard Café Trattoria

$$$ Dinner daily.
6731 No. Lake Blvd., Tahoe Vista.
530-546-7213

The extensive wine selection and glasses are in a mahogany sideboard as you enter, giving credence to the fact that you are in for a taste treat at this elegant restaurant. It is hard to decide among the many appetizers or whether to have the special salad creation before one of the entreés or the risotto of the evening or pasta dishes. When you are seated your server brings crunchy Italian bread baked on the premises with spreads of chick pea and garlic and roasted eggplant.

Captain Jon's

$$$$ Lunch and dinner Tues-Sun.
7220 No. Lake Blvd., Tahoe Vista
530-546-4819

Enjoy your before-dinner drink in the over-the-water lounge and then dine on French country and seafood specials from this notable lakeside restaurant. The desserts are so special that some people come for a late evening dessert and coffee only. A sushi bar on the water is open Friday and Saturday nights and there is often a reasonably priced early-bird dinner from 5:30 p.m. to 7:00 p.m. with entreé, salad and dessert.

Year-Round

Dining Out

$$$$ Dinner daily.
7238 No. Lake Blvd.,
Tahoe Vista
530-546-4464

Le Petit Pier

Dinner in this cozy restaurant directly on the lake features one of the finest French cuisines on the North Shore. Dinner is exquisitely prepared and presented with delicious sauces. The appetizers are varied and a must to complement your dinner entreé. Of particular interest is the lobster ravioli or the escargots. Chef Geno daily prepares a six course complete dinner, or you can choose from the regular entrées. The house specialties are a live Maine lobster steamed to perfection, or the Pheasant Souvaroff for two. The latter must be ordered 24 hours in advance. If you have only one night for a splurge, this is definitely the restaurant to choose. If you want to be assured a table with a view, come off season and early.

$$$ Dinner daily.
7320 No. Lake Blvd.,
Tahoe Vista
530-546-3640

Sunsets on the Lake

Fine Northern Italian and American cuisine can be enjoyed with a panoramic view down the Lake from the restaurant at the North Lake Tahoe Marina. The antipasti are so tempting you might want to try two for dinner accompanied by one of their special salads. A full list of pastas and meat entreés as well as their famous spit roasted garlic chicken fill out the menu. Their pizzas are cooked in an olive wood burning oven.

$ Lunch and dinner daily.
8290 No. Lake Blvd.,
Kings Beach
530-546-2218

Steamers Beachside Bar and Oven

A great place for lunch while watching action on the beach or letting the children play before being served. The clam chowder is among the best there is to complement the salads, sandwiches and, of course, pizza. The old photos on the walls recall the days when steamer ships brought patrons to the door and carried tourists around the lake.

Dining Out

$$ Breakfast, lunch and dinner daily. Dinner wkds. only, winter. Corner Hwys. 267 and 28, Kings Beach 530-546-9495

The Moose's Tooth Café

The Old Brockway Golf Course has built a beautiful new clubhouse with the added attraction of a new restaurant. With both inside and outside dining they offer a full menu of breakfast and lunch specials as well as dinner entrées. Interesting appetizers inlcuding baby back ribs and Dungeness crab cakes are excellent lunch choices.

$$$$ Dinner daily. 9983 Cove Ave., Crystal Bay 530-546-7529

The Soule Domain

The Soule Domain is fine dining in a historic Tahoe building, a log cabin, built by Harry Riley at the same time as the original Cal-Neva Lodge in 1927. The hearth features stones quarried at Crystal Bay and the exposed log beams were cut nearby. The chef-owner, Charles Edward Soule IV, has managed to create a delightful ambience in the two main rooms of the renovated cabin. He calls his cuisine American, but it is a flavorful combination of California, Italy, plus France and the Orient. Many of the dishes present a mixture of taste sensations that are hard to identify, but add up to a meal with "a high flavor component," according to the chef. Soup is included with your entreé. This is an excellent choice for a romantic dinner or before an evening at the casinos within walking distance of the restaurant.

$$$ Dinner daily. 24 State Line Rd., Crystal Bay 775-832-2739

Lakeview Room at Cal-Neva Lodge

At this historic casino, you can dine with an exciting view down the lake. This moderately priced restaurant serves traditional California cuisine including a great prime rib au jus and their special scampi. The wine list is extensive and affordable. After dinner don't miss the Indian Room and its informative Washo Indian exhibit.

Year-Round

Dining Out

Christmas Tree Restaurant

$$$ Dinner Daily. Reservations recommended. 20007 Mt. Rose Hwy. 775-849-0127

Owners Dana and Lisa Emerson have kept the tradition of this historic restaurant overlooking the Carson Valley on the Mount Rose Highway east of the ski area. Fine mahogany grilled meats, including a petite New York steak grilled to perfection for light eaters, are their stock in trade. However, you can have a lobster and meat combination or opt for one or their fine pastas. Appetizers are many and include everything from crab cakes to a smoked seafood platter. There is live jazz on Friday and Saturday nights.

Incline Village

The Big Water Grille at Tahoe

$$$$ Dinner daily. Reservations recommended. 341 Ski Way Incline Village 775-833-0606

The former Spatz with its fabulous views has reopened under the management of a group owning restaurants in Maui. The menu reflects a Hawaiian influence with plenty of fresh fish attractively presented. The appetizers are so enticing that you may just order two and add one of their special desserts featuring Macadamia nuts and Kaanapali estate grown coffee with chocolate truffles. Meat eaters will delight in the selection of duck, pork or venison. The wine list is extensive and you can check it out at the wine rack as you enter.

Yoshimi Japanese Restaurant

$$$ Lunch, dinner, daily. Christmas Tree Village #26, Incline Village 775-831-2777

Sushi and Sashimi afficianados will find a complete and tempting list of these delicacies at this new attractively decorated restaurant. The menu offers a wide selection of combination dinners with nabe, udon or soba. For the less adventurous, the tempura is light and there are many teriyaki offerings. All come with salad, rice and tea.

Dining Out

$$$ Breakfast, lunch daily. Summer, Dinner daily. Winter, dinner Thur. thru Mon. Off season, Dinner Thur., Fri., Sat.
333 Village Blvd., Incline Village
775-832-7333

Café 333

Owner Mary Young personally serves dinner in her small dining room behind the breakfast espresso bar and lunch room. Her personal interest in wine is reflected in the most extensive wine list in the area and the dozen wines by the glass, many moderately priced. The entreé menu changes every couple of weeks, but the meat offerings remain, only with different sauces. The black Angus beef and rack of lamb are regulars, along with seared ahi with wasabi. For starters, try the nightly soup special or the phyllo wrapped wild mushrooms. The dessert menu is a chocoholics dream, with five or six chocolate creations.

$$$$ Dinner daily.
907 Tahoe Blvd., across from Raley's Incline Village
775-832-3007

Jack Rabbit Moon

This recent addition to the gourmet dining scene at Incline Village serves the creations of its two chefs who are graduates of the California Culinary Institute. The dining room and bar are small, which can make it noisy when all tables are filled, but the taste delights offered here are outstanding. Appetizers range from ginger carrot soup to crispy prawns with an Asian dipping sauce and butternut squash ravioli. The entreés are well presented and include Cider Glazed Pork Chops, Goat Cheese Crusted Rack of Lamb, a fish special, roasted salmon and a pasta dish. Leave room for desert or an after dinner drink from the extensive list of single malt scotch, dessert wines and liqueurs.

Dining Out

Lone Eagle Grille

$$$ Lunch, summer only. Dinner daily.
*Country Club Dr. at Lakeshore Dr.
Incline Village*
702-832-3250
After 12/15/98
775-832-3250

The restaurant is on the site of the former Hugo's Rotisserie and is the Hyatt Regency's star restaurant. The dining room graced by two grand stone fireplaces features fabulous views down the lake from south-facing windows. The menu is hearty American but with some Asian and Hispanic influences. Appetizers feature such specialties as spicy crab cakes. The dining room is large and often full, but the service is excellent. This is a great location for a hearty summer lunch on the deck with its million dollar view down the lake.

Ciao Mein Trattoria

$$ Dinner daily.
Hyatt Regency Lake Tahoe, Incline Village
702-832-1234
After 12/15/98
775-832-1234

Located next to the casino in the Hyatt Regency Lake Tahoe, Ciao Mein serves an interesting combination of Oriental dishes with an Italian flare. One would usually expect a coffee shop menu in this location, but the dinner menu is extensive, moderately priced and tasty.

La Fondue

$$$ Dinner, Wed.-Sun. Reservations required.
Country Club Mall
702-831-6104
After 12/15/98
775-831-6104

Owner Karin Busch treats diners as her special guests in this intimate Swiss restaurant. The menu features traditional cheese and meat as well as dessert fondues. The schnitzels are mouth-watering, perfectly breaded with a light texture. Here is a dining treat for those who can't get to Switzerland for their fondue fix or are looking for a dining experience that is a little bit different.

Dining Out

Le Bistro

$$$$ Dinner, daily. Reservations recommended. *120 Country Club Mall, across from the Hyatt.* 775-831-0800

Chef Jean Pierre Doignon, formerly of La Cheminée, offers some of the best French cuisine in the area. The fixed price menu is changed daily and includes soup, salad or appetizer, entreé and the chef's own grand dessert. The restaurant features Acme bread from Berkeley that is in the true country French tradition, dark and crusty. Every course has its own taste sensation, beautifully presented with delicious sauces and just the right amount to leave room for dessert.

Stateline, Nevada
Fine Dining at the Casinos

A plethora of dining possibilities exist at the four major casino hotels in Stateline. We have chosen to review several that offer exceptional service and creative food offerings. The Casino Buffets with their value dining are described on page 247.

Llewellyn's

$$$$ Lunch and dinner daily. Reservations required but not necessary for lunch off-season. *The Penthouse at Harvey's Resort Hotel, Stateline* 775-588-2411

The restaurant on the top floor offers a superb dining experience with one of the best views in town. Every table looks across the lake with Mount Tallac providing the backdrop. The international cuisine with a California flair is beautifully presented, and the attentive service makes dining an enjoyable experience. The appetizers are tantalizingly different. The lunch menu features unusual sandwiches such as a salmon pancetta club. Dinner entreés run the gamut from venison medallons to range chicken and all with unusual sauces. The wine list is extensive. This is the place to choose for that special evening or, if you want the view but not the expense, try lunch.

Year-Round

Dining Out

$$$$ Dinner daily. Reservations required. *Harvey's Resort Hotel, Stateline* 702-588-2411 After 12/15/98 775-588-2411

The Sage Room at Harvey's

Guests at Harvey's have been dining in the Sage Room since 1947. If you're looking for great beef and traditional western food and hospitality, you can't go wrong here. The Black Angus beef is one-inch thick and is topped with their special onion rings. Other specialties of the house include a mixed grill of venison medallons. You can finish your meal with a chocolate port cake and their Viennese coffee for two.

$$$ Reservations recommended. *Harrah's Lake Tahoe, Stateline.* 702-588-6611 After 12/15/98 775-588-6611

Friday's Station Steak & Seafood Grill

With panoramic lake views below, you can enjoy the fine menu of steaks grilled to perfection over a custom hardwood grill or delectable seafood plus a salad bar. Friday's Station also offers a Sunday Brunch, and this might be the best time of all to enjoy the view from the 18th floor.

$$$$ Dinner daily. Reservations required. *Harrah's Casino Hotel, Stateline.* 702-588-6611 After 12/15/98 775-588-6611

The Summit at Harrah's Casino Hotel

The Summit has won numerous awards for its cuisine. Although very expensive, the taste delights that await you are worth the price. With impeccable service, your meal begins with a complimentary appetizer. There is a chef's special selection offered each night that includes appetizer, salad, choice of entreé and dessert. This fixed price meal is a great way to enjoy several menu items economically, and you can always share with your dinner partner. The appetizers are varied, and each is served with an interesting sauce. Entreés include a delicious rack of lamb and a tender Beef Wellington. Save room for desserts, for along with the double chocolate delights, the soufflé Grand Marnier can be ordered to put the final touch to your five star dinner.

Dining Out

The Broiler Room and Empress Court at Caesars

$$$ Dinner daily. Reservations required. Caesars, Stateline 775-586-2044

You'll find all your favorite steaks and seafood cooked to perfection and served in the quiet, elegant dining room of the Broiler Room which has been expanded at this long-time Tahoe favorite.

For a fine dining experience with an oriental flair, try the Empress Court. Featuring specialties of authentic Mandarin, Cantonese and Szechuan preparations, the selection of dishes will please the most discriminating diners with a desire for gourmet Chinese food.

Josh's at the Horizon Casino Resort

$$ Dinner daily. Horizon Casino Resort, Stateline 775-588-6211

If you're looking for an elegant dining experience that is a bargain, this is an excellent choice. The dinner menu features beef, seafood and pasta entreés served with soup or salad at a very reasonable price.

Other Stateline Dining

Edgewood Terrace Restaurant

$$$$ Dinner $$$ Lunch Lunch and dinner daily. Reservations for dinner recommended. At Edgewood Golf Course, Lake Parkway, Stateline 775-588-2787

Dine at lake's edge in the imposing Edgewood Golf Course Clubhouse where you feel as though you could reach out and touch the mountain landscape across the lake. Attentive service adds to a fine dining experience. Lunch choices at affordable prices include a daily special as well as unique salads and sandwiches. The dinner menu is varied, with suggested wine selections for each entreé. Savor the view of Lake Tahoe from sunset to moonglow while you dine on the delicious offerings from their gourmet kitchen.

Year-Round

Dining Out

The Chart House

$$$ Dinner daily. Reservations recommended. On Hwy. 207 (Kingsbury Grade) 1.5 miles east of U.S. 50. 702-588-6276 After 12/15/98 775-588-6267

Dine here for views of the lake from high up on the Kingsbury Grade. The food is traditional American where you know the lobster, prime rib or steaks will be excellent and the service pleasant. Add the view and you have a winning combination. This is a popular dinner house, so make your reservations early and arrive even earlier to assure yourself a window table.

Ivano's

$$ Dinner daily. 290 Kingsbury Grade, Stateline 702-586-1007 After 12/15/98 775-586-1007

Ivan Constantini has turned an old pizza parlor into a moderately priced classic Italian restaurant. He still serves pizza, but the emphasis is on meat dishes prepared in the Italian style and some pasta. The restaurant is small, but the service is attentive and the food tasty. The wine prices are moderate as well.

South Lake Tahoe

Nephele's

$$$ Dinner daily. Reservations required. 1169 Ski Run Blvd., So. Lake Tahoe 530-544-8130

This small restaurant features creative California cuisine. The food is flavorful and beautifully presented by the chef of eleven years. From an extensive appetizer menu, you can start your meal with a tasty treat before choosing from entreés that run the gamut from salmon poached in California chardonnay then baked and served with a camembert cheese sauce to filet mignon with grilled onions and bacon, served with champagne cognac sauce. If you still have room at the end of the meal, the scrumptious desserts are baked daily.

Dining Out

Café Fiore

$$$ Dinner daily. Reservations required.
1169 Ski Run Blvd. at Tamarack, So. Lake Tahoe.
530-541-2908

Café Fiore is an intimate restaurant serving a complete Italian menu. Antipasto may be followed by insalata or pasta or one of the traditional entreés of veal scaloppine or bistecca alla Fiore. The dinner entreés are served with salad, fresh vegetable and pasta of the day, and the portions are large. The restaurant is very small, but in summer you can dine on the patio when weather permits.

Christiania Inn

$$$$ Dinner daily, 5:30 to 11 pm. Reservations required.
3819 Saddle Rd. across from Heavenly Ski Resort parking lot, So. Lake Tahoe.
530-544-7337

Christiania Inn was built in 1965 to replicate a fine European country inn. The dining room exudes elegant, old-world charm. From the moment your waiter brings your hot, freshly baked bread to the last cup of coffee, he will watch over your every wish. The menu features exciting appetizer choices, including a house-cured salmon carpaccio and beluga caviar. Entreés include a house salad, but you may wish to have your waiter prepare a Caesar salad at the table. The entreés cover the spectrum of veal, beef and poultry with a daily fresh catch, all presented with an eclectic selection of sauces. If you have room, cherries jubilee or any of a number of delicious desserts are available. This is the place for that special night out. If a full a-la-carte dinner is beyond your pocket book, try the "Sunset Specials" between 5:30 and 7:00 p.m. that include choice of three entreés, soup and salad for a very reasonable price. During ski season ask for the "Apres Ski Specials." If you are looking for a unique bed and breakfast at the slopes, Christiania Inn is described on Page 294 in "Historic Inns and B&B's".

Dining Out

Monument Peak Restaurant at Heavenly Ski Resort

$$$ Fee to ride tram; reduced rate after 5pm. Summer: Lunch, dinner and Sunday brunch daily. Winter: Lunch daily.
Take the tram at the end of Ski Run Blvd., So. Lake Tahoe.
Summer phone: 530-544-6263

Skiers can enjoy a sit-down lunch with a view and be treated to sandwiches with an Italian accent. Try the Cervinia chicken sandwich with diavolo sauce and mozzarella, or for the light eater one of the homemade soups and a salad. Service is impeccable and if you've ever dined atop a European ski resort, you will feel right at home here. Summertime lunch or dinner at Monument Peak is an experience not to be missed. If you are inclined, walk the Tahoe Vista trail before dining. As you linger over a cup of Italian espresso after enjoying one of the authentic Northern Italian dinner selections, you can watch the sun set over the distant peaks of Desolation Wilderness.

Riva Grill and Bar

$$$ Breakfast, lunch and dinner daily. Sun. brunch. Reservations recommended.
Ski Run Blvd. So. Lake Tahoe
530-546-2600

As part of the Ski Run Marina redevelopment, Tom Turner of Gar Woods Grill and Pier, has opened a South Shore dining establishment with the same flair. The ambiance of course is boating, with beautiful paintings of Italian Riva runabouts for which the restaurant is named. The fare is Italian with a Mediterranean touch including many Gar Woods favorites such as conchiglie with grilled chicken, smoked Gouda, pancetta and artichoke hearts. Along with an extensive California wine list they also serve their famous Wet Woody drink of three rums in a fruit slush. You will be able to sit on the deck in the summer and watch the Tahoe Queen and other boating action. South Shore has long needed this fine dining experience with a lake view. The restaurant and service are a class act.

Dining Out

Swiss Chalet Restaurant

$$$ Dinner Tue.-Sun.
2544 Lake Tahoe Blvd., So. Lake Tahoe
530-544-3304

Kurt and Ruth Baumann came to Lake Tahoe in 1957, bought the original Schmidt's Bakery and converted it into a little bit of Switzerland at the South Shore. With four generations of restaurant experience in the family, they offer gourmet Swiss cuisine with impeccable service. A collection of beer steins adorn one alcove and huge cow bells hang from the ceiling, creating a decor that transports you to Zurich or Zermatt. Here you can indulge in fondue for two or any number of traditional Swiss dishes, such as bratwurst with spaetzli, or delectable, tender sauerbraten served with red cabbage. The menu also includes daily fish and pasta specials as well as house-baked Swiss pastries to finish your meal.

Fresh Ketch

$$$ Lunch and dinner daily. Reservations recommended.
Dockside at Tahoe Keys Marina, 2435 Venice Dr., So. Lake Tahoe
530-541-5683

Dine among the yachts at Fresh Ketch where fresh seafood is the fare of the day. Lunch offerings include traditional clam chowder along with fish specials, burgers and salads. Pastas and meat entreés are included in the dinner menu. The bar features beers from around the world as well as from many micro breweries in the west. The wine list is also extensive with offerings from France and California.

The Beacon Restaurant

$$ Lunch and dinner daily. Closed Nov. 1 to mid Dec.
Camp Richardson's Resort, Hwy. 89 north of the South Tahoe Y.
530-541-0630

This is a fine place to take the family for dining on the lake. With moderate prices for lunch and plenty of burger choices as well as sandwiches, omelettes and pastas. Since you can walk along the beach to Valhalla, this would be an excellent dinner spot before or after the performance. The dinner menu includes daily fish specials and cioppino as well as homemade soups meat or pasta.

Year-Round

Dining Out

$$$$ Dinner, Mon.-Sat. Reservations required.
536 Emerald Bay Rd., So. Lake Tahoe
530-542-1990

Evan's American Gourmet Cafe

Evan's, named for chef and owner Evan Williams, is possibly the finest dining experience in the Tahoe Basin. Attentive service complements an extensive menu including a long list of nightly gourmet specials. Evan has named his cuisine "Gourmet American," but his sauces and presentation speak of continental training mixed with a unique California touch. Appetizers include a daily pasta or one-person pizza. It is difficult to choose from the long list of entreés, but each meat dish features a special sauce. The wine list is as extensive as the menu. Save room for one of the delectable desserts. Evan's wife, Candice, bakes lavish desserts to test your will power. If you're celebrating a birthday or anniversary, or just want a special night out with a loved one, you would do well to choose Evan's. They are closed for three weeks every November so the chef and his wife can take a vacation.

$$$ Dinner daily.
Hwy. 89 at 10th St., So. Lake Tahoe
530-544-1233

The Cantina

Evan Williams has transformed the former Cantina Los Tres Hombres into a gourmet Sante Fe style restaurant. He still serves the usual burritos, enchiladas, fajitas and tacos, but he has added his own European touches to Southwestern cuisine. This is not your traditional Mexican fare. You can choose from Texas crab cakes or smoked chicken polenta or an astounding array of nightly specials which your waiter will explain to you.

Dining Out

Carson Pass

Sorensen's

$$$ Dinner daily. Reservations recommended. On Hwy. 88 just east of the intersection with Hwy. 89. 530-694-2203

Sorensen's has been providing food and accommodations for weary travelers since 1926. The lodge and cabins are now a full-scale resort with year-round activities for wilderness-loving tourists. See page 295 in "Historic Inns and B&B's." The dining room is not large but the round tables can seat up to eight if you have a large group and want a delicious satisfying meal after skiing or hiking. A fine wine list complements an array of hearty stews and nightly fish specials, and you can get the recipe for items you enjoyed from the front desk. Some evenings a guitarist will accompany your dinner. If they are busy, you may be asked to share your table with others, a great opportunity to meet new folks.

Caples Lake Resort

$$$ Dinner Wed.-Sun. Reservations recommended. At Caples Lake Resort, 4 miles west of Carson Pass on Hwy. 88. 209-258-8888

The resort dining room has one of the most spectacular views in the Sierra combined with lots of history. Caples Lake is on the Carson route of the Emigrant Trail and was settled by a '49er who decided this would be an excellent location for summer pasture. The lodge only dates back to the 1940s, but John Voss has been pleasing the palates of his guests for more than ten years. You can choose from any number of steak or chicken entreés, as well as pasta and nightly specials. However, save room for their house cheesecake. Kirkwood skiers will find this a special place for dinner out. For information about accommodations at the lodge, see page 296 in "Historic Inns and B&B's."

Year-Round

# Dining Out

Kirkwood Inn

$$ Breakfast, lunch and dinner, daily. *Five miles west of Carson Pass on Hwy. 88.* 209-258-7304

The Kirkwood Inn has been in continuous operation feeding locals and travelers over Carson Pass since the late 1800s. The hand hewn beams that support the ceiling are originals, installed by the Kirkwood and Taylor families in the 1860s. Hearty breakfasts and great hamburger lunches are the daily fare, but dinner offerings include pastas, fish specials and baby back ribs or steak. This is a great place to stop after skiing, or to try a hearty breakfast before hitting the slopes. It is also a favorite stopping place for people driving Highway 88 to see the fall color.

The Kirkwood Inn.

© Ellie Huggins

Dining Out

The Casino Hotel Buffets

If you have a hungry crowd, and you want lots of good food, the casino hotel buffets offer the best dining bargain on the South Shore.

Caesars Casino Hotel, Stateline, Nevada 775-588-3515 24-hour menu available.

Caesars Roman Feast Buffet

The selections at this buffet are fit for a Roman emperor, with such offerings as rotisserie prime rib, pasta and brick oven pizzas. There is a salad bar and desserts galore.

Horizon Casino Resort, Stateline 775-588-6211

Le Grande Buffet at the Horizon Casino Resort

Every night Le Grande Buffet at the Horizon Casino Resort puts on a complete, all-you-can-eat buffet dinner that includes prime rib for less that $10 per person. On the weekends there is brunch with many specialties to choose from.

Harvey's Resort Hotel, Stateline 775-588-2411

Harvey's Garden Buffet

Breakfast and brunch buffets are offered daily. Themed dinner menus include Mexican, Basta Pasta, BBQ, German and Seafood as well as salad bar, fresh fruit, dessert, and yogurt. The weekend buffets feature prime rib, steak and fish entrees plus the salad, fruit, dessert and yogurt bars.

Harrah's Casino Hotel, Stateline 775-588-6606

The Forest Buffet at Harrah's Casino Hotel

On the 18th Floor with a view of the mountains you can get brunch or dinner daily that includes a complete salad bar and wide choice of meat, pasta and fish entrees. A fabulous seafood buffet is served every Friday from 4:30 p.m. to 10:00 p.m.

The former C.B. White House in Truckee, now Jordan's.

Kids at Casinos

Many of the casino hotels offer some of the best room rates in town with restaurants and buffets serving excellent food at moderate prices. If you are skiing, shuttles to the slopes allow you to leave your car in the covered parking garages, a real plus if a snow storm occurs.

Since no children under 18 years old are allowed in the casinos, the casino hotels have special arcades where youngsters can play video games or even watch free movies. Each casino hotel listed below offers something for the kids to do while you gamble or have dinner.

Crystal Bay

Cal-Neva:
702-832-4000
Crystal Bay:
702-832-0512
Biltmore:
702-832-0660
After 12/15/98
area code 775

Cal-Neva Lodge and Crystal Bay Club
Tahoe Biltmore Lodge and Casino

All casinos have video arcades to amuse the kids while you hit the tables.

Incline Village

Reservations required.
Must be guests of the Resort.
702-832-1234
Ext. 3214
After 12/15/98
775-832-1234

Hyatt Regency Lake Tahoe Resort and Casino

Camp Hyatt is a program designed just for kids 3 to 12 years old. From mid June to Labor Day your children can participate in their own indoor and outdoor activities, from trips to Ponderosa Ranch or scavenger hunts to bingo and arts and crafts. The camp operates from 9:00 a.m. to midnight in two sessions. The rest of the year day sessions are on weekends only. Evening sessions are from 4:00 p.m. to midnight. One other caveat, your three-year-old must be potty trained with no pull-ups. This is an activity oriented program to stimulate kids, not a baby-sitting service and is open only to guests of the hotel.

Year-Round

Kids at Casinos

South Lake Tahoe

Harrah's Lake Tahoe

Fee for all games.
775-588-6066

Harrah's has opened a completely new Family Fun Center. An indoor playground features ball pools, climbing areas and two levels of slides. Of course there are also video and pinball games and you can win points to redeem for gifts. This is a safe, well lit, non-smoking and alcohol free place, but small children will need to be accompanied by an adult or older child. Harrah's also offers bonded babysitting for hotel guests.

Harvey's Resort Hotel

Fee for all games.
775-588-2411

There is no doubt that this is the most up-to-date and fancy arcade at South Shore. It is centrally located in its own grotto near the hotel. There are special extra fee attractions as well as a family fun center with virtual reality ski and car racing.

Horizon Casino Resort

Fee for all games.
775-588-6211

The Horizon Hotel has an arcade in the convention center. Families must go outside the hotel to reach the arcade, since the other entrance is through the casino. There are games for all ages, but your youngest children will need supervision.

Caesars Lake Tahoe

Fee for all games.
775-588-3515

Caesars has a state-of-the-art video arcade with all kinds of games and virtual reality rides to keep junior guests occupied.

Art Galleries

There is an extensive art community in the Truckee-Lake Tahoe region and many galleries show the works of local artists. In order to find out what is showing, check the local newspapers for information about current shows. *Artifacts*, a free publication about the arts scene, is published quarterly and is distributed around the lake. Galleries are listed below starting in Truckee. Every July, Tahoe ARTour holds a three-day, self-guided tour of 30 artists' studios in the North Tahoe-Truckee area. There are three artists' studio galleries that welcome visitors by appointment.

Downtown Truckee

Artruckee

Daily, 10am-5:30pm.
Downtown Truckee
530-587-5189

Artruckee recently moved to the Loading Dock building features the works of local artist, Audrey Dygert, and others. Interesting carved bears, jewelry and other gift items are also for sale.

The White Buffalo

Daily, 10am-5:30pm.
Downtown Truckee
530-587-4446

This shop features authentic Southwest Indian art, jewelry and pottery as well as clothes, moccasins and cookbooks for hot chili food.

Art Galleries

The Backstreet Framemakers and Gallery

Mon.-Sat., 10am-5:30pm.
Jibboom St., Truckee
530-587-1409

This interesting upstairs store has posters and Edward Curtis prints, plus works of local artists.

Kathleen Curtis Studio

Visitors welcome by appointment.
Studio: 530-582-8673
Home: 530-587-3198

Mythical creatures in a sculpture garden greet the visitor to her downtown Truckee studio — a place to find earthen figures large and small, baskets and notecards. Co-author of *Weavers of Tradition and Beauty: Basketmakers of the Great Basin*, Kathleen also makes modern equivalents and gives workshops in papermaking sculpture and basketry.

Kathleen Curtis' Deer Woman and other earth sculptures.

Courtesy of Kathleen Curtis

Art Galleries

Daily except Tues. 10am-5pm.
Capitol Building upper level, Downtown Truckee
530-587-8460

James Hacker Sculpture

The bronze cast and welded sculptures are specially designed to hang on walls and over fireplaces. His outdoor pieces and fountains will enhance your garden.

Frank Rossback Glasforms

The custom glass blowing and sculpture of Frank Rossback shares the space in the upstairs room of the Capitol Building where you can watch the artist at work.

Highway 89 South and Tahoe City

Wed.-Sun. 10am-6pm.
1600 Squaw Valley Rd., Squaw Valley
530-583-6468

Squaw Valley Trading Post

Here's your chance to see the largest and best collection of Zapotec Indian rugs in the country and at wholesale prices.

Wkds., 10am-10pm
Wkdys., 10am-6pm.
Resort at Squaw Creek, Squaw Valley
530-581-6639

Gallery at Squaw Creek

Discerning collectors can find an eclectic and exciting collection at this gallery located in the shopping arcade. This sister gallery to Sierra Galleries at Lake Tahoe has traditional oil landscapes as well as modern impressionists and colorful contemporary cowboys by Thomas Charles. They also sell old photos of the Tahoe-Truckee area.

Daily. 10am-5:30 pm.
255 No. Lake Blvd., Tahoe City
530-583-0553

Pogan Gallery

This upstairs gallery features ceramic pieces, contemporary and traditional realism, and original fine art in a variety of media. They display local and national artists.

Year-Round

Art Galleries

Suzanne Riley Studio and Gallery

Visitors welcome by appointment.
530-581-3554

Suzanne creates unique, colorful and contemporary prints all about nature and the Northwest. She welcome visitors by appointment to her log cabin studio, or you can see her work at Douglas Taylor Gallery in Tahoe Vista (see page 255) or when you dine at Wolfdales, listed in "Dining Out" on page 227.

North Tahoe Art Center

Thur.- Sun. 11am-4pm.
380 No. Tahoe Blvd., Tahoe City
530-581-2787

The works of local artists are displayed in a changing exhibit at the art center. The shop and gallery are run by volunteer artists who are members of the cooperative.

Frames by Ryrie

Mon.-Sat., 10am-5pm.
Cobblestone Mall,
Tahoe City
530-583-3043

An exciting gallery with posters, etchings of the Sierra, wood blocks and original water colors. They also do custom framing.

Mother Nature's Wildlife Art

Mon.-Sat., 10am-6pm.
Sun., 10am-5pm.
521 No. Lake Blvd., Tahoe City
530-581-4278

This gallery next to Porter's sells fine art prints, photos and sculptures of wildlife by such artists as Lyman Doolittle, Redlin, Wysocki, Bateman, Brenders, Franca Calley and more.

High Country Silverworks

Daily, 10am-6pm.
600 No. Lake Blvd.,
Tahoe City
530-583-1600

This shop features the work of 60 artists using different media and materials. It is also a working jewelry studio.

Art Galleries

Freeman Photo Gallery and Custom Framing

The gallery has original photographs and hand-colored black and white archival prints, pen-and-ink sketches and vintage Tahoe photographs.

Mon.-Sat., 10am-5:30pm.
620 No. Lake Blvd.,
Tahoe City
530-581-4310

Sierra Galleries

This is a large gallery that features the original paintings, sculpture, and limited edition graphics of local, national and international artists.

Daily,
Summer, 10am-10pm.
Winter, 10am-6pm.
Boatworks Mall,
Tahoe City
530-581-5111

North Shore

Douglas Taylor-Art and Framing

Douglas Taylor shows the works of over 20 contemporary print makers and photographers along with works in other media, vintage Tahoe photographs and unique gifts. There are shows three times a year featuring various artists and occasional art workshops.

Mon.-Fri., 10am-6pm.
Sat., 10am-5pm.
6883 No. Lake Blvd.,
Tahoe Vista
530-546-7794

Timeless Sculptures

You'll see sculptures created on the spot — humorous, abstract, caricature and realistic. Stop by and see the bears guarding the entrance; you many want one for your garden.

Daily, 10am-5:30pm.
8626 No. Lake Blvd.,
Kings Beach
530-546-8480

Kilim Hand Woven Rugs

This store is not unlike an art gallery with its handmade old and new Oriental rugs, kilims and contemporary rugs, mats and wall hangings.

Daily, 10am-5:30pm.
8675 No. Lake Blvd.,
Kings Beach
530-546-4011

Year-Round

Art Galleries

Lakeside Gallery and Gifts

Mon.-Sat., 10am-5pm.
8636 No. Lake Blvd.,
Kings Beach
530-546-3135

Established in 1978, the gallery shows landscapes, seascapes, impressionist paintings and still lifes, as well as fine art prints and gift items.

The Potter's Wheel

Thurs.-Mon., 10am-6pm.
8331 No. Lake Blvd.,
Kings Beach
530-546-8400

The Potter's Wheel is back. Formerly in the Watson Cabin, the shop-gallery features water colors by Betty Layton, designer ceramic sinks and other handcrafted pottery as well as glass, woodwork and gift items.

Artists of Tahoe An Arts Desire

761 Northwood,
Incline Village
702-831-3011
After 12/15/98
775-831-3011

Cynthia Ashe frames art work and shows originals by local artists.

Art Attack Gallery

Mon.-Sat., 10am-6pm.
Christmas Tree Village,
Incline Village
702-832-7400
After 12/15/98
775-832-7400

This gallery in the Christmas Tree Village features the work of William and Judith Vrooman as well as an "Artist of the Year." There are special exhibits with lectures by visiting artists throughout the year. Watch the *North Tahoe Truckee Week* or *Artifacts* for listings of these shows.

South Lake Tahoe, Meyers and Stateline

There are numerous galleries in the area that offer eclectic choices for browsing or buying. The casino hotels have galleries in their shopping malls. The area has an active artists' group that sponsors special shows and summer workshops at the Tallac Historic Site. The gallery shop there features local artisans' work for sale.

Art Galleries

The Magic of Tahoe

*Plexus Center
Meyers
530-577-6635*

Along with gifts of the earth, the gallery in Myers shows works of local sculptors and painters.

Hanifin's Art and Antiques

*Tue.-Sun.
10am-5pm.
855 Emerald
Bay Rd.,
So. Lake Tahoe
530-542-4663*

Hanifin's features oils and watercolors by local artists and interesting sculptures. He also sells fine oak and pine European and American antiques.

Eagle Valley Frames and Art Gallery

*Mon.-Sat.,
10am-6pm
2660 Lake
Tahoe Blvd.,
So. Lake Tahoe
530-544-4099*

This gallery features investment art as well as prints and posters with particular emphasis on local scenes and artists.

Lake Tahoe Community College

*Daily,
8am-5pm.
One College Dr.,
So. Lake Tahoe
530-541-4660*

The college hangs changing exhibits of faculty and student art.

Stateline, Nevada

Augustine Arts

*164 Glen Ct.,
Stateline
702-588-3525
After 12/15/98
755-588-3525*

If you're a Marilyn Monroe fan, you'll want to browse through the photographs at this gallery, which also displays paintings and sculptures.

Year-Round

Art Galleries

A Frame of Mind Gallery

Mon.-Thur., 9am-9pm.
Fri.-Sat., 9am-11pm.
Caesars Tahoe
702-588-8500
After 12/15/98
775-588-8500

The newest gallery in the South Lake region features the vibrant and stunning photographs of the renowned Robert Glenn Ketchum. Several of Ketchum's photographs can be seen in Robert Redford's new movie, "American President." The gallery also shows historical works by William Henry Jackson, Edward S. Curtis and others.

Sierra Galleries

Daily, Hours vary.
At Caesars Tahoe
702-588-8081
After 12/15/98
775-588-8081

The gallery is filled with original paintings, limited-edition sculpture and antique carousel horses.

Addi Galleries

Daily, 9am-10pm.
Harrah's Casino Hotel
702-588-1505
After 12/15/98
775-588-1505

The Addi Galleries features works by Red Skelton, their celebrity artist for 15 years. They also publish the work of marine artist David Miller. Other unique items here are burlwood furniture and clocks.

Legends

Daily, 10am-4pm.
Horizon Casino Hotel
702-588-8598
After 12/15/98
775-588-8598

Here you will find limited edition prints of wildlife and wilderness. They also do framing.

Zephyr Cove, Nevada

Jerome Evans

By appointment.
702-588-6486
After 12/15/98
775-588-6486

You can make an appointment to see an interesting collection of antique and contemporary art of the native peoples of Africa, Oceania and North and South America.

Shopping

Truckee

Historic Downtown Truckee along Donner Pass Road is a perfect place to spend a morning or afternoon looking for unusual gifts. Among the many offerings are: **The Cooking Gallery** with everything imaginable for the cook and kitchen; **Cabona's**, selling casual clothing since the early 1900s; and **Truckee River Llama Ranch** with imported sweaters and clothing. **Joanne's Stained Glass** sells fascinating gifts of glass. There's a Christmas shop and homemade candy store, as well as places for T-shirts, ice cream and numerous restaurants. You can sit and watch the action from the balcony of **Café Meridian** while you sip your latté or have lunch. **Andy's 24-Hour Diner** across the railroad tracks serves real milkshakes, meatloaf sandwiches and other fare from the 1950s. **Jordan's Collectibles** in the C.B White House sells antiques and women's clothing.

The **Gateway Shopping Center**, at the corner of Donner Pass Road and Highway 89, is home to Safeway and Payless Drugs. Stores of interest are **Sugar Bowl Ski and Sports** and **The Bookshelf at Hooligan Rocks**, a full service bookstore with books on tape, cards, and magazines and **Pacos Truckee Bike and Ski** for all your biking and cross country skiing needs.

Mountain Hardware and Sports is more than a hardware store, carrying kitchenware and linens, sports supplies for fishing and hunting, snowshoes and skis to rent or buy, plus books and maps.

Next door, the former Ace Hardware is now **Granite Chief**, the Truckee store for the famous Squaw Valley ski service center.

The Factory Stores are located on Donner Pass Road just east of the Donner State Park Interstate 80 exit. The shops offer clothing, household items, jewelry and shoes at marked-down prices.

Year-Round

Shopping

Squaw Valley

The **Squaw Valley Olympic House Mall** features boutiques and ski shops, while the **Resort at Squaw Creek** shopping promenade offers up-scale shopping for clothing, art and jewelry. **Sweet Potato Deli** has delectables to eat and a full line of cookbooks as well. Even if you don't buy, it's a great place to window-shop.

Tahoe City

For plants and other garden items, books, house decorations and Jeb's Mountain Gallery of nature and wildlife prints, don't miss the **Tahoe Tree Company** at 401 West Lake Boulevard south of the Tahoe City Y. Nearby, look in at **Girasole** that sells Irish country furniture, dishes and other decorations for the home.

Five malls offer a variety of shopping experiences. **Cobblestone Mall** shops sell clothing, jewelry, quilts and art. The **Boatworks Mall** has a collection of gift and clothing shops, galleries and the **Bookshelf at Boatworks**. The **Tahoe Marina Mall**, west of the Boatworks also has a variety of shops including **Sports Tahoe** featuring beautiful resort wear. At the **Lakehouse Mall** the **Alpine Bookstore** carries a complete collection of regional and Lake Tahoe books and sells used books.

Next door to Safeway in the **Lighthouse Mall**, **The Store** sells gifts, cards, books and other necessities.

The Watermelon Patch is an interesting gift shop at 3225 North Lake Boulevard near Dollar Point. It features unusual clothing, gifts and cards. In the summer they sell plants for your garden and are the site for a farmers' market that sells fresh produce every Thursday.

Shopping

Incline Village

You'll find **Hallmark Village Cards and Books** has a large collection of books and of course cards for all occasions, while **The Potlatch** offers a complete line of Southwest and Indian art, artifacts and jewelry. **The Christmas Store** in The Christmas Tree Village is the perfect place to pick up decorations and other gifts all year.

South Lake Tahoe

If you are visiting the **Tallac Historic Site** you will definitely want to check out the Art Store in front of Valhalla that sells unusual artifacts and jewelry by local artists along with interesting ornaments from around the globe.

You will find numerous **Factory Stores** around the South Tahoe *Y*. **Mikasa** is a nice place to look for bargains in china and pottery and chocolate lovers will want to visit the **Rocky Mountain Chocolate Factory**. Well-made knits at **Cape Isle Knitters** and **Oneida Silver** are among the many outlets on both sides of U.S. 50.

At the *Y*, on the west side of Highway 50, you'll also find the **Sierra Bookshop**, crammed full of books, cards, games and calendars and an excellent collection of hiking and skiing guides and maps. Their second store is at the Bijou Shopping Center where you will find even more gift and specialty shops.

The casinos have shopping galleries that offer everything from sports essentials to sculptures and paintings by renowned artists, as well as T-shirts and other attire. Be sure to visit **Heavenly Sports** across the street from Harvey's Casino for all your sporting gear and attire.

The redeveloped **Ski Run Marina** features a stylish shopping area next to the Riva Grill that includes a gallery, womens clothing and jewelry shops.

Year-Round

The Watson cabin in Tahoe City.

Museums

The area's history is rich in tales of pioneer grit and Bunyanesque feats to fell and transport lumber and build the first transcontinental railroad across the granite slopes of the Sierra Nevada. Whether you want a diversion on a winter afternoon or are curious about the colorful history of the region, there are many museums and historical sites worth a visit. "Historical Walks" on page 113 describes places in the area where you can follow the trails of the emigrant wagons or see remnants of Lake Tahoe's nineteenth century tourist splendor.

Truckee and North Lake Tahoe

The Western America Ski Sport Museum

Open Wed. thru Sun. Boreal Ski Area, at the Castle Peak exit off I-80. 530-426-3313

The Western America Ski Sport Museum, operated by the Auburn Ski Club, features the history of winter sports. Of special interest to Sierra history buffs are the statue of Snowshoe Thompson and the 20-foot skis he used. He was a fearless Norwegian skier who carried the mail free of charge over the Sierra from Genoa to Hangtown (Placerville) between 1856 and 1876. The exhibits include old photos of the days when skis, called snowshoes, were just wooden boards strapped to your boots, and examples of the evolution of boots to today's high-tech models. There are photos of the West's greatest skiers and on weekends, old ski movies are shown continuously to provide an afternoon of entertainment. During the week, the movies are show upon request.

Museums

Sierra Nevada Children's Museum

Fee. Wed., Thurs., Sat. 10am-4pm.
11400 Donner Pass Road, Truckee
530-587-KIDS

You may have to drag your child away from the fascinating hands-on activities that help children learn about their natural environment. Helpful volunteers guide children in art activities as well.

Donner Memorial State Park and Museum

Fee per person. Museum: Daily, Summer, 9am-5pm. Winter, 10am-4pm. Slide shows on the hour.
On Donner Pass Rd. just west of the Donner State Park exit off I-80.
530-582-7892

This park is a memorial to the Donner Party and all pioneers who made the trek west. The Emigrant Trail Museum's exhibits display artifacts from the Donner Party and show the life of the Paiute tribes who summered in the area for several thousand years. Dioramas depict the construction of the Central Pacific Railroad over the Sierra Nevada between 1864 and 1869. A slide show about the tragic story of the Donner Party is shown several times a day. The bookstore in the museum sells a wide variety of titles on natural history of the area as well as many books about the Donner Party and other emigrant history.

The imposing Pioneer Monument just east of the museum was built to commemorate all who struck out across the trackless land to reach California. Note the height of the monument's base. The snow was that deep in 1846-47, when the Donner Party camped here.

A trail from the museum leads to the site of the Murphy family cabin, one of the families of the Donner Party. A bronze plaque attached to the rock that formed one wall of their shelter lists the survivors and deceased of that ill-fated group. Of eighty-nine who had set out from Missouri in May 1846, only forty-seven lived to see California's fertile valleys.

Museums

The park is open all year. For information about other activities at the park, see "Beaches," "Bicycling," "Special Hikes," "X-Country Skiing," "Just for Kids," and "Ranger Programs."

Donner Day Camp of the U.S. Forest Service

Open in Summer.
On the east side of Hwy. 89 three miles north of I-80.

The tragedy of the Donner Party has fascinated historians and tourists ever since C.F. McGlashan, editor of the Truckee Republican, published his *History of the Donner Party* in 1880. A sign at the edge of the parking lot tells the tragic story of the Donner Party. The sites of makeshift shelters of the families of Jacob and George Donner are marked along a path around the meadow.

During the summer of 1990, volunteers under the guidance of the University of Nevada, Reno undertook an intensive archeological search to uncover artifacts that might confirm the exact locations of the Donner family camps. Bone fragments, pieces of china and metal wagon parts were unearthed in the meadow nearby confirming the presence of the group here. However, nothing was found under the fire-scarred pine tree that was originally thought to be the location of George Donner's family tent.

There is a Commemorative Emigrant Trail built by the U.S. Forest Service that leads north to Prosser Dam. You might want to consider a short hike on this. The whole trail — open to hikers, cyclists and equestrians — traverses 12 miles between the Donner Camp and Stampede Reservoir and is described in "Bicycling" on page 96.

Museums

Open daily in Summer, 11am–5pm. Wed.-Sun. May 15-June 15, and Labor Day-Oct. 1. On Hwy. 89 just south of the Tahoe City Y. 530-583-1762

The Gatekeeper's Cabin

This museum, operated by volunteers of the North Lake Tahoe Historical Society, tells the story of Lake Tahoe. Exhibits include exquisite Washo baskets and several collections of obsidian arrowheads. You can learn about important pioneer settlers of the area and buy books and items of historical interest at the museum store. The newest exhibit at the museum is an accurate scale model of the steamer *Tahoe* that plied the waters of Lake Tahoe delivering mail and passengers to destinations around the lake before roads were built.

Next door, the Marion Steinbach Indian Basket Museum displays the $1.5 million collection that was donated to the Historical Society upon Marion's death in 1991. In addition to the baskets she collected between 1935 and 1957 from Alaska to the Plains, there are over 100 Indian dolls, examples of basket starts, carvings and other art.

Between 1916 and 1968 the Gatekeeper's log cabin served as home for the official regulator of Lake Tahoe's water level. After 1968, the Federal Watermaster's Office in Reno controlled the dam. However, it is still necessary for someone to hand turn the gates of the dam. Special agreements between California and the Nevada irrigation districts determine the amount of water to be released into the Truckee River. The water flows downstream to Reno and its reservoirs. The river finally turns north at Wadsworth, east of Reno, and empties into Pyramid Lake.

Museums

The Watson Cabin Living Museum

Daily, Summer, noon-4pm. Holiday weeks and wknds. only the rest of the year.
560 No. Lake Blvd., Tahoe City
530-583-8717

This turn-of-the-century log cabin stands on its original site overlooking the Commons Beach in Tahoe City. It was built by Robert Montgomery Watson, a Tahoe City pioneer and its first constable. He served the town for 28 years and could often be seen riding around town or into the mountains on his horse Pinto. His son Rob moved into the cottage with his bride in 1909. The Watsons were one of the first families to live in Tahoe City year round. Their daughter Mildred lived in the cabin until 1950 when the building was leased for a gift shop, and then an artisans' gallery. In 1979 the North Lake Tahoe Historical Society purchased the building and placed it on the National Register of Historic Places. The cabin has been restored as a "living museum" depicting the life of a Tahoe pioneer family.

For more information about Tahoe City's past, you may wish to purchase a copy of *Tahoe City's Yesterdays*, gathered and edited by Carol Van Etten. This pictorial history of the town is filled with interesting stories about the people and places of historical importance in Tahoe City. The book is available at both museums and local bookstores.

California State Parks Museums

Summer only. Fee per vehicle.
Sugar Pine State Park, Nine miles south of the Tahoe City Y.
530-525-7982

During the summer, at Sugar Pine State Park and Emerald Bay, the state parks open two mansions for your enjoyment. Step back to Victorian times in the Ehrman Mansion in Sugar Pine State Park. The house is open with living history docents to show you around the rooms of this elegant summer residence built in 1902 by Isaias W. Hellman, a San Francisco financier. For a description of the bicycle ride to the park, see page 89 in "Bicycling."

Year-Round

Museums

Summer only. Must hike or boat to the location. *Eight miles north of the So. Tahoe Y.* 530-541-3030

See page 138 in "Special Hikes" for a description of the hike to **Vikingsholm** on the shores of Emerald Bay. Tours are held during the summer months of this replica of a 9th century Norse fortress, built by Mrs. Lora J. Knight in 1929. Her tea house on Fannette Island can be visited on Tahoe Whitewater Tours kayak trip to Emerald Bay (on page 62 in "Boating") or from your own canoe or boat.

South Lake Tahoe

Fee to enter. Summer, daily, 11am-4pm. Winter, wknds., noon-4pm. *3058 Hwy. 50, So. Lake Tahoe* 530-541-5458

Lake Tahoe Historical Society Museum

Step back in time for an hour or two with Lake Tahoe's interesting history, from the time when Washo tribes called the lake their summer home to Stateline's first gambling casinos. The museum is the product of dedicated volunteers of the Lake Tahoe Historical Society who have assembled exhibits depicting all periods of the area's history. Learn about Washo Indian basketry and pioneers who settled here when Lake Valley was a crossroads for the Bonanza Road from California to Nevada's silver mines. There is an exhibit about the Pony Express and the story of the lake's famous steamers and lumber operators of the late nineteenth century who felled, shipped and flumed their logs to Nevada to shore up the silver mines of Virginia City. There are oral histories on tapes and three different videos for hours of interesting viewing. The museum shop sells books and posters about Lake Tahoe. When you leave, be sure to look at the two buildings behind the museum: the oldest log cabin in the region which was the Society's first museum and Osgood's Tollhouse, built in 1859.

Museums

Tahoe Douglas Chamber of Commerce Visitor Center

Mon.-Fri., 9am-6-pm.
Wknds., 9am.-5pm.
Round Hill
702-588-4591
After 12/15/98
775-588-4591

Be sure to drop in and see the interpretive panels at this new Visitor Center. Here you can learn the story of Lake Tahoe, from the earliest Washo settlements to the new casinos. You can read about the success story of Harvey's Casino Resort that started in 1947 as a small coffee shop with a few slot machines. Harvey's wife Lewellyn brought the food over from their home next door. There are books, jewelry and lots of brochures about the activities mentioned in this book.

Celio Ranch

Drive west on U.S. 50 from the So. Tahoe Y to Upper Truckee Rd. then south on Upper Truckee Rd. about one mile. The Celio Ranch is on both sides of the road. A historic marker is on the right side of the road.

The Celio family has been in Lake Valley since 1863, when Carlo Celio established a ranch south of present day U.S. 50. The family expanded their holdings in 1903 when they purchased most of the land of today's Meyers and Yank's Station Hotel. They operated a lumber company here from 1905 until 1952, furnishing much of the lumber for summer homes in the surrounding areas. They also raised beef cattle and operated a dairy. Across the road is the original milk house. The present-day Celio ranch house was built in 1915 on the foundations of the old house that had worn out. Descendants of the Celio family still live in this lovely structure with its encircling porch that provides shade in summer and protection from snow in the winter.

Year-Round

Photo and Vista Points

The Donner Lake area has three vista points from which to view the pass, lake and railroad and to take photographs.

Lake Tahoe, often referred to as the "Lake of the Sky" or "Jewel of the Sierra," has many locations that offer excellent photo opportunities for camera enthusiasts. The best time to photograph from the East Shore is in the early morning. A trip around the lake from east to west is highly recommended, finishing at the Emerald Bay Overlook. On the way, several restaurants on the North Shore have beautiful vistas. The places listed below are particularly fine points from which to create your photograph and can all be reached by automobile.

Donner Lake and Donner Pass

Donner Lake Vista Points

Vista points are located off Interstate 80 about three miles east of Donner Summit and three miles west of Truckee. The two vista points on the interstate east or west offer magnificent views of Donner Lake, Donner Pass and Schallenberger Ridge. Display maps point out the railroad line, old roads and the emigrant wagon routes used between 1844 and 1870. Without guides or maps, and with precious little knowledge of what lay ahead, these intrepid people dragged their wagons over the precipitous granite walls to the west of the lake.

Donner Lake Overlook and McGlashan Point

Drive west on Donner Pass Road from Donner Lake to the overlook just before the Rainbow Bridge. This classic view of Donner Lake makes a wonderful photo, especially at sunset. The range of mountains to the east is the Carson Range, a spur of the Sierra Nevada. The Rainbow Bridge has been restored and rebuilt and if you walk up the road from the bridge, you can frame the lake through the bridge.

Photo and Vista Points

Lake Tahoe

Logan Shoals Vista Point

The Logan Shoals Vista Point is on U.S. 50, north of Stateline 7.2 miles. Here you can frame a photo of the lake with one of the many beautiful Jeffrey pines at this spot. You may want to climb around on the point to find the perfect location for your photograph.

Memorial Point

About two miles south of Lakeshore Boulevard on Highway 28, the Lake Tahoe Nevada State Park has built a beautiful vista point. Interpretive signs describe the lake, its history and locations of the various overlooks along the lake. Several paths get you close to the emerald water, where your photographs may be able to reflect the granite boulders shimmering just beneath the surface.

Mount Rose Highway Overlook

Take Mount Rose Highway (Highway 431) east from Highway 28 in Incline Village. Drive 3.5 miles to the overlook. The vistas from this point are among the best in the region. The blue-green of the shallow water at the lake's edge contrasts vividly with the azure blue of the deeper water beyond.

Stateline Fire Lookout

From Highway 28 in Crystal Bay take Reservoir Road, across from the post office, and turn right on Lakeview. The Forest Service road is on the left in about one half mile. One of the gates on the road may be closed, but the half-mile walk to the top is worth it. At the end of the road is the region's most spectacular view of Crystal Bay and south to high peaks behind the South Shore. A nature trail with interpretive panels encircles the Fire Lookout Station. Plan to spend an hour taking in the views here and learning some history too. The Lookout has been adopted by local citizens.

Photo and Vista Points

Emerald Bay Overlook

The overlook parking area is 9 miles north from the South Tahoe *Y* on Highway 89. The photo images from this spot are unlimited, particularly when the water reflects the brilliant blue of a California summer day. If you feel like taking a short hike, return to the Eagle Falls parking lot and take the trail up to the falls and on to Eagle Lake. There are spots above Eagle Lake where your vista of Emerald Bay is exceptional. The description of the hike is in "Special Hikes" on page 140.

Carson Pass Region

Several vista points on the south side of Highway 88 as it climbs west toward Carson Pass capture views of Red Lake and the Hope and Charity Valleys below. If you are lucky enough to drive this road during the fall when the aspens splash gold across the valleys, some beautiful photos are possible. Driving west on Highway 88 from Highway 89, autumn foliage will provide colorful backdrops for the meandering Carson River.

Summer visitors will find wildflower gardens that produce a palette of color across the landscape. The best and easiest trail to photograph flowers is the Pacific Crest Trail just north of Highway 88 at Carson Pass. Park in the lot just west of the pass on the north side of the highway. The trail is described in "Special Hikes" on page 160. You don't have to hike far before your camera will be clicking around every corner. Don't miss the opportunity to photograph the giants of the Sierra, those gnarled forms of Sierra juniper that have been around for many centuries.

Special Events

The North Tahoe-Truckee area promotes many annual special events. The North Shore and Truckee papers each list events in their special entertainment sections. Dates vary from year to year, so check with the Visitor Bureaus or the *North Tahoe Truckee Week* magazine for exact dates of the events listed. The South Lake Tahoe and Carson Pass area offer a bonanza of special events including a summer-long music festival. Since specific dates vary from year to year, check the *Tahoe Daily Tribune* "Lake Tahoe Action" section as well as Tourist Information Centers for exact dates. The list below was current at printing time, but new events are planned each year, so this may only be a partial list of the possibilities.

Ski areas in the region have so many ski and snowboard events during the season that it is impossible to include them here. We have listed only those that have been held at the same time during the last few years. In addition, more and more mountain bike races are being scheduled at the resorts with mountain bike parks. If you are interested in these kinds of events, check with the resorts for information.

January   **Winter Celebration**

A torchlight parade, fireworks and ski races at **Heavenly Ski Resort**, including the Hard Corps Ski Challenge, the Celebrity Ski Classic and a Tournament of Champions, gives you a chance to watch the likes of Franz Klammer, Stein Eriksen, Christin Cooper and Bill Johnson.

March   **Coors Light Top Gun on Gunbarrel at Heavenly**

Billed as one of the top mogul competitions in the country you can watch how the pros of bump skiing do it on the famous Gunbarrel run.

Year-Round

Special Events

March	**Snowfest**

A week-long winter carnival for **North Lake Tahoe and Truckee** starts with a torchlight ski parade at Squaw Valley and is followed by races, spaghetti feeds and pancake breakfasts, plus dances and dress-up contests.

During Snowfest	**The Great Race**

This 30 km cross-country race from Tahoe City to Truckee attracts locals and world-class skiers alike. Be sure to watch the skiers finish at Hilltop then join the Wild West Celebration in Truckee. In-shape intermediate skiers should consider doing the race.

March	**Longboard Races**

Celebrating the miners who started the skiing tradition in the 1860s in the northern Sierra Nevada, men and women put on their ten foot wooden skis to speed down the hill at speeds that defy credibility. Costumes of the day are prevalent making this a great spectator event.

Today's racers try to emulate these 1860s champions of La Porte, California.

Special Events

May	**Jazz Festival on the West Shore**
	A collection of jazz groups entertain at a variety of sites along the lake. Usually held on Mother's Day weekend, the organizers are hoping to move it to June.
Memorial Day weekend	**Windows on History**
	All of downtown Truckee becomes a stage with a wandering barbershop quartet, an entertainment stage, the Virginia City Gunslingers and Saloon Girls and other strolling acts.
Early June	**Renaissance Festival**
	Come participate in medieval festivities with food, dancing and art at **Camp Richardson's Resort**.
June or July	**Donner Lake Triathlon**
	Watch them swim, run and ride bicycles up Donner Pass Road. This event draws hundreds of competitors.
July	**Northstar-at-Tahoe Beer Festival**
	Spend an evening tasting beer from Northern California's microbreweries. The event often supports a local charity.
June to August	**Valhalla Summer Arts and Music Festival**
	The Tahoe Tallac Association sponsors a summer-long festival of art and music. Starting with the Renaissance Festival in early June and ending with Jazz Nights at the end of August, there is music every Thursday night at Valhalla and a Potpourri Concert every Tuesday.
July 4th	**July 4th Celebrations**
	Truckee has a real, small town parade including floats, drill teams, horses and floats. Fireworks are also produced at North and South Lake Tahoe.

Year-Round

Special Events

Second Saturday in July

The Death Ride

Bicycle riders gather in **Markleeville** to begin a 128-mile death ride over five alpine passes returning to Markleeville. The riders are off at 6:00 a.m., but if you can't get there at that hour, come in the afternoon and stay to see the first riders return. You can start your day in Alpine County with a hike at Grover Hot Springs followed by a dip in the hot pools there, then repair to Markleeville for the end of the race.

During July and August

Valhalla Sunset Concert Series at Heavenly

Sounds of music will fill the air from the top of the tram at Heavenly, one of the most spectacular sites in the world for a mountain amphitheater. Internationally-known entertainers will play folk, rhythm, blues and jazz.

July

Western States 100-mile Endurance Run

Watch runners leave from the base of **Squaw Valley** ski area and run up the mountain on the first leg of this demanding marathon that ends in Auburn.

July

Wa She Shu Edeh Native American Festival

Come to the **Tallac Historic Site** for basket weaving demonstrations, art exhibits and traditional dances.

Wed. thru Sat. July and August

Tahoe Mountain Musicals

Bring the family, a blanket, and a picnic to watch a Broadway musical at the Lakeview Amphitheater in **North Tahoe Regional Park** in Tahoe Vista.

Ongoing July and August

Lake Tahoe Summer Music Festival

Musical groups play at various locations around the lake.

Special Events

August	**Shakespeare at Sand Harbor**
	Shakespearean plays are presented in an outdoor theater on the beach at Sand Harbor. Bring a blanket, picnic and warm jacket to enjoy the Bard's plays under the stars.
August	**Great Gatsby Festival**
	Relive Lake Tahoe's gilded era at the Great Gatsby Festival at the **Tallac Historic Site**.
August	**Wooden Boat Week in Tahoe City**
	Enjoy a Concours d'Elegance of Lake Tahoe's antique wooden boats.
Second weekend in August	**Truckee Championship Rodeo**
	Serious rodeo competition with out-of-town as well as Truckee riders.
July and August	**Summer Music Festival at Squaw Valley**
	Nationally famous groups play in the valley and on the mountain.
September	**Northstar Splendor of the Sierra Fine Arts Show**
	Artists from around the West display their work for sale.
September	**Bijou Park Bash**
	For one day in September the Lake Tahoe Community Orchestra and the community welcome you to a day of music, performances and cultural exhibits.
September	**Truckee Railroad Days**
	Celebrate Truckee's connection to the railroad since its founding in the 1860s. Hand car races, model railroads, a parade and more fill the weekend.

Year-Round

Special Events

End of September	**Northstar Autumn Jubilee Food and Wine Festival**

California wines are matched to food from 30 local restaurants for tasting and comparing.

October **Donner Party Hike Weekend**

Learn more about the Donner Party history on hikes and presentations in the Truckee/Donner Summit area.

October **Oktoberfest**

Dining, dancing and fine Bavarian libations are offered at **Alpine Meadows.**

October **Kokanee Salmon Festival**

When the salmon are spawning at Taylor Creek, come to the **U.S. Forest Service Visitor Center** to watch the strange behavior of these fish as they return to the creek to lay their eggs. See page 62 in "Boating" for information about viewing the fish on a special kayak tour.

December **Genoa Christmas Faire**

On the first weekend in December the town of Genoa welcomes you to their Christmas Faire. Here's a chance to finish your Christmas shopping in Nevada's oldest town.

December **Tiny Tim's Christmas Fair**

Arts and crafts are on sale at the Truckee Recreation and Parks District building. A good place to do some early Christmas shopping.

Inns and B & B's

North Lake Tahoe and Truckee have been tourist meccas since the Central Pacific started service in 1869. The region boasts of several historic lodges and bed and breakfast inns that offer delightful accommodations. South Lake Tahoe and the Carson Pass/Hope Valley region have been welcoming summer tourists since the late 1800s. We have listed 24 inns that offer unique overnight experiences year-round with fine dining on the premises or nearby. The inns are listed by area.

Soda Springs and Truckee

Royal Gorge's Rainbow Lodge

Take I-80 to the Rainbow Rd. exit. Drive east one-half mile to the lodge. Reservations and information: 530-426-3871

The Big Bend of the Yuba River is filled with history. The original part of this beautiful mountain lodge was built in the 1880s and served as a stage stop on the Dutch Flat to Donner Lake Road. When the Lincoln Highway and later U.S. 40 were built, additions to the hotel were made in 1931 to accommodate the growing number of visitors to the area. The current lodge, operated by Royal Gorge Cross Country Ski Area, retains the feeling of the past while offering comfortable lodging and excellent cuisine in the Engadine Cafe. There are 32 cozy rooms, a bridal suite and a family suite for two adults and two children. The historic location on the banks of the Yuba offers spectacular hiking, fishing and skiing right from the front door. Free shuttle buses take cross-country skiers to Royal Gorge, where experienced skiers can take the 22-mile interconnect trail from the summit direct to the lodge at the end of the day. Four Donner Summit downhill areas are but 20 minutes away. After your day of activity, you can sit in the guest lounge by a roaring fire, or visit the bar with the original spittoon at its base.

 _____ Inns and B & B's

Sugar Bowl Lodge

Take the Magic Carpet Gondola on Donner Pass Rd. one-half mile east of Donner Summit.
530-426-9000

The Bavarian-style lodge was built in 1939 for this first destination resort in the Sierra Nevada. In the 1940s skiers, including some famous Hollywood stars, boarded the "Snowball Express" train from San Francisco to Norden where a tractor-drawn sleigh took them on a 40-minute ride to the resort. Today guests ride the Magic Carpet Gondola from the parking garage on Donner Pass Road to a world away from the hustle, bustle and stresses of today's life. When you stay here, no waiting for buses, or chaining up the car in the morning. You can hit the slopes as soon as they open. Ski weeks are described in "Downhill Skiing" on page 173. Photos of early-day skiing at Sugar Bowl adorn the walls of The Belt Room bar where you can relax after a day on the slopes, while the dining room serves up sumptuous meals at dinner.

The Traverse Inn

*P.O. Box 1012
Soda Springs
530-426-3010*

Located on the banks of the Yuba River in old Soda Springs, this small inn is open during ski season and weekends during the summer. One room with a queen bed has a private bath, another shares a bath down the hall with the owner. A bunk room with six beds offers an economical overnight for outdoor enthusiasts who want a full breakfast to start the day. This hostelry is only minutes from the four Donner Summit downhill ski areas and the extensive Royal Gorge cross-country trails.

Inns and B & B's

Donner Pass Rd., Norden
530-426-9108

Donner Spitz Hütte

Bela and Mimi Vadasz have transformed an old Cal Trans building into a comfortable and affordable European style bunk and breakfast for mountain adventure skiers, hikers, mountain bikers and rock climbers. If you have signed up for one of their courses, the accommodations are included, but you can stay here very reasonably without being registered for a class. The clean mini dorms and a few private rooms share a bath down the hall. The social and dining rooms invite camaraderie, while the sunny back deck with a view of Donner Peak is perfect for relaxing after a day of mountain activities. Their mountain cuisine has become famous and they sell select beer and wine. Dinner is included for course registrants, but they only serve dinner for guests if they sign up in the morning. Guests must purchase this meal. For a description of Alpine Skills International courses see page 214 in "Winter Adventures."

Donner Spitz Hütte.

Inns and B & B's

The Truckee Hotel

At the corner of Hwy. 267 and Bridge Street in Truckee.
Reservations:
800-659-6921
530-587-4444

The Truckee Hotel in downtown Truckee has been in continuous operation since the 1870s. The new owners have completely renovated the building to reflect its Victorian heritage and were awarded the prestigious 1994 California Heritage Council Award of Merit for historic preservation. You really can step back into Truckee's past in rooms that are uniquely decorated in nineteenth-century style. Eight rooms or suites have private baths. The rest of the rooms come with sink, mirror and towels in the room and share a bath across or down the hall. Breakfast is served every day in the parlor on the first floor. On weekends and holidays there are hors d'oeuvres and wine to be enjoyed before dinner. The management thoughtfully provides ear plugs for those unaccustomed to a downtown location next to the railroad, but then that is part of the charm of the place.

The Richardson House where you can sit on the porch and sip your Sunday coffee while watching the action below in downtown Truckee.

Inns and B & B's

Corner of Spring and High Sts., Truckee
530-587-5388

Richardson House

The Richardson House was built in the 1870s by Warren Richardson, a lumber baron of Truckee. The Victorian residence has undergone a complete restoration to bring the property back to its nineteenth century splendor. Much of the beautiful woodwork is original, as is the wainscot created to look like tooled leather in the front hall and up the stairs. Located high on Spring Street, the rooms overlook the town and the surrounding mountains. The beautiful garden with its gazebo is designed for weddings and guests' enjoyment during summer. Eight rooms feature genuine antiques, and each with a different theme. The Tamsen and George Donner Room has a queen bed and private bath with a claw foot tub for two. There are two two-room suites that share a bath. All other rooms have private baths. A full continental breakfast with baked goods and a hot dish is served in the Victorian dining room, complete with a breakfront that used to belong to Mr. Florsheim of Florsheim shoes. Wine and cheese are in the parlor that features a player piano as well as a modern TV with VCR. However, on a summer afternoon you may wish to take your wine onto the front porch to rock in the wicker chairs there and watch the action in downtown Truckee. You can walk to dinner in any of the many wonderful restaurants there. See "Dining Out" starting on page 220 for suggestions.

# Inns and B & B's

10064 South East River Rd., Truckee
530-582-1923

Bocks 10064 House

Kent and Monica Bocks invite you into their newly constructed Victorian home on the banks of the Truckee River. They have three rooms, each with private bath. Two bedrooms have double beds and the master bedroom features a queen-size bed. They offer a full breakfast as well as wine and cheese in the afternoon. The Bocks are outdoor enthusiasts and can give advice about hikes, bike rides and skiing. While you are out enjoying your skiing or hiking, they will make dinner reservations for you. Their home is just across the river from downtown Truckee with its many dining and shopping opportunities.

10098 High St., Truckee
530-582-5775
888-600-3735

Hania House

You can stay with Hania in her lovely white house with blue trim on High Street overlooking Truckee. Hania speaks English, Polish, German and Russian and offers very special American and European breakfasts with many specialties such as Polish-style potato pancakes with vanilla sugar or crêpes with cinnamon apples or cream cheese. She will also serve you breakfast in bed from her extensive menu. Three rooms have log furniture, queen beds, private baths and TV with VCR.

Highway 89 South and Tahoe City

Squaw Valley
530-583-3451
800-334-3451

Christy Inn

This is truly an historic lodge. Formerly the home of the Poulsens, who founded Squaw Valley and built the home for their large family with one of the choicest views in the valley of the mountain. The inn has seven rooms, each decorated in a different theme with many homey touches.

Inns and B & B's

One large room with a king-size bed plus a trundle has its own electric fireplace. Four rooms have queen-size beds and private bathrooms with showers, and two rooms have two queens and bathrooms with tub and shower. There is at present no breakfast service, but Graham's restaurant is in the front of the building and can handle wedding parties of up to100 people, particularly in the summer when the deck is available. See "Dining Out" on page 224.

River Ranch Lodge

Hwy. 89 and Alpine Meadows Rd.
530-583-4264
In California:
800-535-9900

This historic lodge on the Truckee River dates back over 100 years when the Deer Park Inn became a fashionable watering place on the narrow gauge railway from Truckee to Tahoe City. The Great Depression brought hard times until 1950 when the old timbers of the rundown structure were cleared for a new summertime fishing lodge. During the 1960 Winter Olympics, diplomats and other officials stayed here. Now completely renovated with Early American antiques, you can stay on the banks of the Truckee River in an atmosphere of "Old Tahoe." You can access the Tahoe City to Truckee Bike Trail, or take the bus

The Mayfield House in Tahoe City. See next page for description.

Year-Round

Inns and B & B's

to Alpine Meadows Ski Area just up the road. Summer afternoons will find guests on the riverside patio, where musical groups play on weekends. The dining room is described in "Dining Out" on page 225.

236 Grove St., Tahoe City
530-583-1001
888-518-8898

Mayfield House

Built in 1928 as the home of Norman Mayfield, a pioneer contractor at Lake Tahoe, Mayfield House and its new owners Colleen McDevitt and Stan Scott welcome guests to enjoy the quiet charm of this old Tahoe home on a quiet side street in Tahoe City. There are six newly decorated rooms, three with Queen beds and private baths. Julia's room is where famous architect, Julia Morgan, a personal friend and associate of Norman Mayfield, stayed. It has a king size bed and private bath. The Mayfield Room is a suite with large sitting area, dining area, king size bed and private bath with jacuzzi. The small cottage in back with a queen bed offers a secluded location. Wine and cheese or tea and cookies are served every afternoon and wine and brandy are available in the evening. The inn is within walking distance of Tahoe City's finest restaurants and all the activities of the harbor. Stan and Colleen continue the tradition that, "there are no strangers at Mayfield House, only friends who have not yet met."

1690 W. Lake Blvd., Tahoe City
530-581-4073
800-581-4073

The Cottage Inn at Lake Tahoe

The Cottage Inn features a group of renovated cottages, each with a distinctive exterior and decor clustered under century-old pine trees. The cottages dating back to 1938, were built by the Pomin family and are in "Old Tahoe" style, which means lots of knotty pine, stone fireplaces and the feeling of having retreated from the world. With 15 cabins to choose from, there is something for every taste.

Inns and B & B's

The Bit O' Bavaria, for instance, offers a two-room fireplace, kitchen, private balcony with a view, and even a sofa bed for an extra person. The Bird Nest, a suite with a lake view, has a loft bedroom for two extra persons. Honeymooners or couples looking for a romantic weekend will find the solitude they desire in a suite with a two-story fireplace and natural rock jacuzzi with a waterfall. The hearty country breakfast is served in the dining room or on the deck in summer. A sauna is available to relax muscles after your day of activity, and best of all, the guests can walk to one of Tahoe's finest private beaches. If all you want to do is stay in front of the fire and read or watch a video, the management will leave breakfast on your doorstep, hold any messages in the office and provide a fine selection of books and videos to borrow.

The Chaney House. See next page for description.

Year-Round

# Inns and B & B's

West Shore

Chaney House

4725 West Lake Blvd., Homewood
530-525-7333

Lori and Gari Chaney's bed and breakfast is truly their own home. You will be treated like a valued guest in this historic Old Tahoe house nestled in a grove of Jeffrey pines. Stone masons for the house were the same who built Vikingsholm at Emerald Bay. The house has eighteen-inch-thick stone walls, Gothic arches and a massive stone fireplace in the livingroom. Furniture to fit the scale of the room is just right for relaxing with afternoon wine or to read a book on a quiet evening. The beautiful dining room, used for breakfast in winter and cooler seasons, features a mahogany table and sideboard filled with the family's own silver, which Lori uses to serve you. Three rooms in the house formerly were used by the Chaney's children. One suite has a king-size bed and sitting area. All have private baths. The Honeymoon Suite is a one-bedroom apartment over the garage with a separate sitting area, TV, kitchen, queen bed and bath. In summer the guests eat breakfast on the side patio with a view of the lake. The house has its own private pier and beach. It is hard to imagine a more dignified and elegant place to stay.

Rockwood Lodge

5295 West Lake Blvd., Homewood
800-Le-Tahoe
530-525-5273

Here is a chance to stay in one of Tahoe's grand 1930s summer chalets, built of rock and knotty pine with hand-hewn beams. The stonework was done by Austrian stone masons who had finished working on the Kaiser Estate, now Fleur du Lac. Step back in time to a gracious home — removing your shoes at the door — and enjoy the hospitality of Lou Reinkins and Connie Stevens who have operated their lodge since 1985. They lovingly restored the

Inns and B & B's

house, put in modern bathrooms and decorated it with antiques. The spacious livingroom beckons for a chat in front of the stone fireplace with a glass of Riesling or Cabernet that is always available. All guest rooms have private baths, with feather beds and down comforters on the queen beds. Room decorations feature Laura Ashley prints that are matched on the tiles above the pedestal sinks. One room has a Russian Marriage Bed. The knotty pine throughout the house displays the original finish. The house is set back from the road and across the street from the lake. The front patio has an outside fireplace to take off the chill of early summer evenings at the lake. For those with an interest in wildlife, Connie has been operating the Wildlife Rescue for the Lake Tahoe region for several years in a small building at the back of the property.

Tahoma Meadows Bed and Breakfast

6821 West Lake Blvd., Tahoma
800-355-1596
530-525-1553

Nestled among sugar pines on the west shore are eleven historic cabins of the Tahoma Meadows Bed and Breakfast. Lovingly redecorated with themes of local wildflowers, most have queen-size beds and all have TV. Some bathrooms have claw foot bath tubs to bring back memories of grandmother's house. One cabin with two bedrooms sleeps six, but does not include breakfast. However, have no fear, because the Stony Ridge Café out front offers scrumptious breakfast and lunch. The Tahoma location is close to Sugar Pine and Bliss State Parks with all the beautiful beaches and trails that they offer.

Year-Round

 _____ **Inns and B & B's**

Norfolk Woods Inn

6941 West Lake Blvd., Tahoma
530-525-5000

The inn and cabins have been renovated and redecorated to bring out the charm of this "Old Tahoe" inn. Plenty of knotty pine will take you back in time to relaxed mountain vacations of a former era. Two rooms in the inn share a bath — perfect for a family. Two suites each have two bedrooms, bath, kitchen and living room with TV. On this beautiful wooded property with heated swimming pool and spa for summer guests, there are five separate cabins, four with fireplaces, that can accommodate up to six people. Amy's Cottage is a historic 100-year-old log cabin, updated to make the perfect honeymoon hideaway. After a day of active pursuits in the area, be sure to check out the homemade pastries, fruit smoothies and shakes, espresso or capuccino at the Ice-House. Your stay should always include a romantic dinner in the gourmet restaurant, described on page 230 in "Dining Out."

Knotty Pine Bed and Breakfast

6779 West Lake Blvd., Tahoma
530-525-1023
877-280-8915
Non-smoking inn.

New owners Vaughn and Dan Hollingsworth reopened the inn adding their own personal touches to the charming house with its knotty pine walls. A suite upstairs has a king bed, private bath, sitting room with a couch and a private deck. Another room with a queen has a private bath. Two rooms downstairs have queen beds and in-room pedestal sinks, but share a bath with a claw-foot tub. These are perfect for two couples traveling together or for two singles. Gourmet breakfasts of Vaughn's homemade breads, fruit and main dish are served outside in the summer. They serve complementary hot and cold drinks and baked treats all day, plus a wine hour in the afternoon. You can borrow all the accoutrements for a day at the beach as well.

Inns & B and B's

North Shore and Incline Village

Shooting Star Bed and Breakfast

315 Olive Street, Carnelian Bay
530-546-8903
Non-smoking inn.

Bill and Nancy Matte, former members of the Cal Marching Band at UC Berkeley, have come to the North Shore and built a lovely two-story home as a bed and breakfast. The two downstairs rooms are large, each with a queen bed. One bath has a six-foot spa tub and the other and large shower, big enough for two. A library on the guest floor features only part of Bill's extensive collection. The upstairs great-room has a telescope the better to see the action on the lake, just a block away. Boat fans are that close to the famous Gar Woodies and Riva runabouts. A special feature of their inn is a customized breakfast menu, from which you may order the night before.

The Shore House

7170 No. Lake Blvd., Tahoe Vista
530-546-7270
800-207-5160

Located on the spectacular North Shore with its own private pier, this new bed and breakfast offers all the best of Tahoe. Nine rooms are decorated with modern log furniture and comfortable beds, private baths and lots of knotty pine. One room, the Studio, invites you to use the easel and pastels to recreate the mountain scenery out your window. All rooms come with a journal to record your thoughts. A full mountain breakfast is served in the dining room with a view down the lake. You can enjoy wine and cheese in the afternoons or cookies before bed in the sitting area with a river rock fireplace and lots of comfortable log furniture. Your hosts, Marty and Barb Cohen, have lived at Lake Tahoe for more than 20 years can recommend outdoor adventures to fill your days and dining possibilities for the evening. However, you may choose just to relax and sit on the lawn watching the lake.

Year-Round

Inns and B & B's

593 N. Dyer Circle,
Incline Village
800-731-6222

Haus Bavaria

You don't have to travel to Bavaria to be stay in an Alpine Chalet. Haus Bavaria was built in 1980 to be a European-style guest house, complete with German bric-a-brac in the panelled living room offering views of the surrounding mountains. The inn is located in a residential area high above Incline Village. There are five rooms, each with private bath, two with king beds and three with queen beds and all with private balconies. Your host, Bick Hewitt, serves beverages when you arrive, and a breakfast of home-baked goods and fresh fruit in the pleasant dining room each morning. He is happy to hold small weddings in his lovely Alpine chalet.

Haus Bavaria.

Courtesy of Haus Bavaria

Inns and B & B's

South Lake Tahoe

Camp Richardson's Resort

On Hwy. 89 two miles north of the South Tahoe Y.
530-541-1801
800-544-1801

Richardson's Resort has been in operation continuously since 1921, when Captain Alonzo Richardson leased a large parcel from the Comstock and Lawrence families to set up a stage service between Placerville and Lake Tahoe using his Pierce Arrow touring cars. In 1924 he bought the property and built cabins, naming many after automobiles of the day. In 1927 when the neighboring Tallac Hotel was torn down, Richardson brought the Tallac post office to Richardson's and built a hotel, dining room and many other buildings. He also built a pier so that the steamer *Tahoe* and other vessels could bring passengers, mail and freight to the resort. Present-day operation is under an agreement with the U. S. Forest Service that now owns the land, but the traditions of the Richardson family continue. The cabins have been renovated and winterized, so that winter guests can choose between a hotel room or cabin. With cross country skiing across the street, numerous summer activities available just outside the front door at Camp Richardson's Resort Marina and a moderately priced restaurant within walking distance, your family could easily become one of those who wouldn't miss a summer at Richardson's.

Year-Round

Inns and B & B's

3819 Saddle Rd., So. Lake Tahoe
530-544-7337

Christiania Inn

The inn is a replica of a fine European hostelry, complete with an elegant gourmet restaurant with fireplaces, cozy bar and six unique rooms and suites. Located just 500 yards from the California Base Lodge of Heavenly, it is as close to ski in, ski out accommodations as possible here. From the moment of your arrival you will be pampered by their attentive staff. The European decor features antiques and wood-burning fireplaces. Each of the four suites has a separate living room. Two suites are two story, with living rooms on the first floor along with wet bar, dry sauna and bath, and second floor bedrooms with king-size beds, sitting room and fireplaces. One other two story suite features a queen sized bed with overhead mirror in the loft. The fourth suite, decorated with a Victorian flavor, comes with king-size bed and a bath/shower steam bath combination. The other two rooms have a dinette or dining nooks. A continental breakfast is brought to you every morning and a decanter of brandy is supplied with each room. In summer the snow gives way to a beautiful garden among the pines. Their advertisement is "all the grace of yesterday, in harmony with the comforts of today." See page 241 in "Dining Out" for a description of the restaurant.

Inns and B & B's

Carson Pass

Sorensen's

Just east of the intersection of Hwys. 89 and 88.
530-694-2203.
800-423-9949

From sheep camp to stopping point for early automobile enthusiasts, Sorensen's Resort was officially opened in 1926. In a beautiful aspen grove beside the West Fork of the Carson River, a group of homey cabins among the trees offer relaxation and all the forms of recreation Hope Valley and Carson Pass have to offer. Now in the capable hands of John and Patty Brissenden, the resort offers romantic cabins for two with wood burning stoves, group cabins that can sleep up to eight, homes on the Carson River and even some cabins where dogs are allowed. You can cross-country ski from your door, or indulge in one of the many workshops offered here. Classes are given in everything from wildflower identification or watercolor painting to fly-fishing instruction. There is some kind of workshop every month of the year. So, call for the schedule and plan a special overnight or two in one of their unique cabins. There is a sauna to warm after-ski muscles and a café that serves scrumptious, hearty food at the end of the day. See "Dining Out" on page 245 for restaurant information. You don't need to be an overnight guest to enjoy Sorensen's cuisine.

Year-Round

Inns and B & B's

*On Hwy. 88
four miles west
of Carson Pass.*
209-258-8888

Caples Lake Resort

For those who want simple, rustic accommodations for a fishing, hiking or skiing holiday, the setting of Caples Lake Resort in the historic Carson Pass area cannot be matched. The environs beckon for hikes to Emigrant Pass or Lake Winnemucca, fishing in Caples Lake or any of the dozen alpine lakes within a day's hike. Or you may just want to sit on the rocks in front of the lodge to drink in the serenity of the view. The lodge itself has been there only since the 1940s, but the area has been settled ever since the first emigrants struggled over Carson Pass. James "Doc" Caples, who passed through in 1849, recognized the advantageous setting. He returned to build a cabin and brought his cattle for summer pasture for the next thirty years. He became a prominent citizen of the new state of California, representing his district in the Constitutional Convention.

The lodge rooms overlooking the lake share a bathroom, and the housekeeping cabins that sleep up to six people are great for a weekend of cross-country skiing or a few days of fishing or hiking in this glorious wilderness. You can end your days with a delicious meal in the lodge dining room, then relax in front of the fire or watch the sun cast alpenglow on Round Top Peak from the deck. There are few finer views in all of the Sierra. The restaurant is described on page 245 in "Dining Out."

Lodging Reservations

When you are planning a trip to Lake Tahoe, Truckee or Carson Pass there is now a resort association with three central numbers to call for information about hotels, motels and condominiums. When you call the following numbers, you can ask for the summer or winter planners that have detailed information on most of the resorts, hotels and condominiums.

For North Shore Reservations:
800-824-6348 — www.tahoe-4-u.com

For South Shore Reservations:
800-288-2463 — www.virtualtahoe.com

For Incline Village/Crystal Bay
800-468-2463 — www.gotahoe.com

If you know what price range, location and kind of facility you want, this may be the only call you need to make.

Truckee, Squaw Valley, Northstar-at-Tahoe, and Kirkwood also have central reservations, and will gladly send brochures or connect you to a property management service that handles private homes.

Truckee Chamber of Commerce
530-587-2757 — www.truckee.com

Northstar-at-Tahoe - Central Reservations
800-466-6784 — www.skinorthstar.com

Squaw Valley - Central Reservations
800-545-4350 — www.squaw.com

Kirkwood - Central Reservations
800-967-7500 — www.skikirkwood.com

Lodging Reservations

Lake Tahoe

Vacation Station — 800-841-7443

The 100 homes and condominiums with Vacation Station are located in Incline Village and Crystal Bay. The company leaves gift packages including champagne to honeymooners or wedding parties and in winter plows the drive and turns on the heat.

Lake Tahoe Accommodations — 800-544-3234

This company has the largest selection of luxury vacation rentals around the lake. They have four offices, in South Lake Tahoe, Stateline, Incline Village and Tahoe City. The office in South Lake Tahoe is open seven days a week. The units are located in prime locations. Deluxe accommodations have access to pools, jacuzzis, tennis courts and beaches.

Lake Tahoe Lodging — 800-654-5253

The company has 100 special units ranging from cabins to corporate or celebrity retreats, some on the lake or with fabulous lake views. Their homes have from one to eight bedrooms, and can accommodate from two to 20 guests. They offer concierge service and discount packages for skiing and other activities.

Lake Tahoe Lodgings — 800-242-5378

The company manages 200 privately owned properties on the South Shore. Their properties can handle from two to 24 people in executive homes, condominiums and chalets, some with lake views and some with hot tubs.

Lake Tahoe Reservations Tours and Adventures
North Shore — 800-424-8988 South Shore — 800-533-4743

Lake Tahoe Reservations features 85 properties at the lake, including lakefront homes. Their specialty is complete packages for skiing, boating, fishing or golfing, and they will arrange your transportation by airline and a car rental.

Lodging Reservations

Squaw Valley, Truckee and Donner Summit

Squaw Valley Accommodations — 800-330-3451 is run by Squaw Valley Realty, and books the Christy Inn and manages about 70 homes and condominiums in the valley. When you arrive, your home will be heated and the driveway plowed.

Donner Lake Realty — 800-392-5253 specializes in mountain homes on and around Donner Lake. Many homes have privileges at the private beach and some have their own docks on the lake.

Martis Valley Vacation Rentals — 800-287-7685 specializes in Northstar homes and condominiums with access to all the Northstar facilities.

Ski West Vacation Rentals — 800-339-5535 manages 110 homes and condominiums at Tahoe Donner and Northstar.

Soda Springs Rentals — 530-426-1031 manages properties on one of the Serene Lakes or other woodsy retreats in the Soda Springs area. If you love cross-country skiing or hiking, you will want to book at Soda Springs.

Castle Peak Vacation Rentals — 888-253-5551 specializes in homes at Serene Lakes, some on the lakes. They offer tender loving care, shovel the driveway and entrances, turn on the heat and even leave a bottle of wine in the refrigerator.

Second Home Care — 530-582-0220 specializes in homes in the Tahoe Donner area.

Truckee Mountain Vacation Rentals — 800-805-8199 manages homes in the Tahoe Donner area.

Vacation Property Management — 800-748-6725 specializes in homes in the Tahoe Donner area. Each home is opened before you arrive, preheated in winter with driveways plowed. They offer a welcome package of information about the area to all renters.

Beauty is before me
Beauty is behind me
Beauty is below me
Beauty is above me
I walk in beauty
  Navajo Prayer

Index

All-Terrain Vehicle Rides 36
Alpine Meadows
  Dining Out
    River Ranch 225
  Downhill Ski Area 175
  Historic Inns and B&B's
    River Ranch 285
  Horseback Riding 100
  Special Events
    Oktoberfest 278
  Special Hikes
    Five Lakes 136
Art Galleries 251

B&B's 279
Back Country Skiing 193
Balloon Rides 32
Beaches 48
Bicycle Paths 88
Bicycle Rentals 86
Bicycling 88
Big Bend
  Dining Out
    Rainbow Lodge 220
  Historic Inns and B&B's
    Rainbow Lodge 279
  Historical Walks
    The Emigrant Trail 113
Boat Launch 60
Boat Rentals 46
Boating 58
Bungee Jumping 36
Bus Service 2
Bus Tour Companies 44

Camp Richardson
  Beaches 54
    Kiva Beach 54
    Pope Beach 54
    Resort Beach 54
  Bicycle Rentals 87
  Boat Launch 59
  Boat Rentals 46
  Cross Country Skiing 191
  Cruising Lake Tahoe
    Tahoe Para-dice 64
    Woodwind 66

Camp Richardson
  Dining Out
    Beacon Restaurant 243
  Fishing Charters 78
  Historic Inn 293
  Historical Walks
    Tallac Historic Site 120
  Horseback Riding 101
  Parasailing 32
  Sleigh Rides 212
  Special Events
    Renaissance Festival 275
  Water Ski School 61
  Water Sports Rentals 46
Caples Lake
  Boat Launch 59
  Boat Rentals 47
  Fishing 74
  Historic Inns and B&B's
    Caples Lake Resort 296
Carnelian Bay
  Beaches
    Patton Beach 50
  Boat Launch 59
  Boat Rentals 46
  Dining Out
    Gar Woods 231
  Fishing Charters
    Mickey's Big Mack 78
  Historic Inns and B&B's
    Shooting Star 291
  Miniature Golf
    Magic Carpet 112
Carriage Rides 36
Carson City
  Excursions
    Bowers Mansion 40
    Nevada State Museum 40
    Railroad Museum 40
Carson Pass
  Bicycle Rentals
    Hope Valley Outdoor Center 99
  Boat Rentals 47
  Cross Country Skiing 192

Carson Pass
  Dining Out
    Caples Lake Resort 245
    Kirkwood Inn 246
    Sorensen's 245
  Dog Sled Rides
    Husky Express 216
  Downhill Ski Areas
    Kirkwood Resort 182
  Fishing 74
  Fly-Fishing Guides
    Horse Feathers Fly-Fishing School 81
  Historic Inns and B&B's
    Caples Lake Lodge 296
    Sorensen's 295
  Historical Walks 123
  Horseback Riding
    Kirkwood Stables 102
  Just For Kids
    Kirkwood Explorers 165
  Mountain Bike Parks
    Kirkwood Resort 95
  Mountain Bike Roads
    Blue Lakes 98
    Burnside Lake 99
  Photo and Vista Points 272
  Sleigh Rides
    Kirkwood Resort 214
  Sno-Park Trails 197
  Special Hikes
    Meiss Pass 160
    Winnemucca Lake 158
  Special Ski Classes
    Sierra Ski Touring 216
Carson Pass and Hope Valley 21
Carson River
  Fishing 73
Cascade Creek
  Horseback Riding
    Cascade Stables 101
Casino Hotel Buffets 247
Cave Rock
  Boat Launch 59
  Fishing 71

Index

Climbing Walls 34
Cross Country Skiing 185
Cruising Lake Tahoe 63
Crystal Bay
  Dining Out
    Lakeview Room 233
    Soule Domain 233
  Kids at Casinos 249
  Photo and Vista Points 271

D.L. Bliss State Park
  Beaches 53
  Just For Kids 164
  Special Hikes
    Rubicon Trail 138
Dining Out 220
Dog Sled Rides 216
Donner Lake
  Beaches
    Donner Memorial State Park 48
    West End Beach 49
  Bicycling 88
  Boat Launch 60
  Boat Rentals 46
  Boating 60
  Fishing 68
  Historic Inns and B&B's
    Donner Country Inn 282
  Special Events
    Donner Lake Triathlon 275
  Tennis
    West End Beach 103
Donner Lake and Donner Pass
  Photo and Vista Points 270
Donner Party 12
Donner Pass, I-80
  Downhill Ski Areas
    Boreal 170
  Museums
    Western America Ski Sport Museum 263
  Sno-Park Trails 195

Donner Pass, I-80
  Snowplay
    Boreal 208
  Special Hikes
    Pacific Crest Trail 129
    Summit Lake 132
Donner Summit
  Downhill Ski Areas
    Donner Ski Ranch 173
    Sugar Bowl 172
  Historic Inns and B&B's
    Donner Spitz Hütte 281
    Sugar Bowl Lodge 280
  Historical Walks
    Emigrant Trail 114
  Rock Climbing
    Alpine Skills International 34
  Special Hikes
    Anderson Peak 130
    Donner Peak 132
    Mount Judah Loop Trail 131
    Pacific Crest Trail 129
  Special Ski Classes
    Alpine Skills International 214
    North American Ski Training Center 215
Downhill Ski Areas 170

Echo Lakes
  Boat Launch 59
  Boat Rentals 47
  Fishing 72
  Ranger Programs 167
  Sno-Park Trails 197
  Special Hikes
    Pacific Crest Trail 157
Echo Summit
  Downhill Ski Areas
    Sierra-at-Tahoe 181
  Sno-Park Trails 196
Emerald Bay
  Beaches
    Emerald Bay Beach 53
  Museums
    Vikingsholm 268

Emerald Bay
  Special Hikes
    Cascade Falls 141
    Eagle Lake 140
    Granite Lake 141
    Vikingsholm 138
Excursions 38

Fallen Leaf Lake
  Boat Launch 59
  Boat Rentals 46
  Fishing 70
  Special Hikes
    Angora Lakes 143
Fishing 67
Fishing Charters 76
Fly-Fishing Guides 80

Gaming at the Lake 19
Gardnerville
  Balloon Rides
    Dream Weavers 32
Genoa, NV
  Excursions
    Genoa and the Mormon Station 41
  Historic Inns and B&B's
    Walley's Hot Springs 42
  Special Events
    Christmas Faire 278
Glenbrook
  Golf 110
Glider Rides 33
Golf 106
Guided Hikes 37

Hay and Carriage Rides 36
Historic Inns and B&B's 279
Historical Walks 113
Homewood
  Bicycle Rentals 86
  Boat Launch 59
  Boat Rentals 46
  Dining Out
    Swiss Lakewood 229
    West Shore Café 230
  Downhill Ski Areas
    Homewood 177

Index

Homewood
  Fishing Charters
    Kingfish 77
  Fly-Fishing Guides
    Riffleworks 80
  Historic Inns and B&B's
    Chaney House 288
    Rockwood Lodge 288
  Water Ski Schools
    High Sierra 61
Hope Valley. *See* **Carson Pass**
Hornblower Cruises
  Water Taxi 2
Horseback Riding 100

Ice Skating 203
Incline Village
  Art Galleries
    Art Attack Gallery 256
    Artists of Tahoe 256
  Back Country Skiing
    Climb to Mount Rose 200
    Tahoe Meadows 200
  Beaches
    IVGID Beaches 52
    Sand Harbor 57
  Bicycle Paths
    Lakeshore Boulevard 90
  Carriage Rides
    Truckee Carriage and Coach Company 37
  Cross Country Skiing
    Diamond Peak Cross Country 190
  Cruising Lake Tahoe
    Krinnit Yacht Charters 64
    Sierra Cloud Catamaran Cruises 64
    Tahoe Sailing Charters 63
  Dining Out
    Big Water Grille 234
    Café 333 235
    Christmas Tree 234
    Ciao Mein 236
    Jack Rabbit Moon 235
    La Fondue 236

Incline Village
  Dining Out
    Le Bistro 237
    Lone Eagle Grille 236
    Yoshimi 234
  Downhill Ski Areas
    Diamond Peak 179
    Mount Rose 178
  Excursions
    Ponderosa Ranch 39
  Golf
    Championship Course 107
    Executive Course 108
  Historic Inns and B&B's
    Haus Bavaria 292
  Just For Kids
    Tahoe Trips and Trails 164
  Kids at Casinos
    Hyatt Regency 249
  Parasailing
    Action Water Sports of Tahoe 31
  Photo and Vista Points
    Mount Rose Highway Overlook 271
    Memorial Point 271
  Shopping 261
  Snowplay
    Golf Driving Range 210
    Tahoe Meadows 211
  Special Events
    Shakespeare 277
  Special Hikes
    Mount Rose 156
    Tahoe Rim Trail 155
  Tennis
    Incline High School 104
    Incline Village Tennis Complex 104
    Lakeside Tennis Club 105
Inns and B&B's 279

July 4th Celebrations
  Special Events 275

Just For Kids 162

Kaspian Recreation Area
  Sno-Park Trails 195
Kayaking 62
Kids at Casinos 249
Kings Beach
  Art Galleries
    Kilim Hand Woven Rugs 255
    Lakeside Gallery 256
    The Potter's Wheel 256
    Timeless Sculptures 255
  Back Country Skiing
    Martis Peak 198
  Beaches
    Coon Street 51
    Kings Beach State Recreation Area 51
    North Tahoe Beach Center 51
    Secline Beach 51
  Bicycle Rentals 86
  Boat Launch 59
  Boat Rentals 46
  Dining Out
    Moose's Tooth 233
    Steamers Bar 232
  Golf
    Old Brockway 108
  Miniature Golf
    Boberg's 112
  Parasailing
    King Beach Aqua Sports 31
  Snowmobiling
    Brockway Golf Course 205
    Mountain Lake Adventures 205
    Snowmobiling Unlimited 204
  Tennis
    Kings Beach Elementary School 104
  Water Ski Schools
    Goldcrest Resort 61
  Water Sports Rentals 46

Index

Kirkwood
  Cross Country Skiing 192
  Dining Out
    Kirkwood Inn 246
  Downhill Ski Areas
    Kirkwood Resort 182
  Fly-Fishing Guides
    Trout Creek 82
  Horseback Riding
    Kirkwood Stables 102
  Just for Kids 165
  Mountain Bike Park 95
  Sleigh Rides 214

Lake Lapper Bus 2
Lake Tahoe
  Bank Fishing 70
  Fishing 71
  Just For Kids
    Tahoe Trips and Trails 164
  Photo and Vista Points 271
Lake Tahoe Facts 27
League to Save Lake Tahoe 20
Lodging Reservations 297

Maps
  Historic Downtown Truckee 120
  South Lake Tahoe Bike Paths 91
Markleeville
  Excursions
    Grover Hot Springs State Park 39
  Special Events
    The Death Ride 276
Meeks Bay
  Beach 53
  Boat Launch 59
  Special Hikes
    Crag Lake 137
Meyers
  Art Galleries
    Magic of Tahoe 257

Meyers
  Back Country Skiing
    Grass Lake Meadows 201
  Bicycling
    Pioneer Trail to Meyers 92
    Upper Truckee Road 92
  Museums
    Celio Ranch 269
  Special Hikes
    Big Meadow and Round Lake 147
    Hawley Grade 145
Minden, NV
  Scenic Flights
    High Country Soaring 34
Miniature Golf 112
Mountain Bike Parks 94
Mountain Bike Roads 96
Museums 263

Naming Lake Tahoe 21
Nifty 50 Trolley 3
North Lake Tahoe
  Special Events
    Snowfest 274
    Summer Music 276
Northstar-at-Tahoe
  Bicycle Rentals 86
  Climbing Wall 34
  Cross Country Skiing 189
  Dining Out
    Timbercreek 223
  Downhill Ski Area 177
  Golf 106
  Horseback Riding 100
  Just For Kids 163
  Mountain Bike Park 94
  Sleigh Rides 212
  Snowplay 209
  Special Events
    Autumn Jubilee 278
    Fine Arts Show 277

Parasailing 31
Photo and Vista Points 270

Rafting 84
Ranger Programs 166
Reno
  Excursions
    National Automobile Museum 43
    Nevada Historical Society 44
Road Conditions Phone 169
Rock Climbing 34
Round Hill
  Beaches
    Nevada Beach 56
    Round Hill Pines 55
  Boat Rentals 47
  Fishing Charters
    Don's 79
  Museums
    Visitor Center 269

Sand Harbor
  Beach 57
  Boat Launch 59
  Fishing 72
  Special Events
    Shakespeare 277
Scenic Flights 33
Seaplane Tours 33
Secret Harbor
  Beaches 56
Shopping 259
Skunk Harbor
  Beaches 154
  Special Hikes 154
Sleigh Rides 212
Sno-Park Ski Trails 194
Snowmobiling 205
Snowplay 208
Soda Springs
  Cross Country Skiing
    Clair Tappaan Lodge 186
    Royal Gorge 186
  Downhill Ski Areas
    Soda Springs Ski Area 171
  Historic Inns and B&B's
    The Traverse Inn 280

Index

Soda Springs
  Snowplay 208
South Lake Tahoe
  All Terrain Vehicle Rides
    Lake Tahoe Adventures 36
  Art Galleries
    Eagle Valley 257
    Hanifin's Art and Antiques 257
    Lake Tahoe Community College 257
  Balloon Rides
    Balloons Over Lake Tahoe 32
    Lake Tahoe Balloons 33
  Beaches
    Baldwin 53
    Connolly 55
    El Dorado 55
    Thomas Reagan Memorial Beach 54
  Bicycle Paths
    Pioneer Trail to Highway 89 92
  Bicycle Rentals 87
  Bicycling
    Bicycle Routes 90
    Pope-Baldwin Bike Path 92
    Upper Truckee Road 92
  Boat Launch 59
  Boat Rentals 47
  Bus Tours
    Adventures Unlimited 44
    Tahoe Tours 44
  Cross Country Skiing
    Lake Tahoe Winter Sports Center 190
    South Lake Tahoe Parks and Recreation 191
  Cruising Lake Tahoe
    Tahoe Para-dice 64
    Tahoe Queen 65
  Dining Out
    Beacon Restaurant 243
    Café Fiore 241
    Christiania Inn 241

South Lake Tahoe
  Dining Out
    Evan's 244
    Fresh Ketch 243
    Monument Peak Restaurant 242
    Nephele's 240
    Riva Grill and Bar 242
    Swiss Chalet Restaurant 243
    The Cantina 244
  Downhill Ski Areas
    Heavenly Ski Resort 180
  Fishing
    Sawmill Pond 72
    Tahoe Trout Farm 73
    Taylor Creek 71
    Trout Creek 71
  Fishing Charters
    Blue Ribbon 79
    Captain Hernandez 78
    Tahoe Sports Fishing 79
  Fly-Fishing Guides
    A-Action High Sierra 81
    Alpine Fly-Fishing Service 81
  Golf
    Bijou Municipal Course 110
    Lake Tahoe Golf Course 111
    Tahoe Paradise Golf Course 111
  Historic Inns and B&B's
    Christiania Inn 294
  Horseback Riding
    Sunset Ranch 102
  Ice Skating 203
  Just For Kids
    Camp Tadaka 165
    U.S. Forest Service Programs 165
    Woodsey Rangers 165
  Kayaking
    Kayak Tahoe 62

South Lake Tahoe
  Miniature Golf
    Fantasy Kingdom 112
    Magic Carpet Golf 112
  Mountain Bike Roads 97
  Museums
    Lake Tahoe Historical Society Museum 268
  Parasailing
    Action Water Sports of Tahoe 31
    South Shore Parasailing 32
  Ranger Programs 166
  Scenic Flights
    Alpine Lake Aviation 33
  Shopping 261
  Ski Shuttles 3
  Sleigh Rides
    Sunset Ranch 214
  Sno-Park Trails 196
  Snowmobiling
    Lake Tahoe Winter Sports Center 206
    Sunset Ranch 206
  Snowplay
    Hansen's Resort 210
  Special Events
    Bijou Park Bash 277
    Coors Light Top Gun on Gunbarrel 273
    Great Gatsby Fetival 277
    Heavenly's Run for the Rim 275
    Kokanee Salmon Festival 278
    Valhalla Summer Arts and Music Festival 275
    Valhalla Sunset Concert Series 276
    Wa She Shu Edeh Festival 276
    Winter Celebration 273

305

Index

South Lake Tahoe
  Special Hikes
    Heavenly Tahoe Vista Trail 150
    Mount Tallac 142
    Rainbow Trail and Stream Profile Chamber 143
  Special Ski Classes
    Adventures Unlimited 215
  Tennis
    South Tahoe High School 105
    South Tahoe Middle School 105
  Water Ski Schools
    Werley's 62
  Water Sports Rentals 47
Special Events 273
Special Hikes 127
Special Ski Classes 214
Spooner Lake
  Cross Country Skiing
    Spooner Lake 191
  Fishing 72
  Mountain Bike Roads
    Marlette Lake 97
  Special Hikes
    Spooner Lake Nature Trail 153
Spooner Summit
  Snowplay 211
  Special Hikes
    Tahoe Rim Trail from Spooner Summit 152
Squaw Valley
  Art Galleries
    Gallery at Squaw Creek 253
    Squaw Valley Trading Post 253
  Bicycle Paths
    Truckee to Squaw Valley 88
  Bicycle Rentals 86
  Bungee Jumping
    Bungee Squaw Valley 36

Squaw Valley
  Climbing Wall 34
  Cross Country Skiing
    Squaw Creek 188
  Dining Out
    Alexander's 225
    Graham's 224
    Plumpjack 224
    Resort at Squaw Creek 225
  Downhill Ski Areas
    Squaw Valley USA 174
  Excursions
    Squaw Valley High Camp Bath and Tennis Club 38
  Golf
    Resort at Squaw Creek 106
  Historic Inns and B&B's
    Christy Inn 284
  Horseback Riding 100
  Ice Skating
    Resort at Squaw Creek 203
    Squaw Valley High Camp 203
  Just For Kids
    Resort at Squaw Creek 163
    Ten Little Indians 163
  Mountain Bike Park 94
  Shopping 260
  Sleigh Rides
    Truckee Carriage 212
  Snowplay 209
  Special Events
    Summer Music Festival 277
    Western States 100-mile Endurance Run 276
STAGE bus service 2
Stateline, NV
  Art Galleries
    A Frame of Mind Gallery 258
    Addi Galleries 258
    Augustine Arts 257
    Legends 258

Stateline, NV
  Art Galleries
    Sierra Galleries 258
  Carriage Rides
    Borges Carriage Rides 36
  Casino Hotel Buffets 247
  Dining Out
    Broiler Room, Empress Court at Caesars 239
    Chart House 240
    Edgewood Terrace Restaurant 239
    Friday's Station at Harrah's 238
    Ivano's 240
    Josh's at the Horizon 239
    Llewellyn's 237
    Sage Room at Harvey's 238
    Summit at Harrah's 238
  Downhill Ski Areas
    Heavenly Resort 180
  Fly-Fishing Guides
    Smiling Trout 82
  Golf
    Edgewood Golf Course 108
  Hay Rides
    Borges Hay Rides 36
  Kids at Casinos 250
  Sleigh Rides
    Borges Sleigh Rides 213
Sugar Pine Point
  Back Country Skiing 199
  Beaches 52
  Just for Kids 164
  Museums
    Ehrman Mansion 267
  Tennis 103
Summer Activities 29
Summer Adventures 31
Sunnyside
  Beach 52
  Boat Launch 59
  Dining Out
    Sunnyside Restaurant 229

Index

Sunnyside
Water Ski Schools
High Sierra Ski School 61

Tahoe City
Art Galleries
Frames by Ryrie 254
Freeman Gallery 255
High Country Silverworks 254
Mother Nature's Wildlife Art 254
North Tahoe Art Center 254
Pogan Gallery 253
Sierra Galleries 255
Suzanne Riley Studio and Gallery 254
Back Country Skiing
Paige Meadows 199
Tahoe City to Alpine Meadows 199
Beaches
Commons Beach 49
Lake Forest 50
Pomin Beach 50
Skylandia Park 50
Sunnyside Beach 52
Tahoe State Recreation Area 49
William Kent 52
Bicycle Paths
To Dollar Point 89
To River Ranch 89
To Sugar Pine Point State Park 89
Bicycle Rentals 86
Boat Launch 59
Boat Rentals 46
Cross Country Skiing
Granlibakken 190
Lakeview 189
Cruising Lake Tahoe
Tahoe Gal 63
Dining Out
Christy Hill 227
Fiamma 228
Grazie! 227

Tahoe City
Hacienda del Lago 228
Jake's 228
Pfeifer House 226
Tahoe House 226
Truffula 228
Wolfdale's 227
Downhill Ski Areas
Granlibakken 176
Fishing Charters
Reel Deal 77
Reel Magic 78
Golf
Tahoe City Course 108
Guided Hikes
Tahoe Trips and Trails 37
Historic Inns and B&B's
Cottage Inn 286
Mayfield House 286
Just For Kids
Little Peoples' Adventures 164
Tahoe Trips and Trails 164
Kayaking
Tahoe Whitewater Tours 62
Mountain Bike Parks
Lakeview 95
Museums
Gatekeeper's Cabin 266
Watson Cabin 267
Parasailing
Lake Tahoe Parasailing 31
Lighthouse Watersports 31
Rafting
Tahoe Whitewater Tours 84
Truckee River 84
Seaplane Tours
Commodore Seaplanes 33
Shopping 260
Sno-Park Trails 195
Snowmobiling
T C Sno Mo 205

Tahoe City
Snowplay
Granlibakken 209
South of the Y 211
Special Events
Snowfest 274
The Great Race 274
Wooden Boat Week 277
Special Hikes
Eagle Rock 136
Tennis
Granlibakken 103
Kilner Park 103
North Tahoe High School 104
Tahoe Marina Lodge 104
Water Ski Schools
Captain Kelly's 61
Water Sports Rentals 46
Tahoe Conservancy 20
Tahoe Keys
Balloon Rides
Lake Tahoe Balloons 33
Boat Launch 59
Boat Rentals 47
Cruising Lake Tahoe 64
Tahoe Para-dice 64
Dining Out
Fresh Ketch 243
Fishing Charters
Blue Ribbon Fishing Charters 79
Water Ski Schools
Werley's 62
Tahoe Meadows
Special Hikes
Mount Rose 156
Tahoe Rim Trail 155
Tahoe Vista
Art Galleries
Douglas Taylor 255
Beaches
Agatam Beach 50
Moondunes Beach 50
National Ave. Beach 50

307

Index

Tahoe Vista
  Bicycling
    North Tahoe Regional Park 90
  Boat Launch 59
  Boat Rentals 46
  Cross Country Skiing
    North Tahoe Regional Park 189
  Dining Out
    Boulevard Café 231
    Captain Jon's 231
    Le Petit Pier 232
    Sunsets on the Lake 232
  Fishing Charters
    Mac-A-Tac 78
  Historic Inns and B&B's
    Shore House 291
  Snowmobiling
    North Tahoe Regional Park 204
  Snowplay
    North Tahoe Regional Park 210
  Special Events
    Tahoe Mountain Musicals 276
  Tennis
    North Tahoe Regional Park 104
  Water Sports Rentals 46
Tahoma
  Dining Out
    Chambers Landing 230
    Norfolk Woods Inn 230
  Fishing Charters
    Johnson Guide Service 77
  Fly Fishing Guides
    Johnson Guide Service 81
  Historic Inns and B&B's
    Norfolk Woods Inn 290
    Knotty Pine 290
    Tahoma Meadows Bed and Breakfast 289

Tallac Historic Site
  Beaches 54
  Historical Walk 120
  Valhalla 122
TART 2
Taylor Creek
  Sno-Park Trails 196
Tennis 103
Truckee
  Art Galleries
    Artruckee 251
    Backstreet Framemakers and Gallery 252
    Frank Rossback Glasforms 253
    James Hacker Sculpture 253
    Kathleen Curtis Studio 252
    White Buffalo 251
  Back Country Skiing
    Old Henness Pass Road East 198
  Balloon Rides
    Mountain High Balloons 32
  Bicycle Paths
    Truckee to Squaw Valley 88
  Bicycle Rentals 86
  Boating 60
  Cross Country Skiing
    Martis Peak 198
    Tahoe Donner Cross Country 187
  Dining Out
    Cottonwood 221
    Jibbooms Café 223
    O.B.'s Pub and Restaurant 221
    Pacific Crest 222
    Pianeta 222
    The Passage 220
    Truckee Trattoria 223
  Downhill Ski Areas
    Northstar 177
    Tahoe Donner 174

Truckee
  Fishing
    Boca Reservoir 69
    Little Truckee River 69
    Martis Creek Lake 68
    Prosser Creek Reservoir 68
    Sagehen Creek 70
    Stampede Reservoir 69
    Truckee River 69
  Fishing Charters
    Clearwater Guides 77
  Fly-Fishing Guides
    California School of Fly-Fishing 80
    Thy Rod and Staff 80
  Glider Rides
    Soar Truckee 33
  Golf
    Ponderosa Golf Course 107
    Tahoe Donner 107
  Historic Inns and B&B's
    Bocks 10064 House 284
    Hania House 284
    Richardson House 283
    Truckee Hotel 282
  Historical Walks
    Boca Historic Town Site 118
    Historic Downtown Truckee 116
  Horseback Riding
    Tahoe Donner 100
  July 4th Parade 275
  Just For Kids
    Donner Memorial State Park 162
    Tahoe Donner Equestrian Camp 162
  Mountain Bike Roads 96
  Museums
    Donner Day Camp 265
    Donner Memorial State Park 264
    Sierra Nevada Children's Museum 264

308

Index

Truckee
  Scenic Flights
    Todd Aero 34
  Shopping 259
  Sleigh Rides
    Truckee Carriage 212
  Sno-Park Trails 195
  Snowmobiling
    Eagle Ridge 205
  Snowplay
    Downtown 211
    Tahoe Donner 209
  Special Events
    Donner Party Hike Weekend 278
    Northstar Beer Festival 275
    Railroad Days 277
    Snowfest 274
    Tiny Tim's Christmas Fair 278
    Truckee Rodeo 277
    Windows on History 275
  Special Hikes
    Donner Memorial State Park 133
    Mt. Lola 134
  Tennis
    Truckee Regional Park 103
    West End Beach 103
Truckee Donner Land Trust 20
Truckee History 13
Truckee Trolley 2
Tubing
  Boreal 208
  Northstar-at-Tahoe 209
  Soda Springs Ski Area 208
Tubing
  Squaw Valley 209

Unofficial Sledding Hills 210

Water Ski Schools 61
Water Sports Rentals 46

Wilderness Permits 128
Winter Activities 168
Winter Adventures 212
Winter Driving 169
Year-Round Activities 218

Yuba Gap
  Cross Country Skiing
    Eagle Moutain 185
  Mountain Bike Parks
    Eagle Mountain 94

Zephyr Cove
  Art Galleries
    Jerome Evans 258
  Beaches 56
  Boat Launch 59
  Boat Rentals 47
  Cruising Lake Tahoe
    M.S. Dixie 65
    Woodwind 66
  Fishing Charters
    First Strike Sport Fishing 79
    O'Malley's Fishing Charters 79
  Fly-Fishing Guides
    Trout Creek 82
  Horseback Riding 102
  Parasailing
    Captain Kirk's 32
  Snowmobiling 206
  Tennis
    County Park 105
    Whittel High School 105
  Tour Companies
    Eco Adventures 45
  Water Sports Rentals 47

NOTES

Publisher's Note

Lake Tahoe and Truckee are tourist communities, and as such, shops can change owners or go out of business, or chefs can leave and restaurant menus change.

We have tried to be as complete and up-to-date as possible for the revised and expanded 1998-1999 edition of *What Shall We Do Tomorrow at Lake Tahoe.* If you discover something that could be included in the next edition, please write and let us know. If you would like to order a copy of this book for a friend, use the order blank on the next page.

Other Books by Coldstream Press

All Roads Lead to Yosemite: Where to Stay and Play In and Near the Park has just been released. It is a complete guide to lodging, dining and recreation for the gateway communities of Oakhurst, Mariposa, Groveland, Lee Vining/June Lake and Yosemite National Park.

Coldstream Press has a book about the history of downhill skiing in the Sierra Nevada — *Mountain Dreamers: Visionaries of Sierra Nevada Skiing* by Robert Frohlich, with photographs by Carolyn Caddes and Tom Lippert. This book chronicles the memories of 26 extraordinary men and women who share with us their deep love for the Sierra Nevada. The modern black and white portraits of the dreamers by Carolyn Caddes catch the essence of these pioneers of Sierra Nevada skiing. Aerial photographs of the ski areas are by Tom Lippert, and over 80 historical photos illustrate the text. With a Foreword by Andrea Mead Lawrence and an Epilogue by Stu Campbell, this is a must read for anyone who loves the Sierra Nevada and has skied those perfect days of new snow sparkling under azure skies.

Northwest Passages from the Pen of John Muir in California, Oregon, Washington and Alaska, is a reprint of the 1988 Ben Franklin Award book featuring original woodcuts by Andrea Hendrick that illustrate Muir's inspirational words.

Coldstream Press
P.O. Box 9590
Truckee, CA 96162

I wish to order:

___ What Shall We Do Tomorrow at Lake Tahoe $12.95

___ All Roads Lead to Yosemite: Where to Stay and Play
     In and Near the Park $13.95

    Mountain Dreamers: Visionaries of Sierra Nevada Skiing
___   Soft Cover $29.95
___   Hard Cover $50.00

___ Northwest Passages from the Pen of John Muir $15.00

        Subtotal $_____

        California residents add 7.875% sales tax $_____
        Total $_____

We pay shipping to U.S. destinations.

Please charge my Visa or MasterCard

Card No. _____

Expiration Date _____

Signature _____

Order by phone: 800-916-7450, by fax: 530-587-9081 or on the internet at www.coldstreampress.com

Name _____

Address _____

City _____ State ____ Zip _____

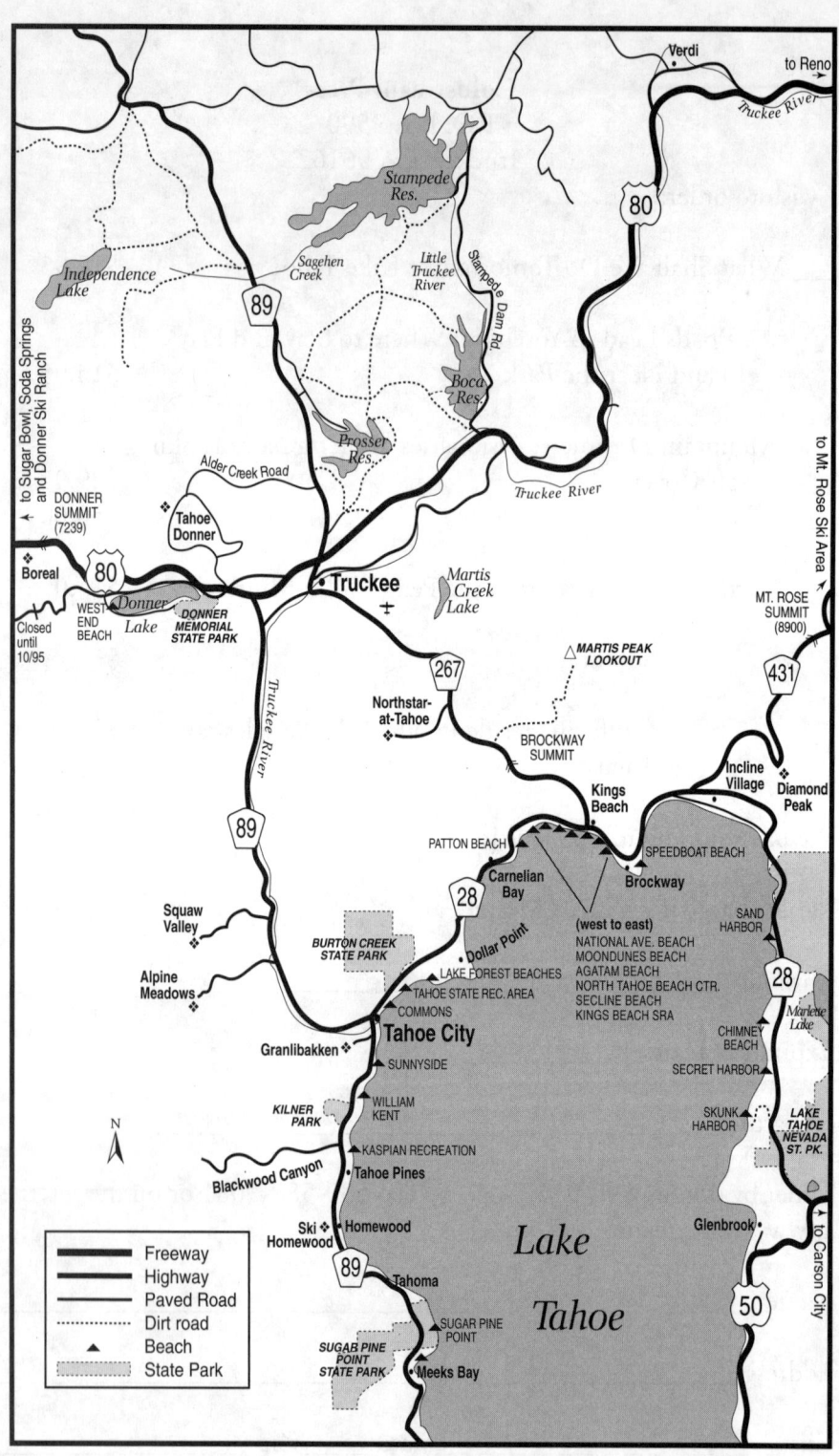